This Book Comes With Lots of
FREE Online Resources

Nolo's award-winning website contains thousands of articles on everyday legal and business issues, plus a plain-English law dictionary, all written by Nolo experts and available for free.

You'll also find more useful **books, software, online apps, downloadable forms,** plus a **lawyer directory.**

GET DISCOUNTS ON NOLO PRODUCTS. Get discounts on hundreds of books, forms, and software.

READ BLOGS. Get the latest info from Nolo authors' blogs.

LISTEN TO PODCASTS. Listen to authors discuss timely issues on topics that interest you.

WATCH VIDEOS. Get a quick introduction to a legal topic with our short videos.

LAW for ALL

www.nolo.com

NOLO # The Trusted Name
(but don't take our word for it)

"In Nolo you can trust."
THE NEW YORK TIMES

"Nolo is always there in a jam as the nation's premier publisher of do-it-yourself legal books."
NEWSWEEK

"Nolo publications…guide people simply through the how, when, where and why of the law."
THE WASHINGTON POST

"[Nolo's]…material is developed by experienced attorneys who have a knack for making complicated material accessible."
LIBRARY JOURNAL

"When it comes to self-help legal stuff, nobody does a better job than Nolo…"
USA TODAY

"The most prominent U.S. publisher of self-help legal aids."
TIME MAGAZINE

"Nolo is a pioneer in both consumer and business self-help books and software."
LOS ANGELES TIMES

17th Edition

Everybody's Guide to
Small Claims Court

Attorney Cara O'Neill

SEVENTEENTH EDITION MARCH 2018

Editor	CARA O'NEILL
Cover Design	SUSAN PUTNEY
Book Design	SUSAN PUTNEY
Proofreading	ROBERT WELLS
Index	RICHARD GENOVA
Printing	BANG PRINTING

ISSN: 2328-9848 (print)
ISSN: 2328-9856 (online)
ISBN: 978-1-4133-2490-7 (pbk)
ISBN: 978-1-4133-2491-4 (epub ebook)

This book covers only United States law, unless it specifically states otherwise.

Please note

We believe accurate, plain-English legal information should help you solve many of your own legal problems. But this text is not a substitute for personalized advice from a knowledgeable lawyer. If you want the help of a trained professional—and we'll always point out situations in which we think that's a good idea—consult an attorney licensed to practice in your state.

Thank You

Thanks must go to Ralph Warner, the cofounder of Nolo and the original author of this book. While working as a Legal Aid lawyer in the late 1960s, it occurred to him that most Americans—not just the poor—were alienated from and oppressed by the legal system. Deciding to make a career out of working to provide better legal services, he cofounded Nolo in 1971. Ralph authored and coauthored a number of Nolo books, including *Save Your Small Business: 10 Crucial Strategies to Survive Hard Times or Close Down and Move On*. Without Ralph, this book, and many others, wouldn't exist today.

About the Author

Cara O'Neill is a bankruptcy attorney in Northern California and a legal editor with Nolo. She has been practicing law in California for over 20 years. Prior to joining Nolo, she served as an administrative law judge, litigated both criminal and civil cases, and taught law courses as an adjunct professor. She earned her law degree in 1994 from the University of the Pacific, McGeorge School of Law, where she served as a law review editor and graduated a member of the Order of the Barristers—an honor society recognizing excellence in courtroom advocacy. Cara has authored and coauthored a number of Nolo books, including *How to File for Chapter 7 Bankruptcy*, *The New Bankruptcy*, *Money Troubles*, and *Credit Repair*.

Table of Contents

Your Small Claims Court Companion

Filing a case in small claims court is a highly cost-effective strategy for resolving all kinds of disputes. In most states, the maximum amount you can sue for has increased substantially in recent years, and court judgments have become far easier to collect. In addition, many states have implemented innovative mediation programs for small claims, which can spare you the time and tension of presenting your case to a judge. Although more can and should be done to make small claims court a true people's court, it is an efficient forum that gives participants an opportunity to resolve many personal consumer and small business disputes.

The goal of this book is to give people bringing a case and those defending one all the information they need to make the best possible use of small claims court. From deciding whether you have a case through gathering evidence, arranging for witnesses, planning your courtroom presentation, and collecting your money, you will find everything here.

> **TIP**
> **From the bench.** *Everybody's Guide to Small Claims Court* is the only guide to include practical suggestions from former small claims court judges. You'll see their comments throughout the book.

Everybody's Guide to Small Claims Court has now been in print for more than 30 years. Our goal is to make it the best possible tool to help you answer such questions as:

- How does small claims court work?
- Do I have a case worth pursuing or defending?
- How do I prepare my case to maximum advantage?
- What witnesses and other evidence should I present?
- What do I say in court?
- Can I appeal if I lose?
- How do I collect my judgment?

Proper presentation of your small claims action can often mean the difference between receiving a check and writing one. This isn't to say that we can tell you how to take a hopeless case and turn it into a blue-ribbon winner. It does mean that with the information contained here, and with your own creativity and common sense, you will be able to develop and present your legal and factual position as effectively as possible. In short, this book will show you how a case with a slight limp can be set on four good legs.

Just as important as knowing when and how to bring your small claims court action is knowing when not to. Clearly, you don't want to waste time and energy dragging a hopeless case to court. And even if your case is legally sound, you won't want to pursue it if your chances of collecting from the defendant are poor.

In addition to studying the information you'll find here, it's important that you review the materials made available by your state's small claims court. Crucial technical details such as when and where court is held, what types of evidence are allowed and prohibited, and how much it will cost to collect a judgment are covered in more detail in those materials than we can possibly do in this 50-state guide. Fortunately, accessing this material is easy—it's usually available online as well as in free pamphlets available at your small claims court clerk's office. You'll find information about your state's small claims court and website in the appendix.

Finally, I'd like to say a few words about the many referrals to other Nolo self-help law books and Nolo's website. Lest you think the only goal is to try to sell you another book, let me make three points. First, Nolo is by far the most comprehensive publisher of self-help law materials in the United States. As a result, there are many legal areas where Nolo publishes the only decent materials aimed at nonlawyers. Second, because a huge variety of legal issues can be litigated in small claims court, information in many other Nolo books and on Nolo's website may be useful (and is far too voluminous to repeat here). Third, as Nolo's books are available at most American libraries, it shouldn't be hard to look up any needed information at no cost.

Basics of Small Claims Court

Why Use Small Claims Court?

Small claims procedures are established by state law. This means there are differences in the operating rules of small claims courts from state to state, including the maximum amount for which you can sue; who can sue; and the what, where, and when of filing papers. There are even differences in what small claims court (or its equivalent) is called in the different states, with justice, district, municipal, city, county, and magistrates court among the names commonly used.

Although the details of using small claims courts vary from state to state, the basic approach necessary to prepare and present a case is remarkably similar everywhere. But details are important, and you should do three things to make sure you understand how small claims court works in your state:

- Look up the summary of your state's rules in the 50-state appendix to this book.
- Obtain your local small claims rules from your small claims court clerk's office.
- Check out your state's small claims rules online. See the appendix for information on how to find your state's small claims court.

The purpose of small claims court is to hear disputes involving modest amounts of money, without long delays and formal rules of evidence. Disputes are normally presented directly by the people involved. Lawyers are prohibited in some states, including Michigan and California, but are allowed in most. However, the limited dollar amounts involved usually make it economically unwise to hire a lawyer. The maximum amount of money for which you can sue (in legal jargon, the "jurisdictional amount") is set by state law, too. While these amounts vary state by state, the range is from as low as $2,500 (Kentucky) to as high as $15,000 (Delaware).

> CAUTION
> **Check your state's jurisdictional amount before you file.** We provide the most up-to-date information available at the time this book was published. But these amounts change, so be sure to check the rules for your state before filing. An excellent resource for 50-state small claims court information is www.freeadvice.com/resources/smallclaimscourts.htm.

There are three great advantages of small claims court:

- You get to prepare and present your own case without having to pay a lawyer more than your claim is worth.
- Filing, preparing, and presenting a small claims case is relatively easy. The gobbledygook of complicated legal forms and language found in other courts is kept to a minimum. To start your case, you need only fill out a few lines on a simple form (for example, "Defendant owes me the sum of $4,000 because the 2012 Neon he sold me on January 1, 2017, in supposedly 'excellent condition,' died less than a mile from the car lot"). When you get to court, you can talk to the judge in plain English without any legal jargon.
- Small claims court doesn't take long. Most disputes are heard in court within two or three months from the time the complaint is filed. The hearing itself seldom takes more than 15 minutes. The judge announces a decision either right there in the courtroom or mails it within a few days.

Will Small Claims Work for You?

Before you decide that small claims court sounds like just the place to bring your case, you will want to answer a basic question: Will the results you expect to achieve balance out the effort you will have to expend? Even in small claims court, a successful case will probably take ten to 20 hours to prepare and present and, depending on your personality, may actually cause a few sleepless nights.

In order to assess whether your dispute is worth the effort of bringing to court, you will want to understand the details of how small claims court works, starting with being clear about who can sue, where, and for how much. You will also want to do the following:

- Learn a little law to answer such important questions as whether you are likely to win and, if so, how much; what types of papers you must file and when; and who can sue (and be sued). Part of this involves knowing the different legal rules for different types of cases—for example, a personal injury claim versus a security deposit dispute.

- Once you conclude you do have a winning case, understand how best to prepare and present it.
- Finally, and most importantly, determine whether you will be able to collect the money if you win. This is an important detail that so many people overlook, to their later dismay. Assuming that you prepare and present your case brilliantly and get a judgment for everything you request, it's to little avail if you can't get paid. Unfortunately, many plaintiffs who go through the entire small claims procedure and come out winners have no chance of collecting a dime because they have sued a person who has neither money nor any reasonable prospect of getting any.

This book covers of all of these. The first several chapters will help you decide whether or not you have a case worth pursuing; these are not the chapters where grand strategies are brilliantly unrolled to baffle and confound the opposition—that comes later. Here we are more concerned with such mundane tasks as locating the person you want to sue, suing in the right court, filling out the necessary forms, and properly delivering the forms to the person you're suing.

TIP

Defendants may want to file their own lawsuit. In addition to their right to defend themselves, defendants also have the opportunity to file their own case against the plaintiff. (See Chapters 10 and 12.) If you are sued, you'll want to do this if you believe that you lost money due to the same events the plaintiff is complaining about and the plaintiff is legally responsible for your loss. Defendants' claims commonly develop out of a situation in which both parties are negligent (for example, in a car accident) and the question is who was more at fault. If your claim is for less than the small claims court maximum, you can file there. But if it is for more, you will want to check your state's rules. Typically, you'll learn that you should file your case in a different court (and have your opponent's case transferred there), but your state may use a different system. (See Chapter 10.)

Below are preliminary checklists of things ("Initial Stage Questions") you will want to think about at this initial stage—depending on whether you are the plaintiff or the defendant. This book goes into each of these areas in more detail, and provides targeted advice for both plaintiffs and defendants in small claims cases.

Initial Stage Questions for a Plaintiff

☐ 1. Do you have a good case? That is, can you establish or prove all the key pieces of your claim? (See Chapters 2, 14–22.)

☐ 2. How much is your claim for? If it is for more than the small claims maximum, do you wish to waive the excess and still use small claims court? (See Chapter 4.)

☐ 3. Have you made a reasonable effort to contact the other party and settle the case? (See Chapter 6.)

☐ 4. Are you within the deadline (statute of limitations) by which you must file your suit? (See Chapter 5.)

☐ 5. Whom do you sue and how do you identify this person or business on your court papers? In some types of cases, especially those involving businesses and automobiles, this can be a little more technical and tricky than you might have guessed. (See Chapter 8.)

☐ 6. Which small claims court should you bring your suit in? (See Chapter 9.)

☐ 7. If mediation is offered or encouraged by your small claims court, do you understand how it works and how best to use it? (See Chapter 6.)

☐ 8. Can you make a convincing courtroom presentation? (See Chapter 15.)

☐ 9. And, the most important question: Assuming you can win, is there a reasonable chance you can collect? (See Chapters 3 and 24.)

Initial Stage Questions for a Defendant

☐ 1. Do you have legal grounds for a countersuit against the plaintiff? Or put another way, does the plaintiff really owe you money instead of the other way around? (See Chapters 10 and 12.)

☐ 2. Do you have a partial or complete defense against the plaintiff's claim? Or put another way, has the plaintiff filed a bogus lawsuit? (See Chapters 2 and 12.)

☐ 3. Is the plaintiff's money demand reasonable, or excessive? (See Chapter 4.)

☐ 4. Has the plaintiff brought the suit within the proper time limit? (See Chapter 5.)

☐ 5. Has the plaintiff followed reasonably correct procedures in bringing suit and delivering the court papers to you? (See Chapters 11 and 12.)

☐ 6. If mediation is offered or encouraged by your small claims court, do you understand how it works and how to use it? (See Chapter 6.)

☐ 7. Have you made a reasonable effort to contact the plaintiff in order to arrive at a settlement? (See Chapters 6 and 12.)

☐ 8. Assuming you'll fight the case in court, you'll normally need proof that your version of events is correct. Can you collect evidence and witnesses to accomplish this? (See Chapters 13–15.)

☐ 9. Are you prepared to present your side of the case convincingly in court? (See Chapter 15.)

How to Use This Book

This guide covers the procedures that both plaintiffs and defendants should use to successfully bring or defend a small claims case. Unlike other guides, it also contains step-by-step instructions for preparing particularly common small claims cases, along with examples from real cases.

Chapters 2 and 3 help you answer the basic question of whether you should sue in the first place by asking two crucial questions: Do you have a good case? Can you collect any money from the defendant if you win?

If your answer to either of these questions is "no," then you should read Chapter 6 to see whether you might be able to settle your dispute without going to court, or you should consider dropping the idea of a lawsuit.

Chapters 4–9 walk you through the procedural details. Small claims court is meant to be easy, but it still has rules about how much money you can sue for, whom you can sue, what court you should bring your lawsuit in, and so forth.

Chapters 10 and 11 are about the actual paperwork: How do you fill out your papers and deliver them to the defendant once you've decided to bring a small claims lawsuit?

Chapter 12 is for the defendant. You've just been sued; what do you do?

Chapters 13–15 get you ready for your day in court. In Chapters 23 and 24 you'll find out how the judge issues a ruling, how to appeal, and how to collect your money if you're successful.

In Chapters 16–22, we look at the most common types of cases and discuss strategies to handle each. Even if your fact situation doesn't fit neatly into one of these categories, you should read this material. By picking up a few hints here and a little information there, you should be able to piece together a good plan of action. For example, many of the suggestions on how to handle motor vehicle repair disputes can also be applied to cases involving problems with fixing major appliances such as televisions, washers, and expensive sound systems.

Appendix A contains a summary of important small claims court information and rules for every state. For each state, you can easily find the name of the court that handles small claims cases, the relevant state statutes, the link for the small claims court website, dollar limits for bringing a lawsuit, service of process rules, time limits for responding to claims, how to appeal a decision, and more. You will want to check your state's small claims court website early in the process, whether you're a plaintiff or a defendant, for valuable information about how small claims cases are handled in your state. Be sure to also check the local small claims court clerk's office for local rules.

Appendix B is a glossary of some key legal jargon related to small claims cases and court. Fortunately, there is not a lot of it but there are a few terms that may be new to you. If you're stumped by a term that isn't defined in the book, check out the Nolo website, which includes a Free Dictionary of Law Terms and Legal Definitions.

Do You Have a Good Case?

Stating Your Claim

One of the advantages of small claims court is that when you file your case you are not required to present theories of law—instead, you simply state the facts of the dispute, that you have suffered monetary loss and that the person or business you are suing caused your loss. Even so, it's a good idea to understand the legal basis for your claim (more later).

In Chapter 10, we'll go over the forms you must file to start your lawsuit. In your complaint or claim, you will give a simple description of the dispute. Depending, of course, on the facts of your case, you will state your claim more or less like this:

- "John's Dry Cleaners ruined my jacket on December 13, 20xx."
- "His dog bit me on the corner of Rose and Peach Streets in West Covina, California, on April 27, 20xx."
- "The car repairs that Joe's Garage did on my car on July 11, 20xx, were done wrong, resulting in an engine fire."
- "Landlord refused to return the cleaning deposit when I moved out of my apartment on August 11, 20xx, even though I left it clean."
- "The used car I purchased from her on January 26, 20xx, in 'tiptop condition,' blew a gasket the next day."
- "The $5,000 I lent defendant has not been repaid by November 12, 20xx, as promised."

Time to Get Organized

Even before you file your case, you should set up a good system to safeguard key papers and evidence. It's no secret that more than one case has been won (or lost) because of good (or bad) record keeping. One excellent approach is to get a couple of manila envelopes or file folders and label them with the name of your dispute (*Lincoln vs. Williams*). Use one folder to store all documentary evidence, such as receipts, letters, names and addresses of potential witnesses, and photographs. The other is for your court papers. Once organized, make sure you conscientiously store your folders in a safe place.

TIP

Don't argue your case until you get to court. When you state your case on the court papers, your goal is to notify the other party and the court of the issue in dispute. You don't need or want to try to list your evidence or otherwise try to convince anyone that you are in the right or that the law is on your side. Your chance to do this will come later in court.

But Is My Case Any Good?

You might be told that because you are in small claims court, you don't need to have any legal knowledge or understanding about how legal claims work. You might be led to believe that all you will need to be able to do is:

- briefly state the nature of your dispute
- organize any evidence and witnesses you think will help back up your version of events
- come to court on time
- be polite, and
- let the judge decide if your case is any good.

At a very basic level, this is decent advice—you expend little effort or thought and rely on the judge to do the heavy legal lifting. However, the problem with this approach is that the judge will not decide your case based on what seems morally "right" (although it never hurts to seize the high moral ground) or on whose presentation and witnesses are more convincing. Instead, the judge must apply exactly the same legal rules to your case as would be followed if your dispute was heard in a formal court.

JUDGE'S TIP

"Unfair" doesn't automatically mean "illegal." Unfortunately, the mere fact that you have suffered a trauma at the hands of another person does not automatically entitle you to a legal judgment. The law must support your contention that you were harmed by the *illegal* actions of another.

Obviously, this means there are a number of problems with this "stay ignorant and trust the judge" approach. Here are the biggies:

- If you don't understand the legal rules the judge will apply to decide your case, you might waste time and energy pursuing an obvious loser.
- If you don't understand the legal realities that underlie your case, you might prepare irrelevant arguments. In a worst-case scenario, you might not even understand—and therefore fail to fulfill—the key legal requirements necessary to have a judgment entered in your favor.
- If you win—and especially if you lose—you won't know why.

If none of this sounds good to you, perhaps you are open to considering a more informed approach. This consists of taking the time to understand the basic legal—as well as the moral—issues that underlie your case. Or put another way, it means looking at your case in the same way a judge will ultimately view it.

⊙ **TIP**

Defendants need the same legal knowledge as plaintiffs. Every law has several parts, called "elements," that a plaintiff must prove to win a case. A plaintiff who fails to prove an element must lose. To defend a case well, a defendant needs to understand the essential legal elements of the case the plaintiff is attempting to prove. Once armed with this information, the defendant will be in good shape to try to convince the judge that at least one legal requirement is missing.

The rest of this chapter contains a discussion of the legal theories most commonly used to establish legal liability in small claims court. In many instances, this information will be all you need to prepare your case. But occasionally, you will want to do additional legal research, especially if the exact wording of a statute or key court decision has a direct bearing on your case. (See Chapter 25 for more on how to do legal research.)

⊙ **CAUTION**

Check your state's small claims court rules. Many small claims courts limit the types of cases they will decide in addition to restricting the dollar amount of damages you can claim. For example, Rhode Island's small claims court only allows breach of contract claims and claims by consumers for damages connected with retail products or services. Ask your small claims court clerk or review your small claims court's rules to make sure your type of case can be heard. (See the appendix for your state court's website for contact and other information.)

Below is a list of the most common legal theories and what you need to prove to establish each one. The rest of this chapter reviews each key legal theory in detail, so you can see whether the facts of your case fit the requirements of at least one of them.

Bad Debt. A type of contract case. To prevail, you need to prove the debt exists, its amount, when payment was due, and that the person you are suing hasn't paid it or has only partially paid it.

Breach of Contract. One or more terms of a valid contract (written, oral, or implied) has been broken by the person you are suing. As a result, you have suffered a monetary loss.

Breach of Warranty. A written or implied warranty (assurance) extended to you by a merchant has been breached and, as a result, you have suffered a monetary loss—for example, a new or used car suffers mechanical problems while still covered by warranty.

Failure to Return a Security Deposit. Another variety of contract case that commonly arises between tenants and landlords. As discussed in more detail in Chapter 20, the tenant needs to prove that a deposit was made, that it was not returned (or only partially returned), and that the premises were sufficiently clean and undamaged when the tenant left so the landlord owes the tenant some or all of the amount withheld.

Libel or Slander (Defamation). To prove a libel or slander case, you must show that the other party said or wrote something untrue about you or your business, that others heard or read it and understood it was about you, and that it really did damage your reputation. (Public figures must also show that the person defaming them knew the offending statement or writing was false or was made in "reckless disregard of the truth.")

Nuisance. Someone's conduct creates a health or safety hazard to you (and perhaps to other neighbors or nearby property owners) or interferes with your ability to use and enjoy your property—for example, a factory makes so much noise that you and other nearby residents are kept awake all night.

Personal Injury. The negligent (careless) or intentional behavior of the person you are suing has caused you to suffer personal injury.

Product Liability. You or your property were injured by a defective product. If so, you qualify for recovery under the legal doctrine of strict liability, which holds the manufacturer responsible for the damages you suffered, without your having to prove negligence.

Professional Malpractice. A lawyer, doctor, or other professional's failure to use the ordinary skills of members of that profession results in you, as a client or patient, being harmed (in the case of a lawyer or accountant, you must suffer a monetary loss).

Property Damage. The negligent (careless) or intentional behavior of the person you are suing has damaged your personal property.

> CAUTION
> **Other legal theories exist.** The legal theories listed above are involved in more than 99% of small claims cases. There are dozens of more obscure types of lawsuits, each with its own legal requirements. If your case isn't covered here, you will want to do some research to determine whether your case meets the qualifications of some other legal theory.

> TIP
> **How to find other legal theories.** One way to review common causes of action is to thumb through your state's set of civil jury instructions (many of the legal theories will apply in small claims court). The beauty of using the jury instructions is that the elements you'll need to prove will be set forth in plain language, and in many cases you'll find citations to the law as well. You'll find most state's jury instructions online or at your local law library (and don't be afraid to ask the librarian for help).

Now, before we consider each of these legal theories individually, here is an example of why it's so important to establish not only that you have suffered a loss, but also that the defendant is legally required to compensate you.

> **EXAMPLE:** One night, someone entered the garage in Sue's apartment complex, smashed her car window, and stole her custom car stereo worth $600. Upon discovery of the theft, and after reporting it to the police, Sue promptly filed suit against the landlord in small claims court. As part of preparing for her day in court, Sue got several witnesses willing to testify that her car had been vandalized and obtained a copy of the police investigation report. She also got several estimates as to the cost of repairing the damage to the car window and replacing the stereo.

In preparing for her case, Sue overlooked one crucial thing. Under the circumstances, the building owner wasn't liable. He had never promised (either orally or in writing) to keep the garage locked. In addition, he had never locked the garage or otherwise led Sue to believe that he would do so. The judge determined that all the tenants knew or should have known that anyone could gain access to the garage, either from inside or outside the building, and that there had been no previous crimes committed there. The judge concluded that, in failing to lock the garage, the building owner was neither in violation of a contract nor guilty of any negligent behavior. As he explained to Sue when he ruled for the landlord, the legal situation she faced was little different than it would have been if her car had been damaged on the street.

Now let's take this same situation, but change a few facts. Let's assume the lease Sue signed with the landlord stated that Sue would be assigned a parking place in a "secure garage." Let's also assume that the garage had always been locked until seven days before the theft occurred when the lock broke. Finally, let's assume that Sue and other tenants had asked the owner to fix the lock the day after it broke, but that he hadn't "gotten around to it." In this situation, Sue should win. The landlord made a contractual promise to the tenants (to keep the garage locked) and then failed to keep it though he'd had plenty of time to fulfill his obligation. The breach of contract allowed the thief access to the car.

Breach of Contract Cases

A contract is any agreement between individuals or businesses in which one side agrees to do something for the other in exchange for something in return. For example, A asks B to paint his kitchen for $3,000 and B agrees. The agreement can be written or oral (in most situations), or implied from the circumstances. Contracts made by minors can be found invalid if they are made before the minor turns 18. However, in most states, if a minor makes a contract and then honors it after turning 18, the contract is valid and can no longer be annulled.

All contracts come with an obligation that each party carry out its terms in "good faith." This means each contracting individual or business will deal with the other fairly and honestly under the circumstances so that

the common purpose set out in the agreement can be achieved. On the other side of the coin, courts have found "bad faith" when one party does something that evades the spirit of the agreement or violates community standards of fairness and reasonableness. Practically, it's important to understand that all contracts contain an unwritten good faith requirement, because it means that a small claims judge often won't find in favor of a party who sues based on a highly technical—but obviously unfair or unreasonable—interpretation of contract language. For example, if X agrees to landscape Y's yard in two weeks, but on the last afternoon doesn't quite finish because she is called to the bedside of a sick child, a court will not agree with Y's contention that he doesn't have to pay for any of the work because X technically missed the 14-day deadline. Instead, a judge will almost surely rule that Y's duty to carry out the agreement in good faith requires him to allow X to finish the job a few days late.

Common Contract Rules

Here is a short summary of basic contract principles designed to help you understand whether you've got a valid contract in the first place:

- **A gift is not a contract.** As every law student learns on the first day of contracts class, a promise to make a gift is not a contract. The reason is simple: The gift's recipient hasn't promised to do anything in return. Or put another way, an enforceable contract absolutely depends on an exchange—or a promise to exchange—something of value, such as money for services.

 EXAMPLE 1: Marcia tells Steve she is in a bad way financially, so Steve promises to give Marcia $750 on January 1. Later, Steve changes his mind, because he decides he doesn't like Marcia after all. Can Marcia sue Steve for the $750? No. This is not a contract, because Marcia has not promised to do anything for Steve in return for his promise to make a loan. Steve had only indicated that he would give Marcia a gift in the future. A promise to make a gift is not an enforceable contract because there is no reciprocal promise or "quid pro quo," sometimes also called "consideration."

- **A loan is a contract.** By contrast, a loan, or a promise to make a loan, is normally a valid contract. That's because each party provides the other something of value: The lender agrees to advance the borrower the money, and the borrower agrees to pay it back.

- **An agreement to exchange goods, services, or money is a contract.** The most common type of contract occurs when A agrees to pay money to B in exchange for B agreeing to work for A or provide A with valuable goods.

 > **EXAMPLE 2:** Steve promises to pay Marcia $750 on January 31 in exchange for Marcia's promise to tutor Steve's oldest son. This is a valid contract because each person has promised to do something for the other. If Steve fails to pay Marcia on January 31 and Marcia has kept her part of the bargain, then Marcia can go to court, claiming breach of contract.

- **Most oral contracts are valid if proven.** The great majority of spoken agreements are valid and enforceable, assuming their existence can be established to the satisfaction of a judge. But there are several major exceptions to this rule. Generally speaking, oral contracts are not valid if they: (1) can't be accomplished within a year, (2) are for the sale of real estate, or (3) involve the sale of goods or property worth more than $500. (But this third type of transaction needs very little written proof—a faxed order or a letter confirming a deal will be enough.) Because the great majority of oral consumer contracts—whether to fix a kitchen, repair a car, or deliver a bed—can easily be carried out in less than a year (even if it actually takes longer), most oral contracts that can be proven to the satisfaction of a judge can be enforced in small claims court.

- **Someone's unjust enrichment can prove a contract.** A contract can be implied where one party has obviously benefited from the other and the other expects to be paid for goods or services. This is a tricky area of contract law that occasionally surfaces in small claims cases. The judge will be particularly interested in evidence that the party who received the benefit knew that the service provider expected to be paid.

EXAMPLE 3: Paul asks Barbara if she wants her house painted. Barbara says "Yes," and Paul paints her house. After he's done with the work, Barbara refuses to pay, claiming that because they never agreed on a price, there was no contract. Barbara is wrong. A contract exists when one person does work for another in circumstances where payment is normally expected and the second person accepts it. Consent can be stated, as in this example, or even implied, as would be the case if Barbara simply watches Paul paint her house. In other words, even though one or more technical parts of a contract is missing, when work is involved the law will require that a person who knowingly benefits from another person's work pay for it, unless it is absolutely clear the work was donated.

Unpaid Debts

Often, a contract that has not been honored involves a failure to pay money. Hardly a day goes by in any small claims court when someone isn't sued for failing to pay the phone company, the local hospital, a friend (former, probably), a relative, or even late fines to the public library. (See Chapter 18 for more on small claims suits where money is owed.) In many situations, getting a judgment for an unpaid debt involves no more than stating that the defendant made a commitment to buy certain goods or services, that they were, in fact, provided, and that a legitimate bill for X dollars has not been paid.

As a plaintiff, you must normally prove:

- the identity of the debtor
- the existence of a contract with the debtor
- that you kept your promises under the deal (normally that you provided the goods, services, or loan), and
- that the debt hasn't been paid.

If you are a defendant and believe you have a good defense, you'll normally need to prove:

- the goods or services you were supposed to receive were delivered late or not at all or were seriously defective
- the plaintiff never lent you the money in the first place
- you already paid back some or all the money the plaintiff lent you, or
- the plaintiff agreed to a subsequent contract to forgive the debt or give you more time to pay.

If you are sued because you owe money to a company from which you bought consumer goods or consumer services, research your state's consumer protection laws. (See Chapter 25 on painless methods of legal research.) Also, if a seller of consumer goods or services violates a consumer protection law, then you may be able to get your money back or cancel your deal with no obligation to pay.

- If fraud is present as part of a transaction, the deal can be canceled and your money refunded. Fraud can be:
 - intentional misrepresentation (a deliberate, false statement about a product or service)
 - negligent misrepresentation (a statement about a product or service made without investigating its truth)
 - fraudulent concealment (suppression of the truth) or,
 - a false promise (a promise with no intention to perform), or any other act designed to deceive.
- If you make certain types of purchases, you have a "cooling-off" period under federal law during which you can cancel the contract or sale. (See "The Cooling-Off Rule," below.)

Failure to Perform

Sometimes, a breach of contract suit results not from a refusal to pay a bill, but because one party claims that the other failed to carry out one or more of the terms of a contract. Such would be the case if:

- A tenant sued an apartment owner who agreed to rent him or her an apartment but instead rented it to someone else. (Leases and rental agreements are discussed in more detail in Chapter 20.)
- A small business sued a caterer who showed up four hours late with the food and drink for an important party.
- A customer sued a tattoo artist who began an elaborate skull pattern on his back but couldn't find the time or inspiration to finish it— leaving the customer with what looked like a lumpy potato tattoo and the prospect of paying someone else to finish or remove it.

The Cooling-Off Rule

If you buy a product or service from a seller at a location that's not the seller's permanent place of business, you have three business days to change your mind and cancel the sale, as long as the purchase was over $25 and made at your residence. If not made at your residence, the purchase must be over $130. (16 CFR Part 429.)

The Cooling-Off Rule applies if you buy something from a door-to-door salesperson (even if you invited the salesperson to make the presentation), at work, and at temporary sales locations like convention centers, fairgrounds, and restaurants.

The Cooling-Off Rule does not apply to sales of real estate, insurance, securities, motor vehicles sold at temporary locations as long as the seller has at least one permanent place of business, or arts or crafts sold at fairs, shopping malls, civic centers, and schools. The Cooling-Off Rule also doesn't apply to goods or services that:

- cost less than $130 (or $25 if purchased at your residence)
- are not primarily intended for personal, family, or household use
- are sold entirely by mail or telephone
- are sold after prior negotiations at the seller's permanent business location
- are needed to meet an emergency, or
- are made as part of your request for the seller to do repairs or maintenance on your personal property.

The Cooling-Off Rule requires the salesperson to tell you about your cancellation rights at the time of sale and give you two copies of a cancellation form and a copy of your contract or receipt. The contract or receipt must be in the same language used in the sales presentation, be dated, show the name and address of the seller, and explain your right to cancel.

> **TIP**
>
> **In court, you'll need to convince the judge that the contract existed.**
> If the contract is in writing, bring it to court. If it's oral, be prepared to prove its existence through witnesses and circumstantial evidence. Be creative—if you lent money to a debtor using a check, bring a copy. Along with your own testimony that the borrower promised to repay you, this should be all you need to establish the existence of a contract.

Damages resulting from a breach of contract are normally not difficult to prove. After you show that the contract existed and that the other party failed to meet its terms, you should testify as to the dollar amount of damages you have suffered as a result. And when appropriate, you'll also need to introduce evidence to convince the judge that you really did lose this amount.

> **EXAMPLE 4:** Justine and Bob planned a June wedding. Since the families of both prospective spouses were widely dispersed, this was to be a combination family reunion and wedding. As a result, the couple planned a large reception with a meal and arranged to have it catered by Top Drawer Deli. The deli prepared a written list of all food and drink orders, and Justine signed it. When the big day arrived, everything went swimmingly until the 200 guests arrived at the reception to find that, while the band was playing cheerfully, Top Drawer Deli had not shown up with the food and bubbly. The best man hopped into his SUV, drove to the nearest liquor store, and was back in less than 20 minutes with ten cases of champagne. Someone else had the presence of mind to order 30 pizzas. Two hours later, Top Drawer Deli showed up full of apologies. Justine and Bob accepted the cake and turned down everything else. When the bill came, they paid for the cake only. Top Drawer sued the newlyweds for $4,000 for breach of contract. Bob and Justine countersued for $5,000 for emotional distress. The judge agreed with the newlyweds that by being two hours late to a time-sensitive event, Top Drawer had breached its contract and, as a result, Bob and Justine owed them nothing. But the judge also dismissed Bob and Justine's emotional distress claim, stating that the reception went well and that the newlyweds suffered no damage.

The fact that many contract cases are easy to win doesn't mean that all result in victory. In fact, a good number of plaintiffs lose cases that they assumed were open and shut. Why? Usually because they:

- failed to show that a contract existed (see Examples 1 and 5)
- failed to show that a contract was broken (see Example 6)
- failed to sue the right defendant (again, see Example 5), or
- failed to establish that they really suffered a monetary loss (see Example 4).

EXAMPLE 5: Ben, a landlord, sued John, the parent of one of his tenants, for damage John's daughter and her roommates did to their rental unit. John was sued because he had cosigned his daughter's lease. Ben easily convinced the judge that the damage had, in fact, occurred, and the judge seemed disposed toward giving him a judgment for the $980 requested, until John presented his defense. John showed that the lease between his daughter and the landlord had been rewritten three times after he originally cosigned it and that he had not added his signature to any of the revised versions, one of which involved replacing several of his daughter's original roommates with others. The judge agreed that because John had not cosigned any of the subsequent leases, he wasn't liable. The reason was simple: There was no longer a contract between Ben and John. (Leases and rental agreements, including a detailed discussion of the rights and responsibilities of cosigners, are discussed in more detail in *Every Landlord's Legal Guide*, by Marcia Stewart, Ralph Warner, and Janet Portman (Nolo).)

EXAMPLE 6: Sid sued Acme Dry Cleaners for $650, the cost of replacing a pigskin suede jacket that was ruined (it shrank dramatically) by Acme. Sid established that he had taken the jacket to Acme for cleaning and had agreed to pay Acme $80. Acme, by accepting the jacket, clearly implied it would properly clean it, so there was no question that a contract existed. Sid was very sure of his loss. He stood in the courtroom and slowly tried to wriggle into the jacket. The sleeves barely came to Sid's elbows, and the coat itself didn't reach his waist. By putting on the shrunken jacket, he made his point more effectively than he could have with ten minutes of testimony.

Unfortunately for Sid, he overlooked two key things. Sid's first mistake was asking for the full $650, which is how much he paid for the jacket. However, by the time Acme got a hold of it, the jacket was eight months old and had been worn almost every day. Valuation is a common problem in clothing cases. (It's discussed in detail in Chapters 4 and 21.) Sid's jacket was probably worth no

more than $400 (and probably less) in its used condition. Whenever property is damaged or destroyed, the amount of money you're entitled to will be limited to the fair market value of the goods at the time the damage occurred—not their replacement value.

Sid's other mistake was failing to anticipate what Acme might say in its defense. Vijay, Acme Dry Cleaners' owner, testified that he was amazed when he saw the jacket after cleaning. His cleaning shop specialized in leather goods, and the cleaning process should not have resulted in such shrinkage. He also testified that he had examined a number of other items in the same cleaning batch and found no similar problem. He then sent the jacket to an "independent testing laboratory." Their report, which he presented to the court, stated that it was the jacket itself, not the cleaning, that was the problem. According to the report, shrinkage occurred because the leather had been severely overstretched prior to assembly.

The judge was convinced by the testing lab report and felt that Acme had breached no contract as far as the cleaning was concerned. However, the judge also felt that Acme, as a leather cleaning specialist, had some responsibility to notify Sid that the jacket should not have been cleaned in the first place. Therefore, the judge held mostly for Acme but did award Sid $100. He also suggested that Sid might want to consider suing the store that sold the jacket. The judge explained that Sid could claim the store breached an implied warranty by selling clothing made from seriously defective material. He could use as evidence the very lab report that lost him his original case.

RELATED TOPIC
More material concerning contracts:
• How much you should sue for in a breach of contract case (how to value your damages) is discussed in Chapter 4.
• Breach of warranty (based on a written or oral contract) is covered below.
• Leases and rental agreements (a specialized type of contract) are covered in Chapter 20.
• How to collect on contracts involving unpaid bills is covered in Chapter 18.
• If your contract involves fraud, undue influence, or a simple mistake ($2,000 was mistakenly written as $20,000), you may have a right to have the contract ended or rewritten or to get your goods back under the legal doctrine of equitable relief. (See Chapter 4.)

Property Damage Cases

Another category of small claims disputes involves a claim that a defendant negligently (carelessly) damaged the plaintiff's property. Less often, the plaintiff claims that the defendant intentionally damaged his or her belongings.

Negligence

A technical definition of negligence could—and does—fill entire law texts. Here's the short version: If your property is harmed as a result of another person's conduct, and that person didn't act with reasonable care under the circumstances, you have a valid legal claim based on that person's negligence.

> **EXAMPLE:** Jake knows the brakes on his old Saab are in serious need of repair but does nothing about it. One night, when the car is parked on a hill, the brakes fail and the car rolls across the street and destroys Keija's persimmon tree. Keija sues Jake for $225, the reasonable value of the tree. Jake will lose because he did not act with reasonable care under the circumstances.

Negligence can also occur when a person with a duty or responsibility to act fails to do so. For example, an electrician who promises and then fails to check the wiring in a room where you tell him you saw some frightening sparks would be negligent.

Another obvious situation involving negligence would be one where a car or bus swerves into your traffic lane and sideswipes your fender. The driver of the offending vehicle has a duty to operate the car in such a way as not to damage other cars. By swerving into your lane, it is extremely likely that he has failed to do so.

On the other hand, a situation in which negligence could be difficult to show would involve your neighbor's tree that falls on your car while it is properly parked in your driveway. Here you have to be ready to prove that the tree was in a weakened condition for some reason (such as age, disease, or a bad root system), and the neighbor knew about it but was negligent in failing to do something about it. If the tree looked to be in good health, your neighbor probably wasn't negligent, and had no reason to remove it or prop it up.

Here are some additional examples in which a person or business failed to act with reasonable care and as a result was negligent:

- While playing with his kids in his small backyard, Kevin hits a ball over the fence, smashing a neighbor's window.
- While upgrading Eddie's computer, Bill carelessly installs the wrong chip, which crashes Eddie's hard drive and ruins the computer.
- RapidMail Inc., a local courier service, loses several time-sensitive deliveries and fails to notify the sender of the problem.

Negligence exists where more than one person is responsible for the damages you suffer—for example, if two coworkers break your vase while playing keepaway. When dealing with a situation in which more than one person may have contributed to your loss, sue them all.

> **EXAMPLE 1:** Sandy comes home from work one day to find her new fence knocked over and Fred's Chevy Blazer in the middle of her herb garden. Fred admits his vehicle knocked over the fence when his brakes failed. To Sandy, this may at first seem like a simple case against Fred. But what if Fred had just picked up his car from Atomic Auto Repair, where he had his brakes worked on? Fred's liability may be minimal if Atomic is only 50 feet away and Fred just left the shop with the assurance that the brakes were fixed. Or, it may be extensive if Atomic is located across town and at the last two stop signs Fred's brakes acted "funny" but he continued to drive anyway. Although Sandy may not know all these details, if she learns that Fred recently had his brakes worked on, she would be well advised to sue both Fred and Atomic and let the judge sort out who is more at fault.

> **EXAMPLE 2:** Now suppose that Fred's brakes are fine, but he claims he was rear-ended at the stop sign by Dana, whose pickup truck pushed his vehicle through Sandy's fence. Again, Fred's liability may be minimal (Dana was drunk and speeding), or it may be extensive (Fred ran a stop sign while turning and was rear-ended by Dana, who had the right of way). Again, Sandy would be wise to sue both parties and let the judge sort out who was more at fault.

To help you determine whether you have a good case based on someone else's negligence, answer the following questions:

- Did the person whose act (or failure to act) damaged your property behave in a reasonable way? Or to put it another way, would you have behaved differently if you were in that person's shoes?

- Was your own conduct a significant cause of the injury?

If the person who damaged your property behaved in an unreasonable way (ran a red light when drunk) and you were acting sensibly (driving at 30 mph in the proper lane), you probably have a good case. If you were a little at fault (slightly negligent) but the other fellow was much more at fault (very negligent), you can probably still recover most of your losses, because most courts (but not all, so check the law in your state) follow a legal doctrine called comparative negligence. This involves subtracting the percentage of your negligence from 100% to find out how legally responsible the other party is. Thus, if a judge finds that one person (drunk and speeding) was 80% at fault, and the other (slightly inattentive) was 20% at fault, the slightly inattentive party can recover 80% of his or her loss.

RESOURCE

Where to get more information about negligence. It's a good idea to get more details of negligence theory by doing some research online (see Chapter 25 for information on legal research). Or, you can go to your nearest law library and review legal text on torts (wrongful acts or injuries). The law librarian will be happy to help you find a good resource.

Intentional Acts

Not all damage is the result of an accident. You also have the right to recover money if someone intentionally damages your personal property (which includes all property other than real estate).

EXAMPLE: Basil and Shirley are neighbors who can't stand the sight of each other, despite, or perhaps because of, the fact that both are prize-winning rose growers. When Basil took first place in the local exotic rose contest, Shirley was angry, frustrated, and jealous. She left her hose running on purpose and drowned Basil's roses. By bringing a small claims case, Basil should be able to recover the value of his rose bushes from Shirley. He might even get some money for emotional distress, although it's unlikely (see below).

In theory, at least, it may be possible to recover punitive damages—money given to you solely for the purpose of punishing the other person—if your property is damaged by the malicious conduct of someone else. However, in part because public sentiment is running strongly against punitive damage awards, they are seldom awarded in small claims court.

 RELATED TOPIC
More material concerning property damage. To determine how much to sue for, see Chapter 4.

Personal Injury (and Mental Distress) Cases

Most personal injury cases are based on a claim that someone has been negligent (careless), and a few are based on claims of intentional injury. The legal theories involved are the same as those set out in the section just above. To prevail, you must show that your injury was caused by someone's negligent or intentional behavior (unless your injury was caused by a defective product, in which case a different legal doctrine applies—see "Defective Product Cases," below).

CAUTION
Check your state's rules. Remember, in some states you cannot file a personal injury case in small claims court, even if the amount of damages is less than the maximum.

Start by understanding that most personal injury cases involve amounts of money that are clearly over the small claims maximum and should therefore be pursued in formal court. However, occasionally a minor personal injury case will be appropriate for small claims.

EXAMPLE 1: Jenny and Karen are playing softball in a picnic area of a park, where many families are enjoying their lunches in the sun. Jenny, never a star fielder, misses a batted ball that hits seven-year-old Willie in the face and chips his tooth. With the help of his parents, Willie sues Jenny and Karen for the $2,000 it will cost to repair his tooth. Jenny and Karen claim they were just playing a game and shouldn't be held liable. How will a judge decide this case? Almost surely in favor of Willie, who was eating lunch in a picnic area where he had a right to be. By contrast, Jenny and Karen almost surely were careless (negligent). Why? Because as a society, we have decided that picnic areas are for picnickers—not ballplayers— and since Jenny and Karen's game was inappropriate and dangerous to others, they are going to have to pay for their negligence.

EXAMPLE 2: Now, assume that Jenny and Karen move over to a nearby ball field. Their skills haven't improved and Jenny again misses the ball. And again it hits poor Willie—who has escaped his parents and wandered onto the field unobserved—in the mouth. Are Jenny and Karen still liable to pay to fix Willie's tooth? Probably not. Jenny and Karen took reasonable precautions to avoid hitting picnickers by playing on the ball field. Although they may have a responsibility to get little Willie off the field if they spot him, they are probably not legally responsible—that is, negligent—in a situation where he wanders onto the field unnoticed.

TIP
Consider not only your loss but also whether the other party acted reasonably under the circumstances. Before you sue someone for an injury, consider whether it was really caused by negligence. If so, the person is legally liable to make your loss good. If not (you trip and fall down a perfectly safe set of stairs), you have no right to recover, no matter how serious your injury (again, there's one major exception to the rule that you must demonstrate the other side's negligence—when you are injured by a defective product). If in doubt, go ahead and sue, but be prepared to deal with the negligence question as well as prove the extent of your injury. In Chapters 14 and 15 you'll find some practical advice on how to prove your case.

As discussed in more detail in Chapter 4, you do not have to suffer a physical injury to recover in court based on someone else's negligent or intentionally harmful behavior. Intentional or negligent infliction of mental distress are lawsuits that can be based on nonphysical injuries.

> **EXAMPLE:** Suppose your landlord enters your apartment without notice, permission, or good legal reason. You make it clear that this behavior is highly upsetting and ask her to cease invading your privacy. She nevertheless persists in entering your apartment with no good reason, causing you to become genuinely upset and anxious. You file a small claims case based on the intentional infliction of mental distress. Assuming you can convince the judge that you were truly and seriously upset, your chances of winning are good.

Obviously, not every act of another person that upsets you merits a lawsuit. Generally, to support a court case, the other person's behavior must:

- be negligent, violate a law, be outrageous, be intended to cause you harm, or be done in reckless disregard of whether it will cause you harm, and
- cause you emotional distress that is serious (for a negligence case) or severe (for a case where you claim the person's actions were intentional).

This second element is sometimes the hardest to prove in a mental distress case. Proving that you suffered emotional harm can be difficult and often more expensive than a small claims case would warrant. But if you have seen a doctor or therapist and you can get a written statement that you've suffered emotional distress, you could use that for evidence. Of course, your own testimony will probably be your primary form of proof.

RESOURCE
More information on personal injury. See the Accidents and Injuries section of Nolo.com for dozens of free articles on personal injury, from proving liability to hiring a personal injury lawyer. Nolo also publishes a book on the subject: *How to Win Your Personal Injury Claim*, by Joseph Matthews.

One area in which the number of small claims cases is growing involves sexual harassment in the workplace, which is illegal under both federal and state law. Small claims court is a particularly helpful option for people having trouble finding an attorney because their cases will be hard to prove or not worth much in damages. Before going to court, you must file a formal complaint, with either the federal Equal Employment Opportunity Commission (EEOC) or your state's equivalent. Wherever you file, your object before going to small claims court is to get a "right to sue" letter, meaning that the agency will not pursue the matter on its own—a likely outcome, given that these agencies get numerous complaints. Once you've got that letter, you can proceed to court.

RESOURCE

More information on sexual harassment. See the website of the U.S. Equal Employment Opportunity Commission (www.eeoc.gov) for information on laws prohibiting sexual harassment and filing a claim. Nolo's Employment Law section also includes useful articles on the subject.

Defective Product Cases

If your vacuum cleaner, hair dryer, steam iron, lawn mower, or other product malfunctions and you are injured as a result, you are entitled to recover from the manufacturer or other defendant (usually the person you bought or rented the product from) without proving that the defendant was negligent.

When an injury is serious, product liability cases are always filed in formal court. Now and then, however, a defective product will cause a more minor injury, in which case a small claims court lawsuit may be appropriate. It's best to sue both the manufacturer and seller of the defective product. Be prepared to prove:

- the product really did malfunction
- you were using the product as the manufacturer or seller intended or as they should have foreseen, and
- you were injured as a result.

Breach of Warranty Cases

> **RELATED TOPIC**
> **Car warranties.** Chapter 17 discusses warranties as they apply to problems with new and used cars.

In simplest terms, a warranty is a promise by the manufacturer or seller of a product that the product is of a certain quality or that they will repair the product for a stated period of time. The manufacturer or seller is legally obligated to live up to its promise if the product turns out to have a defect that's covered by the warranty. Warranty law is extremely confusing, even to lawyers. A principal reason for this is that three separate warranty laws can apply to the retail sale of consumer goods. The unhappy result is that, short of presenting you with a major legal treatise, it's impossible to thoroughly explain warranty law. The best I can do in this short space is to review the basic rules.

Types of Warranties

There are a number of different types of warranties that might apply to your defective product.

Express Written Warranty

If a new or used consumer product comes with an express written warranty, you have the right to rely on what it says. The express warranty may be the seller's written description of the product that you relied on when deciding to purchase it (for example, a promise that a car is defect free). Or, the express warranty may be the manufacturer's or retailer's written promise to maintain the performance of the product (for example, a promise to repair or replace defective parts for a stated period).

Express Oral Warranty

If a seller makes an oral statement describing a product's features (for example, "these tires will last at least 25,000 miles" or "this car is in running condition") or what it will do ("it will work for two years"), and you rely

on the statement in deciding to purchase the product, the oral statement is a warranty that you have the right to rely on. It is important to understand that this is true even though a more limited written warranty printed on the package states there are no other warranties. You must be able to prove that the seller made the oral statement; if you can't, the written warranty and its limitations may be effective.

Warranty Law: Where Does It Come From?

The Magnuson-Moss Warranty Federal Trade Commission Improvement Act (15 U.S.C. § 2302) is a federal law that applies in every state. In addition, every state has a commercial code, which includes similar laws regulating retail sales and warranty protections for consumers. Some states have enacted separate consumer protection and warranty laws that go beyond the Magnuson-Moss Act and these commercial codes. For example, in California, a warranty or guarantee is still good even if the buyer doesn't fill out and return the manufacturer's form (Cal. Com. Code § 2801), and in Kansas an implied warranty exists even for goods sold "as is," unless the consumer has knowledge of the exact defects in the merchandise (Kan. Stat. Ann. § 50-639). To find out about your state's warranty laws, search your state statutes for "commercial code," "consumer protection," or "warranty" (see Chapter 25 for more on how to do this), or get in touch with your state consumer protection agency.

Implied Warranty

In most retail sales of consumer products, an implied warranty exists stating that the product is fit for the ordinary purposes for which it is used (for example, that a lawn mower will cut grass, a tire will hold air, and a calculator will add and subtract). This warranty exists in addition to any express written and oral warranties to maintain the product's performance. This applies even if there is a statement (often called a "warranty disclaimer") printed on the product or packaging saying no warranties exist beyond the express written warranty, or that no warranty exists at all, or that all implied warranties are specifically disclaimed.

When a Breach of Warranty Occurs

If you believe any warranty has been breached—for example, a computer with a one-year warranty on parts and labor breaks the month after the purchase—you should notify the seller and manufacturer in writing, keeping copies of both letters. Give them a reasonable chance to make necessary repairs or replace the defective product. Thirty days to accomplish this is usually considered reasonable. If they fail to do so, it's time to think about filing in small claims court.

In considering whether and how to pursue a breach of warranty case, realize that small claims court judges tend to evaluate warranty disputes based on their own broad view of what is fair under the circumstances. In other words, if you purchase goods that are clearly defective or do not accomplish the task the seller claimed they would accomplish (either in an advertisement or a personal statement to you), and you have made and documented a good faith effort to give the seller or manufacturer a chance to either fix or replace the goods or refund your money, your chances of winning are excellent—as long as you can prove:

- the warranty existed in the first place
- the defect is "substantial" (for example, a computer screen that won't light up would be substantial, but a loose letter on the keyboard would not be), and
- you did not cause the defect by misusing the product.

However, realize that proving the existence of a warranty can be difficult when the promises were made orally and the other party will likely deny they were ever made.

> EXAMPLE: Alan purchases a computer and some expensive accounting software from ABC Computer. He thoroughly explains his specialized bookkeeping needs to the salesperson and is assured that the computer and software will do the job. The computer contains a written warranty against defects in parts and labor for 90 days. The warranty statement says that all implied warranties are disclaimed. The software contains no written warranty statement. It is apparent to Alan after a couple of days' work that the software simply is not sophisticated enough to meet the bookkeeping needs he had explained to the salesperson and that the salesperson didn't know what he was talking about when he said it was "perfect for the job."

Two days later the computer has a major crash. Alan calls ABC and asks for the computer to be fixed or replaced and for his money back on the software. When ABC ignores him, Alan sues in small claims court. Alan should have no problem recovering for the price of the computer—it failed within the written warranty period. But the software raises a tougher problem. Alan is claiming a breach of an express oral warranty (the salesperson's statement that the software would meet his needs), and a breach of the implied warranty of general fitness or merchantability. To succeed on the first claim, he must prove that the salesperson did in fact assure him that the software was right for his needs, which may be difficult. Proving the second claim will be even harder, however, because Alan must somehow prove that the software falls below the reasonable standard for sophisticated small business accounting packages. ABC is likely to counter Alan's claim with evidence that the software is in wide use and is generally considered to be adequate to accomplish most accounting tasks. In short, Alan would be smart to focus on trying to prove that in making his decision to purchase the software, he relied on the salesperson's oral statements that the software would meet his specific bookkeeping needs.

How should he do this? If Alan gave the salesperson a written specification detailing his accounting needs and still has a copy, he should show it to the judge. Even better, if he has a witness who heard the salesperson's overly optimistic promises, he should ask this person to testify in court or at least write a letter stating what happened. Unfortunately, if Alan has no convincing evidence as to the salesman's statements, the small claims hearing is likely to come down to his word against the salesperson's, with the judge left to decide who appears to be telling the truth.

Professional Malpractice Cases

An increasing number of small claims cases are being filed against doctors, lawyers, accountants, and other professionals. The main reason is that it can be difficult or impossible to get lawyers to represent you in a formal court action. As a result, the injured person must decide to either file without a lawyer in formal court (that is, a regular state court other than small claims court), or scale down the dollar amount of the claim to fit into small claims court.

To succeed with a malpractice claim, you must establish all of the following facts:

- **Duty.** The lawyer, doctor, dentist, or other professional owed you a duty of care. This is automatic as long as you were a patient or a client.
- **Carelessness.** The professional failed to use at least ordinary professional skills in carrying out the task (unless the person claimed to be a specialist, in which case the standard is higher). This one can be tougher to prove, because unless the mistake is breathtakingly obvious, you'll normally need to get the opinion of one or more other professionals (experts) that your professional screwed up. In theory, you can do this via a letter, but since the professional you are suing will almost surely be in court denying all wrongdoing, it is far better to have your expert witness testify in person.
- **Causation.** The professional's carelessness directly caused the harm or injury you suffered. For most types of malpractice, showing that the professional caused your injury isn't a problem (if a dentist stuck a drill through your cheek, for example). But in the legal field, the causation issue can be tricky. That's because you typically will need to show not only that the professional's mistake caused you to lose but also that you would have won if no mistake had been made. In other words, you need to convince the judge your underlying lawsuit was a winner.
- **Damages.** The harm you suffered at the hands of the professional resulted in actual economic loss to you.

EXAMPLE: You consult a lawyer about an injury you suffered when you tripped and fell at a store. The lawyer agrees to file a lawsuit on your behalf but forgets to do so before the two-year statute of limitations runs out. Several malpractice lawyers you consult won't represent you in suing the incompetent lawyer because your injuries were fairly minor and they aren't sure that even if malpractice is established, you will be able to prove that you would have won your case against the store. (In other words, they believe you may not have been harmed by your lawyer's mistake in failing to file your case on time because your case wasn't so great in the first place.) You sue your lawyer in small claims court. His failure to file your case on time is clearly an act of carelessness (a lawyer using

ordinary legal skills would have filed on time), but to win you'll also have to show that your lawyer's careless act resulted in monetary harm to you. This means convincing the judge that, in fact, your case against the store was a winner and that your injuries were serious enough to qualify for at least the amount of money you are requesting.

RESOURCE

Further reading on malpractice cases. *Represent Yourself in Court: How to Prepare & Try a Winning Case,* by Paul Bergman and Sara Berman (Nolo), explains how to bring a malpractice case in formal court.

Nuisance Cases

In legal theory, what's called a private nuisance occurs whenever someone prevents or disturbs your use or enjoyment of your property. For example, if your neighbor lets his dog bark all night, preventing you from sleeping, that's a private nuisance. If the barking persists and causes you real discomfort after you ask that the dog be kept quiet, you can sue.

To successfully sue someone for causing a private nuisance, you must prove that:

- you own, rent, or lease property
- the defendant created or maintained a condition that was
 - harmful to your health
 - indecent or offensive, or
 - obstructed your free use of your property
- you did not consent to the person's conduct
- the person's conduct interfered with your use or enjoyment of your property
- the conduct would be reasonably annoying or disturbing to an ordinary person
- you were, in fact, harmed (for example, your sleep was disturbed) by the person's conduct, and
- the seriousness of the harm outweighs the public benefit of the conduct.

A public nuisance, by contrast, means that someone is acting in a way that causes a group of people to suffer a health or safety hazard or lose the peaceful enjoyment of their property. For example, lots of noisy airplanes suddenly begin flying low over a residential area, or a chemical plant lets toxic fumes drift over a neighboring property. Public nuisance suits are often initiated by groups of individuals who all file small claims suits at more or less the same time.

To successfully sue a person or group of people for creating a public nuisance, you must prove all the facts listed above relating to private nuisance and also that:

- the condition affected a substantial number of people at the same time
- any social usefulness of the offending conduct is outweighed by the seriousness of the harm, and
- the harm you suffered was different from the harm suffered by the general public (for example, if a chemical plant's fumes are noticeable from the nearby freeway but ashes from the plant's smokestack fall into your swimming pool).

One fairly common example of this phenomenon involves the filing of multiple small claims lawsuits against drug-selling neighbors or their landlords. (See Chapter 20 for more about these types of cases.)

TIP

Try mediation before filing a lawsuit against a neighbor. It is very difficult to put a dollar value on lawsuits against neighbors for antisocial acts, no matter how annoying. In addition, filing suit usually makes long-term relationships worse. For these reasons, disputing neighbors should always try mediation before turning to small claims court. Some local law enforcement agencies provide mediation services for neighborhood disputes. (See Chapter 6 for more on mediation.)

Can You Collect Your Money If You Win?

This is the shortest chapter in the book but one of the most important. It asks you to focus on a very simple question: If I win my small claims case, can I collect the judgment (that is, the decision given by the court)? You may be surprised to learn you don't automatically receive the money when you win a judgment. If the defendant doesn't voluntarily pay, you'll have to use additional legal procedures to collect.

Collecting from solvent individuals or businesses isn't usually a problem, because most will routinely pay any judgments entered against them. If they don't, there are a number of legal ways you can force them to do so. But unfortunately, a goodly number of people and businesses sued in small claims court are either broke (lawyers say "judgment-proof") or so adept at hiding their assets that collecting your winnings may prove impossible. And if a debtor won't pay voluntarily, collecting your judgment can be difficult and require you to spend more money, without knowing if you'll be able to collect enough from the defendant to repay these collection expenses. For example, debtor protection laws prevent you from seizing certain types of property, including the food from the debtor's table, the clothing from the closet, the TV from the living room, or even, in most states, the car from the driveway.

What should these facts mean to you? A significant percentage of people who are not homeless or even "poor" are nevertheless "judgment-proof." You can sue and get judgments against these defendants, but you won't be able to collect a dime.

To investigate whether you might have trouble collecting from the debtor, start by finding out whether the defendant has a job. If so, that's good news—when someone fails to pay a judgment voluntarily, the easiest way to collect is to garnish the person's wages. But usually you can't garnish a welfare, Social Security, unemployment, pension, or disability check. So if the person's income is from one of these sources, red flags should definitely be flying unless you can locate other nonexempt assets.

Wage Garnishments in a Nutshell

Under federal law and in most states, a creditor with a judgment can't take more than 25% of a judgment debtor's net earnings, or the amount by which the debtor's net earnings exceed 30 times the federal minimum wage, whichever is less. (Net earnings are total earnings minus all mandatory deductions for such items as withheld income taxes and unemployment tax.)

The sheriff or marshal's office in your area usually can supply you with your state's rules. If you're a defendant and there's a judgment against you, strategies to cope with wage garnishment are covered in *Solve Your Money Troubles: Strategies to Get Out of Debt and Stay That Way,* by Amy Loftsgordon and Cara O'Neill (Nolo).

What about other collection sources? Can't a judgment be collected from assets other than wages? Sure. Real estate, bank accounts, stocks and bonds, and motor vehicles are other common collection sources. And if you've sued a business, you can often collect by ordering the sheriff or marshal to take the amount of the judgment right out of the debtor's cash register.

But remember, as mentioned above, many types of personal property are legally exempt from attachment. Most states exempt household goods and appliances necessary for everyday living (such as a stove, refrigerator, dishes, or TV); sentimental items and family keepsakes (such as photos, jewelry, or works of art); and tools or machinery the debtor uses to make a living (such as a computer, professional library, or power saw). A debtor's retirement account, life insurance, pension, and certain types of savings accounts are also protected. Even more significant in terms of assets, a portion or all of the equity in a debtor's home is exempt.

What does all this boil down to? Simply this. Before you file your small claims court case, make sure that at least one of the following is true:

- The person or business you wish to sue is solvent and likely to pay a court judgment voluntarily.

- The person is broke now but is very likely to be solvent in the future. Judgments in most states can be collected for five to 20 years (this period can usually be renewed) and earn interest until they are paid. In short, if you are willing to take a chance that a destitute college student will eventually get a job, win the lottery, inherit money, win a personal injury lawsuit, or otherwise become solvent sometime in the next few years, go ahead and sue. You'll have to sit on the judgment for awhile, but eventually it should be collectible.

- You can identify other assets—not protected by debtor exemption laws—that you can levy on, such as a bank account or real property (preferably other than the place where the person lives).

- If the defendant is a business, you can identify a readily available cash source you can collect from—the best source is a cash register. Another good one is a valuable piece of equipment or machinery the judgment debtor owns free and clear, for which you can get an order to have the property sold to pay off your judgment.

- Your lawsuit is based on a motor vehicle accident. In some states, a nonpaying defendant can have his or her license suspended for a period of time. Just the threat of a license suspension can causes some debtors to pay. (See Chapter 24.)

> **CAUTION**
> **Beware of bankruptcy.** If a person or a business declares a straight bankruptcy (under Chapter 7 of the federal Bankruptcy Act) and lists you as a creditor, your right to recover a small claims court judgment outside the bankruptcy is cut off, along with most other debts. There are, however, exceptions to this general rule, such as if your claim arose because you or your property were injured by the fraudulent or malicious behavior of the defendant. In this situation, your right to collect your judgment should survive the bankruptcy, but you may need to intervene in the bankruptcy proceeding. If you had security for the amount owed you on the judgment, as would typically be the case with a car loan, a mechanic's lien, or a real estate mortgage, you should still be able to recover the property that is the security, but the bankruptcy can cause a delay. For more information, see *How to File for Chapter 7 Bankruptcy*, by Cara O'Neil, and Albin Renauer (Nolo).

Now let's look at some situations where you are likely to have a problem collecting:

- The defendant has no job or prospect of getting one.
- You can't identify any property to use as a collection source (for example, your opponent has no real estate, valuable car, or investments).
- If a business is involved, it's a fly-by-night outfit with no permanent address or obvious collection source, such as a cash register or owned fixtures or equipment. (Remember, many businesses lease equipment or take out a secured loan to purchase it, which means you're out of luck.)
- A contractor you want to sue is unlicensed and hard to track down.

RELATED TOPIC

More information on collecting a judgment. In Chapter 24, we deal in detail with the mechanics of collecting after you get your judgment. If you still think that collection may pose a problem, please skip ahead and read that chapter before deciding to sue.

How Much Can You Sue For?

T he maximum amount for which you can sue—or be sued—in small claims court varies from state to state. For example, it's $15,000 in Minnesota, $2,500 in Kentucky, and $5,000 in Florida. You'll find the limits for other states in the appendix, but because these can change, you'll always want to check by calling your local small claims court clerk or checking your local court rules. With some exceptions, small claims courts do not hear cases unless they are for money damages. Thus, you can't use small claims court to get a divorce, stop the city from cutting down your favorite oak tree, change your name, or do many of the thousands of other things that require a solution other than one side paying money to the other.

One exception to the "money only" rule involves equitable relief. This is legalspeak for a court's power to order a person or business to do something specific, such as return a uniquely valuable piece of property or change a contract that contains an obvious mistake. These remedies are discussed in "Equitable Relief (or, Money Can't Always Solve the Problem)," below.

Another exception to the money-only rule involves evictions. In some states, a landlord can use small claims court to evict tenants in certain situations. (See Chapter 20 and the appendix for more information.)

Cutting Your Claim to Fit the Limit

It is legal to reduce a claim that is too large so that it will fit into small claims court. Thus, you could take a $5,300 debt and bring it into small claims court in North Carolina (where the dollar limit is $5,000) asking for only $5,000. (Costs for filing and serving papers are always recoverable in addition to the dollar limit. See "Recovering Costs" in Chapter 15.) But if you do this, you forever waive the $300 difference between $5,000 and $5,300. In legal parlance, this is called "waiving the excess." Why might you want to do this? Because the alternative to small claims court involves filing your suit in formal court with dozens of complicated rules and the likelihood that you'll need to hire a lawyer, who will surely charge considerably more than $300 to represent you.

It is possible to represent yourself in formal court, but doing so requires a good bit of homework. If you do plan to go it alone, check out *Represent Yourself in Court: How to Prepare & Try a Winning Case,* by Paul Bergman and Sara Berman (Nolo).

> **TIP**
> **Check out the court just above small claims.** In most states, there are several levels of courts with different monetary limits. A case that doesn't fit into small claims court may be appropriately filed in an intermediate level court (possibly called circuit, district, or county court, depending on the state). In recent years, these courts typically hear cases worth between $10,000 and $25,000.

Calculating the Amount of Your Claim

Usually, determining the amount to sue for is fairly easy. But for some types of cases it can be a little tricky. Before we get to the tricky part, let's start with a basic rule: When in doubt, always estimate your damages a little on the high side. Why? Because the court has the power to award you less than you request, but can't give you more, even if the judge feels that you are entitled to it. But don't go overboard—if you sue for $2,500 on a $1,000 claim, you are likely to spur your opponent to furious opposition, ruin any chance for an out-of-court compromise, and lose the respect of the judge.

> **TIP**
> **Ask to amend your claim if you belatedly discover you should have requested more.** If you find yourself in court and realize you have asked for too little, ask the judge to allow you to amend your claim on the spot. Some judges will do this and, at the same time, offer the defendant extra time to prepare to defend against the higher claim. Other judges will allow you to dismiss your original case and start over, which is fine as long as your time to file hasn't run out. (See Chapter 5.)

Contract Cases

To arrive at the exact figure to sue for in contract cases, compute the difference between the amount you were supposed to receive under the contract and what you actually received. For example, if Jeannie Goodday agrees to pay Homer Brightspot $4,200 to paint her house but then pays him only $3,000, Homer has a claim for $1,200, plus the cost of filing suit and serving Jeannie with the papers. (Court costs that can be added to your judgment are discussed in more detail in Chapter 15.) The fact that Jeannie and Homer made their agreement orally does not bar Homer from suing. As discussed in

Chapter 2, oral contracts are generally legal as long as they can be carried out in a year and don't involve the sale of real estate, or goods (personal property) worth $500 or more. (Also see Chapter 22 for a discussion of the relatively relaxed written contract requirements for the sale of goods.)

⏣ **TIP**

Write it down. Because people who are embroiled in a dispute almost always remember the details of any oral contract differently, oral contracts can be hard to prove in court. This is one of several good reasons why it is always wise to reduce agreements to writing, even if only by use of an informal note or letter agreement dated and signed by both parties.

Unfortunately, some claims based on breach of contract are harder to reduce to a dollar amount. This is often due to a legal doctrine known as mitigation of damages. Don't let the fancy term throw you. Mitigation of damages means that the person bringing suit for breach of contract must take all reasonable steps to limit the amount of damages he or she suffers.

> **EXAMPLE:** Tillie Tenant moves out three months before the end of her lease (remember, a lease is a contract). Her monthly rent is $950. Can Larry Landlord recover the full $2,850 ($950 x 3 months) from Tillie in small claims court? Maybe not. In many states, Larry must try to limit (or mitigate) his damages by taking reasonable steps to attempt to find a new tenant. If Larry can immediately rerent the apartment to someone else for $950 or more per month, he has suffered little or no damage (he has fulfilled his responsibility to "mitigate damages"). More typically, it might take Larry several weeks or months (unless he had plenty of advance notice, or Tillie herself found a new tenant) to find a suitable new tenant. For example, if it took Larry one month and $75 worth of newspaper ads, he could recover approximately $1,025 (one month's rent + $75) from Tillie, assuming the judge found that Larry had taken reasonable steps to find the new tenant.

The mitigation of damages concept applies to most contracts in which the person damaged has the opportunity to take reasonable steps to limit his or her losses. In the earlier house painting example, if Jeannie Goodday had agreed to pay Homer Brightspot $300 per day for seven days to paint her house and then had canceled after the first day, Homer would be

eligible to sue her for the remaining $1,800, based on Jeannie's violation of the contract. However, in court, Homer likely would be asked whether he had earned any other money during the six days. If he had, it would be subtracted from the $1,800. But what if Homer refused other work and slept in his hammock all week? If Jeannie could show that he had turned down other jobs or had refused to make reasonable efforts to seek available work, the judge would likely consider this a failure to mitigate damages and reduce Homer's recovery accordingly.

Loan Contracts

How much should you sue for if you lent money to a person who promised to repay it but failed to do so? Bring suit for the total you are currently owed, including any unpaid interest (assuming it doesn't result in your claim exceeding the small claims maximum). People sometimes make the mistake of suing for the exact amount of the debt, thinking they could have the judge add the interest when they got to court. This normally can't be done—in most states, the judge doesn't have the power to make an award larger than the amount you request.

> **TIP**
>
> **Don't invent interest if none was provided as part of the loan.** As a general rule, you can only recover interest when it is called for in a written or oral contract. For example, if you loaned a friend $1,000 but never mentioned interest, you can sue only for the return of the $1,000.

> **CAUTION**
>
> **Understand special rules for installment loans.** If you are owed money under the terms of a promissory note (contract) that calls for repayment to be made in installments, you are normally only entitled to recover the amount of the payments that have already been missed (that is, what you are currently owed) and not those that aren't yet due. And this is true even if you are sure future installments will never be paid. But there is an important exception to this rule: You can sue for the entire loan amount plus any interest your contract calls for if your installment contract contains what lawyers call an acceleration clause—language that states that the entire amount of the loan is immediately due if one payment is missed.

Bad Checks

In some situations, a statute (law) establishes your right to receive extra compensation, over and above the amount of the financial loss. The most common of these involves a bad check (or a check on which the writer stops payment in bad faith).

The majority of states have bad check laws, which allow you to recover the amount of the check plus a penalty of two or three times the amount of the check if the person giving it to you does not make it good within the time period allowed by the statute—usually within 30 days of your written demand to do so. In some states, this law is mandatory—the judge must award the penalty.

In addition, there are usually some minimum and maximum penalties allowed:

- You can usually sue for some minimum amount in damages, no matter how small the bad check. Thus, in California, which has a minimum penalty of $100, if you get a $25 bad check, you can sue for $125.
- There is usually a top limit on the damages you can sue for, no matter how large the check. Thus, in California, where the maximum penalty is $1,500, for a $600 bad check, the most you can sue for is $2,100 (the amount of the check plus the $1,500 maximum).

> **TIP**
>
> **Don't forget to demand payment before you sue.** If someone gives you a bum check or stops payment on a check and you want to try to collect the triple damages, start by sending a letter by certified mail demanding payment of the amount of the bad check, plus any applicable service charge and your mailing costs. Wait at least 30 days before filing suit to give the check writer time to pay.

> **RESOURCE**
>
> **Further reading.** *Solve Your Money Troubles: Strategies to Get Out of Debt and Stay That Way,* by Amy Loftsgordon and Cara O'Neill (Nolo), contains the details of every state's bad check law.

TIP

Watch your back if you stop payment on a check. If you write a check and then stop payment because you believe the service or goods you purchased were substandard (or never provided), write a letter to the other party stating in detail why you were dissatisfied. If you are later sued in small claims court, bring a copy of your letter to court and show it to the judge as part of your defense.

Property Damage Cases

When your property has been damaged by the negligent or intentional act of someone else, you usually have a right to recover the amount of money it would take to fix the damaged item.

> **EXAMPLE:** John Quickstop plows into Melissa Caretaker's new BMW, smashing the left rear fender. How much can Melissa recover? Melissa is entitled to recover the amount it would cost to fix, or if necessary, replace, the damaged part of her car if John won't pay voluntarily. Melissa should get several estimates from responsible body and fender shops and sue for the amount of the lowest one. (For more on proving car accident cases, see Chapter 19.)

There is, however, a big exception to this rule, which comes up when the cost of fixing the item exceeds its total value. You are not entitled to a new or better object than the one that was damaged—only to have your loss made good. Had Melissa been driving a ten-year-old car, the cost to fix the fender might have exceeded the value of the entire car. In this situation, she would be entitled to the value of the car, not what it would cost to repair it. In short, the most you can recover is the fair market value of a damaged item (the amount you could have sold it for) figured one minute before the damage occurred. From this amount, you have to subtract the item's scrap value, if any.

TIP

Give yourself the benefit of the doubt when putting a value on property. No one knows exactly how much any piece of used property is worth. Recognizing that reasonable minds can differ, it makes sense to place a fairly aggressive value on property that has been destroyed. But don't demand a ridiculous amount, or you'll likely offend the judge and perhaps even weaken your case.

EXAMPLE: Let's return to Melissa from our last example, assuming now that her BMW is ten years old. If several used car price guides indicated the car was worth $2,800 and it would cost $3,000 to repair the fender, she would be limited to $2,800 compensation, minus what the car could be sold for in its damaged state. If she could only sell the car for $800 for scrap, she would be entitled to $2,000. However, if Melissa had installed an expensive rebuilt engine a few weeks before the accident, she might legitimately argue that the car was worth $3,800. Assuming the judge agreed, Melissa would legally be entitled to recover the entire $3,000 to replace the fender, because the car is worth more than replacing the fender.

Unfortunately, knowing what something is worth and proving it are quite different. A car that you are sure is worth $4,000 may look like it's only worth $3,000 to someone else. In court, you will want to be prepared to show that your piece of property is worth every bit of the $4,000. The best way to do this is to get some estimates (opinions) from experts in the field (like a used car dealer if your car was totaled). One way to present this type of evidence is to have the expert come to court and testify, but in small claims court you can also have the expert prepare a written estimate, which you then present to the judge. Depending on the type of property involved, you may also want to check newspaper ads and the Internet for the prices asked for comparable goods and submit these to the judge. And of course, there may be other creative ways to establish the dollar amount of the damage you have suffered. For tips on proving the dollar amount of damage in particular types of cases, see Chapters 16–21.

! CAUTION

Replacement costs aren't relevant when figuring how much you are owed when property is destroyed. Many people insist on believing they can recover the cost of getting a replacement object when theirs has been totaled. As you should now understand, this isn't necessarily true. If Melissa's $1,200 car was totaled and she claimed she simply couldn't get another decent car for less than $2,000, she would still be limited to recovering $1,200.

Damage to Clothing Cases

Clothing is property, so why treat it separately here? First, because disputes involving clothing are extremely common in small claims court. Second and more important, judges seem to apply a logic to them that they apply to no other property damage cases. The reason for this is that clothing is personal to its owner and often has little or no value to anyone else, even though it may be in good condition. It follows that if a judge strictly applied the rules we just learned (that you are limited to recovering no more than the current market value of a damaged item), plaintiffs would often get little or no compensation. Recognizing this, most judges are willing to bend the rules a little to arrive at a value for damaged clothing that is based on the item's original cost and how long it had been worn.

When suing for damage to new or almost-new clothing, it follows that you should sue for the amount you paid. If the damaged item has already been worn for some time, sue for the percentage of its original cost that reflects how much of its useful life was used up when the damage occurred. For example, if your two-year-old suit that cost $900 new was destroyed, sue for $450 if you feel the suit would have lasted another two years.

To summarize, in clothing cases, most judges want answers to these questions:

- How much did the clothing cost originally?
- How much of its useful life had already passed at the time the damage occurred?
- Does the damaged item still have some value to the owner, or has it been ruined?

EXAMPLE 1: Wendy took her new $250 coat to Rudolph, a tailor, to have alterations made. Rudolph cut part of the back of the coat in the wrong place and ruined it. How much should Wendy sue for? The entire $250, because the coat was almost new. She could probably expect to recover close to this amount.

EXAMPLE 2: The same facts as in Example 1, but the coat was two years old and had been well worn, although it was still in good condition. Here, Wendy would be wise to sue for $175 and hope to recover between $100 and $150.

EXAMPLE 3: This time let's return Wendy's coat to its almost new condition but have Rudolph damage it only slightly. I would still advise Wendy to sue for the full $250. Whether she could recover that much would depend on the judge. Most would probably award her a little less on the theory that the coat retained some value. Wendy should argue that she didn't buy the coat expecting to not be able to wear it in public, and as far as she was concerned, the coat was ruined.

Personal Injury Cases

Because so much money is usually at stake, lawyers quickly take over the great majority of cases in which someone is injured. However, some small personal injury cases do end up in small claims court. Dog bite cases are one common example.

CAUTION
Some small claims courts don't allow personal injury lawsuits. Many states require that personal injury cases be filed in formal court. In other states, a small claims judge can award an injured party only the dollar amount of the person's out-of-pocket losses (doctors' bills, lost time from work), but doesn't have the power to award an additional amount to cover the injury victim's pain and suffering, no matter how legitimate. So before filing even a minor personal injury case in small claims court, be sure you check your local rules.

TIP
Try to settle or mediate your personal injury claims. If you are seriously injured, you'll almost always want to sue for more than the small claims maximum. But to gain a fair recovery, you may not need to sue at all. Many people successfully negotiate or mediate a satisfactory settlement with an insurance company. For information on how to do this, see *How to Win Your Personal Injury Claim*, by Joseph L. Matthews (Nolo).

To determine how much to sue for, add up the dollar amount of the following losses:

Out-of-pocket medical costs, including medical care providers	$_____
Loss of pay, or paid time off, for missing work	$_____
Pain and suffering	$_____
Damage to property	$_____
Total	$_____

Let's look at each of these categories in a little more detail.

Medical/hospital bills. The amount of your medical and hospital bills, including transportation to and from the doctor, is routinely recoverable as long as you have established that the person you are suing is at fault. However, if you are covered by health insurance and the insurance company has already paid your medical costs, you will find that your policy says that any money you recover for these costs must be turned over to the company. Often, insurance companies don't make much effort to keep track of, or recover, small claims court judgments, as the amounts of money involved don't make it worthwhile. Knowing this, many judges are reluctant to grant judgments for medical bills unless the individual can show he or she personally paid out of pocket for the treatment. But if you had uninsured expenses or deductible payments, by all means include them.

Loss of pay. Loss of pay or paid time off as a result of an injury is viewed in a similar way. Assume the cocker spaniel down the block lies in wait for you behind a hedge and grabs a piece of your derriere for breakfast, and as a result you miss a day of work getting yourself patched up. You are entitled to recover any lost pay, commissions, or vacation time. However, if your job offers unlimited paid sick time, and therefore you suffer no loss for missing work, you have nothing to recover.

Pain and suffering. The third area of recovery is for what is euphemistically called "pain and suffering." When you read about big dollar settlements, a good chunk of the recovery almost always falls into this category. No question, recovering from some injuries really is a painful, miserable ordeal for which compensation is reasonable. It is also true that in the hands of an aggressive lawyer, "pain and suffering" can become an excuse for an inflated claim.

Don't Count on Recovering Punitive Damages in Small Claims Court

Formal trial courts have the power to award extra damages (over and above out-of-pocket losses and pain and suffering) if an injury is caused by the malicious or willful misconduct (often a fraudulent or criminal act) of the defendant. When the defendant is wealthy, these damages—which are designed to punish the defendant—can run into the millions. About half the states do not allow punitive damages (sometimes called "exemplary damages") to be awarded in small claims. But even in those states where it is theoretically possible to receive punitive damages, small claims court's low dollar limit largely rules them out, except in a few instances where specific dollar amounts are established for bad checks or failure to return a tenant's security deposit on time (see Chapter 20). If you believe you have been injured by conduct wretched enough to support a claim for hefty punitive damages, see a lawyer.

But suppose that you have suffered a minor, but painful, injury and you do want to attempt to recover compensation for your discomfort in small claims court. How much should you ask for? There is no one right answer. When valuing a client's pain and suffering, a lawyer will typically sue for three to five times the amount of the out-of-pocket damages (medical bills and loss of work). Therefore, if you were out of pocket $500, you might wish to ask for $1,500, the overage being for "pain and suffering." To get this, you'll have to convince the judge that you have suffered real pain and inconvenience. The best way to do this is to present bills for medical treatment. If the judge concludes you suffered a real injury, he or she will be more likely to add an amount for "pain and suffering." This is why lawyers routinely encourage their clients to get as much medical attention as is reasonably possible.

EXAMPLE 1: Mary Tendertummy is drinking a bottle of pop when a mouse foot floats to the surface. She is immediately nauseated, loses her lunch, and goes to the doctor for medication. As a result, she incurs a medical bill of $150 and loses an afternoon's pay of an additional $150. She sues the soda

pop company for $900, claiming that the extra amount is to compensate her for pain and suffering. This may well be considered to be reasonable and, depending on the judge, she will probably recover most of this amount.

EXAMPLE 2: The same thing happens to Roy Toughguy. But instead of losing his lunch, he just tosses the soda pop away in disgust and goes back to work. A few weeks later he hears about Mary's recovery and decides to sue—after all, he could use $900. How much is Roy likely to recover? Probably not much more than the price of the soda pop—because he didn't see a doctor and wasn't too upset by the incident, the judge is likely to conclude he suffered little or no injury.

Property damage. Often a personal injury is accompanied by injury to property. Thus, a dog bite might also ruin your pants. If so, include the value of your damaged clothing when you determine how much to sue for.

Emotional or Mental Distress Cases

There are all sorts of ways we can cause one another real pain without even making physical contact, especially in increasingly crowded urban environments. For example, if Tim lives in the apartment above you and pounds on his floor (your ceiling) for an hour at 6:00 a.m. every day, he will probably quickly reduce you to a raving maniac. What can you do about it short of slashing his tires?

One remedy is for you to sue in small claims court based on the fact that Tim's actions constitute the intentional infliction of emotional distress. (You could also sue for causing a nuisance; see Chapter 2.) But how much should you sue for? Unfortunately, it's impossible to provide a formula. It depends on how obnoxious his behavior is, how long it has gone on, and how clearly you have asked him to cease it (this should be done several times in writing). And if this isn't vague enough, it will also depend greatly on the personality of the judge, who may be very skeptical of all neighbor disputes, thinking they don't belong in court in the first place. At the very least, you'll need to convince the judge you are an extremely reasonable person and your neighbor is a true boor before you will be eligible for any compensation.

One way to try to convince the judge you aren't a hypersensitive complainer is to sue for a reasonable amount. Thus, I would normally advise against suing for your state's small claims maximum, or anything close to it, except in the most extreme cases.

TIP
Choose mediation when neighbors are involved. As discussed in Chapter 6, the process of filing, preparing, and arguing a lawsuit tends to make both sides even madder than they were previously. And, of course, the losing side is likely to stay mad for a long time. This may be fine if you are suing a large company or someone you are never likely to interact with again, but given the high value most people place on good relations with neighbors, it's usually best to at least try to settle your case through mediation before going to court.

Malpractice Cases

In theory, most malpractice cases are worth far more than can be sued for in small claims court. But because legal rules (what it takes to prove liability, for example) are usually tilted to favor professionals and these cases are expensive to bring, it's often hard to find a lawyer to represent you on a contingency-fee basis (meaning that the lawyer doesn't charge you up front but takes a percentage of the settlement). That means that quite a few malpractice cases end up being scaled down to fit into small claims court.

For most types of malpractice you need to prove that the doctor's malpractice harmed you financially as well as physically, and then you can sue for that amount (assuming it is below the small claims court maximum). Thus, if a doctor negligently misdiagnosed an illness and as a result you experienced serious medical problems, you would present the court with:

- all medical, hospital, and drug bills you paid that occurred after the misdiagnosis that you claim could have been avoided
- the opinion of a second doctor that the first doctor's handling of your problem did not measure up to accepted medical standards (or, in plain language, that the first doctor screwed up)
- an estimate for your pain and suffering, and
- proof of loss of any pay or vacation time as a result of the misdiagnosis.

> ⚠ CAUTION
> **Special rules for legal malpractice.** As discussed in Chapter 2, if your suit is based on a lawyer's having failed to handle your case properly, you have to be able to prove not only that the lawyer was a bungler but that you would likely have won your original case if the lawyer had done a reasonably competent job. And you must also show that you would have won at least as much money as you are suing for in small claims court.

Equitable Relief (or, Money Can't Always Solve the Problem)

Many states allow judges to grant relief (provided you ask for it) in ways that do not involve the payment of money, if equity (fairness) demands it. In small claims court, equitable relief is usually limited to one or more of four categories: rescission, restitution, reformation, and specific performance. Let's translate these into English.

> ⚠ CAUTION
> **You may need to do more research.** If you think you may want to sue "in equity," you'll need to look up your state's small claims court law. (You'll find the citation for the law in the appendix; see Chapter 25 for tips on easy legal research.)

Rescission. This is a remedy that is used to wipe out a grossly unfair or fraudulent contract under any of the following conditions:

- it was based on a mistake as to an important fact
- it was induced by duress or undue influence, or
- one party simply didn't receive what was promised, through the fault of the other.

EXAMPLE: If a merchant sues you for failure to pay for aluminum siding, the quality of which you contend the merchant seriously misrepresented, you could ask that the contract be rescinded and that any money you paid be returned to you. Don't hesitate to ask for this remedy whenever you feel you have been unfairly treated in a contract dispute.

Restitution. This is an important remedy. It gives a judge the power to order that a particular piece of property be transferred to its original owner when fairness requires the contracting parties be restored to their original positions. It can be used in the common situation in which one person sells another a piece of property (say a motor scooter) and the other fails to pay. Instead of simply giving the seller a money judgment that might be hard to collect, the judge has the power to order the scooter restored to its original owner. If money has been paid under a contract that is rescinded, the judge can order it to be returned, plus damages. Thus, if a used car purchase was rescinded based on the fraud of the seller, the buyer could get a judgment for the amount paid for the car, plus money spent for repairs and alternate transportation.

Reformation. This remedy is somewhat unusual. It has to do with changing (reforming) a contract to meet the original intent of the parties in a situation where some term or condition the parties agreed to was left out or misstated and where fairness dictates the contract be reformed. Reformation is commonly used when an oral agreement is written down incorrectly.

> **EXAMPLE:** Arthur the Author and Peter the Publisher orally agree that Peter will publish Arthur's 200-page book. They then write a contract, inadvertently leaving out the number of pages. If Arthur shows up with a 3,000-page manuscript and demands that it be published in its entirety, a court would very likely "reform" the contract to include the 200-page provision, assuming the judge was convinced that it should have been included in the first place.

Specific performance. This is an important remedy that comes into play when a contract involving an unusual or one-of-a-kind object has not been carried out. For example, you enter into an agreement with someone to buy a unique antique jade ring for your mother's birthday that is exactly like the one she lost years before. If the seller refuses to go through with the deal, a court could cite the doctrine of specific performance to order that the ring be turned over to you. Specific performance will only be ordered in situations where the payment of money will not adequately compensate the person bringing suit.

> TIP
> **The small claims dollar maximum applies to cases involving equitable relief.** In filling out your court papers for a case in which you want one of the types of equitable relief discussed here, you are still required to indicate that the value of the item in question is under the small claims maximum. Thus, you might describe the nature of your claim as follows: "I want the delivery of my 'one-of-a-kind' antique jade ring, worth approximately $4,000, according to my contract with defendant."

Conditional judgments and equitable relief. In some states, judges have the power to issue conditional judgments in cases involving equitable relief. That is, they can order a party to perform, or stop, a certain act or else pay a money judgment. For example, you agree to sell your baby grand piano for $3,000. The buyer fails to pay, and you sue. The judge orders the buyer to either return the piano or fork over the $3,000. If the piano isn't returned within a short period of time (determined by the judge), then you can enforce the money judgment. (See Chapter 24.)

When Should You Sue?

E ach state's legislature sets up time limits within which lawsuits must be filed. These are called statutes of limitations. Time limits are different for different types of cases. If you wait too long, your right to sue will be barred by these statutes.

Why have a statute of limitations? Because unlike wine, lawsuits don't improve with age. Memories fade, witnesses die or move away, and once-clear details become blurred. In other words, disputes are best settled relatively soon after they develop.

Statutes of limitations are almost always at least one year, so if you file promptly, you should have little to worry about.

> CAUTION
> **Act fast for claims against a government agency.** To sue a city, county, state, or governmental agency (for example, a school district), you first must promptly file a claim with the people in charge (for example, the school board, county board of supervisors, city council). Once your claim is rejected—and it usually will be—you can file in small claims court. Often, your administrative claim must be filed within three to six months after your loss occurred, or you'll be out of luck.

Statute of Limitations

Following is a chart of statute of limitation periods for four of the most common types of lawsuits. But you will probably need to do further legal research to learn about time limits that might affect your specific situation. Even the time limits specified in the following chart can be affected by things like the "discovery rule"—see "How the Discovery Rule Works," below. Also, the time limits in the chart may not cover every situation. For example, claims involving medical malpractice, eviction, child or spousal support, fraud, product liability, consumer sales contracts, or faulty work by builders may all have different statutes of limitations. And some states distinguish between different types of property (usually real and personal property) when establishing statutes of limitations.

Statutes of Limitations

These statutes explain when (in years) you must sue for specific types of claims. However, some states have separate rules for particular situations or injuries. Carefully read your state's statutes, or consult an attorney, to learn the rules for your situation.

State and Statute	Contracts		Personal Injury	Property Damage
	Written	Oral		
Alabama Ala. Code § 6-2-30 et seq.	6	6	2	6
Alaska Alaska Stat. § 09.10.010 et seq.	3	3	2	2 for personal property; 6 for real property
Arizona Ariz. Rev. Stat. Ann. § 12-541 et seq.	6	3	2	2
Arkansas Ark. Code Ann. § 16-56-101 et seq.	5	3	3	3
California Cal. Civ. Proc. Code § 312 et seq.	4	2	2	3
Colorado Colo. Rev. Stat. § 13-80-1021 et seq.	3	3; 6 for short-term debt; 2 for tortious breach	2; 3 for motor vehicle injuries	2
Connecticut Conn. Gen. Stat. Ann. § 52-575 et seq.	6	3	2	2
Delaware Del. Code Ann. tit. 10, § 8101 et seq.	3	3	2	2
D.C. D.C. Code § 12-301 et seq.	3	3	3	3
Florida Fla. Stat. Ann. § 95.011 et seq.	5 (1 year in certain situations, see Fla. Stat. Ann. § 95.11)	4	4	4
Georgia Ga. Code Ann. § 9-3-20 et seq.	6	4	2	4
Hawaii Haw. Rev. Stat. § 657-1 et seq.	6	6	2	2
Idaho Idaho Code § 5-201 et seq.	5	4	2	3
Illinois 735 Ill. Comp. Stat. 5/13-201 et seq.	10	5	2	5
Indiana Ind. Code Ann. § 34-11-2-1 et seq.	10	6	2	2 for personal property; 6 for real property

Statutes of Limitations (continued)

State and Statute	Contracts		Personal Injury	Property Damage
	Written	Oral		
Iowa Iowa Code Ann. § 614.1 et seq.	10	5	2	5
Kansas Kan. Stat. Ann. § 60-501 et seq.	5	3	2	2
Kentucky Ky. Rev. Stat. Ann. § 413.080 et seq.	10	5	1	2 for personal property; 5 for real property
Louisiana* La. Civ. Code Art. 3492 et seq.	10	10	1	1 (real and personal property)
Maine Me. Rev. Stat. Ann. tit. 14, § 751 et seq.	6	6	6	6
Maryland Md. Code Ann. [Cts. & Jud. Proc.] § 5-101 et seq.	3	3	3	3
Massachusetts Mass. Gen. Laws ch. 260, § 1 et seq.	6	6	3	3
Michigan Mich. Comp. Laws § 600.5801 et seq.	6	6	3	3
Minnesota Minn. Stat. Ann. § 541.01 et seq.	6	6	2	6
Mississippi Miss. Code. Ann. § 15-1-1 et seq.	6	3	3	3
Missouri Mo. Rev. Stat. § 516.097 et seq.	10	5	5	5
Montana Mont. Code Ann. § 27-2-202 et seq.	8	5	3	2
Nebraska Neb. Rev. Stat. § 25-201 et seq.	5	4	4	4
Nevada Nev. Rev. Stat. Ann. § 11.010 et seq.	6	4	2	3
New Hampshire N.H. Rev. Stat. Ann. § 508:1 et seq.	3	3	3	3
New Jersey N.J. Stat. Ann. § 2A:14-1 et seq.	6	6	2	6
New Mexico N.M. Stat. Ann. § 37-1-1 et seq.	6	4	3	4
New York N.Y. C.P.L.R. § 201 et seq.	6	6	3	3

* Louisiana: Statute of limitations known as a "liberative prescription," personal injury known as "delictuel action."

Statutes of Limitations (continued)

State and Statute	Contracts		Personal Injury	Property Damage
	Written	Oral		
North Carolina N.C. Gen. Stat. § 1-46 et seq.	3 (1 year in certain circumstances, see N.C. Gen. Stat. Ann. §§ 1-52, 1-54)	3	3	3
North Dakota N.D. Cent. Code § 28-01-01 et seq.	6	6	6	6
Ohio Ohio Rev. Code Ann. § 2305.03 et seq.	8	6	2	4
Oklahoma Okla. Stat. Ann. tit. 12, § 91 et seq.	5	3	2	2
Oregon Or. Rev. Stat. § 12.010 et seq.	6	6	2	6
Pennsylvania 42 Pa. Cons. Stat. Ann. § 5501 et seq.	4	4	2	2
Rhode Island R. I. Gen. Laws § 9-1-12 et seq.	10	10	3	10
South Carolina S.C. Code Ann. § 15-3-510 et seq.	3	3	3	3
South Dakota S.D. Codified Laws § 15-2-1 et seq.	6	6	3	6
Tennessee Tenn. Code Ann. § 28-3-101 et seq.	6	6	1	3
Texas Tex. Civ. Prac. & Rem. Code Ann. § 16.001 et seq.; Tex. Bus. & Com. Code Ann. § 2.725	4	4	2	2
Utah Utah Code Ann. § 78B-2-101 et seq.	6	4	4	3
Vermont Vt. Stat. Ann. tit. 12, § 461 et seq.	6	6	3	3 for personal property; 6 for real property
Virginia Va. Code Ann. § 8.01-228 et seq.	5	3	2	5
Washington Wash. Rev. Code Ann. § 4.16.005 et seq.	6	3	3	3
West Virginia W.Va. Code § 55-2-1 et seq.	10	5	2	2
Wisconsin Wis. Stat. § 893.01 et seq.	6	6	3	6
Wyoming Wyo. Stat. Ann. § 1-3-102 et seq.	10	8	4	4

Calculating the Statute of Limitations

Okay, now let's assume you have found out what the relevant limitations period is. How do you know what date to start your counting from? Start with the day the injury to your person or property occurred, or, if a contract is involved, start with the day the contract was broken. When a contract to pay in installments is involved, start with the day each payment was missed. (See "Tricky Rules for Installment Contracts," below.)

How the Discovery Rule Works

With some types of cases, such as medical malpractice, the limitations period starts from the date the harm was discovered or reasonably should have been discovered. This rule protects people who don't know they have a problem until well after it has occurred.

EXAMPLE: During an operation, a doctor leaves a small clamp in your abdomen. It isn't until a year later that you experience extreme pain and see a different doctor, who orders an X-ray that shows the clamp. In most states, the statute of limitations for suits based on medical malpractice (often three years) begins from the date you learn of the problem, not the date of the original operation. However, if you walked around in pain for several years before seeing a second doctor and getting an X-ray, chances are a court would rule that the limitations period would start before actual discovery, based on the theory that you could and should have discovered the problem sooner.

Voluntary Payment After Limitations Periods

What if the following occurs: After the statute of limitations runs out (say two years on an oral contract to pay for having a fence painted), the debtor voluntarily starts to make payments. Does the voluntary payment have the effect of creating a new two-year statute of limitations period, allowing the person who is owed the money to sue if the debtor again stops paying? In most states, the answer is no. Simply starting to pay on an obligation after the time

to sue has passed doesn't create a new period for suit. All the creditor can do is to keep his toes crossed and hope that the debtor's belated streak of honesty continues. However, if the debtor signs a written agreement promising to make the payments, this does reinstate the contract and create a new statute of limitations period. In legal slang, this is called "reaffirming the debt."

> EXAMPLE: Doolittle borrows $1,000 from Crabapple in 2011 under the terms of a written promissory note. The next month he loses his job and never pays back a penny. Crabapple doesn't file a lawsuit within the applicable four-year statute of limitations. In 2016, Doolittle experiences a burst of energy, gets a job, and resolves to pay off all of his old debts. He sends Crabapple $50. A week later, suffering terrible strain from getting up before noon, Doolittle quits his job and reverts to his old ways of waking up a few minutes before race time. Is the applicable statute of limitations allowing Crabapple to sue reinstated by Doolittle's payment? No. As we learned above, once the applicable limitation period for written contracts runs out, it can't be revived by simply making a payment. However, if after Doolittle sent Crabapple the $50, Crabapple coaxed him into sending a letter saying that he would pay the remainder of the debt, Crabapple would again be able to sue and get a judgment if Doolittle failed to pay. Why? Because a written promise to pay a debt that would otherwise be barred by the statute of limitations has the legal effect of reestablishing the debt.

CAUTION

Debtors—beware of waiving statutes of limitations. If a creditor and debtor discuss an unpaid bill and the debtor asks for more time to pay, to lower payments, or to make some other accommodation, the creditor, assuming he or she is willing to agree, will almost always require that the debtor waive the statute of limitations in writing. This means that if the debtor fails to pay, the creditor will have more time to sue.

Suspending the Statute of Limitations

In a few situations, the statute of limitations is suspended for a period of time (lawyers say tolled instead of suspended). This can occur if the person sued is in prison, living out of the state, insane, or a minor, or occasionally for other reasons. If one of these events suspends the statute of limitations, then the time period that the event lasts doesn't count toward the statute

of limitations, and the counting begins again when the event (prison term, absence from state, and so on) ends.

> **EXAMPLE 1:** Jack borrows money from Tim under a written contract in a state with a four-year statute of limitations for written contracts. Jack fails to pay the money back on the day required. Six months later, Jack is sentenced to a year in jail. The four-year statute of limitations would be suspended during this period and Tim would still have three and a half years after Jack gets out of jail to file suit.

> **EXAMPLE 2:** Ed, age 12, stars in a TV series. Just before he turns 18, an accountant for the show tells Ed's family that Ed wasn't paid all the money due under his contract. Ed wonders if he can still sue the TV production company. The answer is yes. Ed's time to sue is measured from his 18th birthday (that is, the statute of limitations period would be suspended or tolled while he was a minor). If he lives in a state with a four-year statute of limitation for disputes based on written contracts, this means that Ed could file suit at least until his 22nd birthday.

Tricky Rules for Installment Contracts

When an installment contract is involved, the statute of limitations normally applies separately to each installment. For example, assume you lend Larry $5,000 and he agrees in writing to pay back the loan in five installments of $1,000 each beginning on January 1, 2015, and continuing on January 1 of each following year through 2019. The contract is governed by Pennsylvania law where there is a four-year statute of limitations. If Larry fails to make his first payment, then you can sue him in small claims court until January 1, 2019. (Note that you can sue him for only the $1,000 payment he missed, not for the entire $5,000.)

From Larry's point of view, if you don't sue by January 1, 2019, then you cannot sue him for the first missed $1,000 payment because the lawsuit is barred by the statute of limitations.

Because Larry's second installment payment isn't due until January 1, 2016, you have until January 1, 2020 to sue him if he misses that payment, and so on.

There is, however, one important exception to this rule: If the written contract contains an "acceleration clause" stating that if one installment payment is missed, all immediately become due, the statute of limitations expires for a lawsuit to collect all installments on January 2, 2019.

What If the Statute of Limitations Has Run?

What should a defendant do if he or she believes that the statute of limitations period on the plaintiff's lawsuit has run out? Tell the judge. Do this in court as part of stating your defense. Or, if your state requires a defendant to make a written response to the plaintiff's claim before the hearing date (see the appendix), then include in your response a statement that the statute of limitations bars the plaintiff's claim. Sometimes, a judge will figure this out without a reminder, but often he or she won't. Don't ever assume that because the clerk has filed the papers and you have been properly served, this means that the suit was started on time. Clerks rarely get involved in statute of limitations questions.

Settling Your Dispute

Lawsuits should be a last, not a first, resort. In addition to being time-consuming and emotionally draining, lawsuits—even the small claims variety—tend to polarize disagreements into win-all or lose-all propositions where compromise is difficult. It's not hard to understand how this happens. When forced to defend our actions in a public forum, we tend to adopt a self-serving view of our own conduct and to attribute the worst motives to our opponents. When possible, it's best to work out disputes amicably, and to use the court system only after exhausting other options.

> **CAUTION**
>
> **In most states, you are required to ask for the money owed you before filing a small claims lawsuit.** For example, in California the form you fill out to start a small claims lawsuit states, "You must ask the Defendant (in person, in writing, or by phone) to pay you before you sue. Have you done this? If no, explain why not."

As discussed earlier, it is almost always wise to first look for a noncourt solution when the other party is someone you'll have to deal with in the future. Typically, this would include a neighbor, a former friend, or a relative. Similarly, a business owner will almost always benefit by working out a compromise settlement with another established local business, a long-term customer, or a client. For example, an orthodontist who depends on referrals for most new customers should think twice before suing a patient who has refused to pay a bill in a situation where the patient is genuinely upset (whether rightly or wrongly) about the services received. Even if the orthodontist wins in court, the patient is likely to disparage the orthodontist and in the end cost him or her a lot more than what was won in court.

Negotiation

It is rarely a waste of time to try to negotiate a compromise with the other party. Indeed, many states all but require you to make the attempt. For tips on writing demand letters, see "Formal Demand Letters," below.

But, first things first. Before you reach for pen and paper, try to talk to the person with whom you are having the dispute. You might find yourself pleasantly surprised that you're able to reach an agreement.

Keep in mind, however, that safety always comes first. If the tension is such that you're worried about verbal escalation, or even assault, it's best to communicate in writing.

> **TIP**
>
> **A settlement offer is not binding.** It's important to know that an offer to settle a case—whether made orally or in writing—does not legally bind the person making it to sue for that amount if the offer is not accepted. Thus, you can make an oral or written demand for $2,000, then offer to settle for $1,500, and, if your offer is turned down, still sue for $2,000. If the person you are suing tries to tell the judge you offered to settle for less, the judge will not consider this to be relevant.

In an effort to help you arrive at a good compromise, here are a few suggestions that you can modify to fit the circumstances:

- If you are the potential plaintiff, start by offering to settle for about 20% less than your original written demand. Why 20%? If you offer a smaller discount, chances are you won't be taken seriously. Offer a bigger discount and you're giving away too much too soon.
- If you are the potential defendant, and you conclude that the plaintiff probably has a decent case, start by offering to pay about 50% of the amount demanded. This should be enough to start negotiations without conceding too much too soon. Many plaintiffs will ultimately agree to knock as much as one third off their original demand, in order to save the time and trouble of going to court.
- Money isn't always at the root of the problem. If you pay close attention to the other party's concerns, you may find that the key to arriving at an agreement can be found elsewhere. For example, a print shop owner who refuses to repay you $2,000 for a screwed-up job might agree to do the disputed job over and give you a discount on the next one, in exchange for an agreement to continue to work together and speak well of each other in the future.
- The patient negotiator has the edge. Many Americans are in such a big hurry to arrive at a solution that they agree to a bad one. Take your time. If you make a lowball offer and the other person gets mad and hangs up, you can always wait a few days and call back with a slightly sweetened one.

- Good negotiators rarely change their position quickly, even if the other side does. Instead, they raise or lower their offer in very small increments. For example, if your opponent counters your original offer of a 20% reduction in exchange for a settlement by offering to pay 50% of what you originally asked for, you'll do best by not jumping to accept or even agreeing to split the difference. Instead, counter by reducing your original demand by an additional 5%–10%. Often this will result in your opponent further improving his or her offer.

> **TIP**
>
> **Splitting the difference.** One of the hallmarks of negotiation is that each side makes a new offer until they reach an amount that they can both agree on. Typically, negotiations start to slow or stall when one or both sides get close to their settlement tolerance. A common way to solve the problem is by offering to meet halfway by "splitting the difference." Many times, your opponent will see the wisdom of relinquishing a bit more if you're giving up the same amount and it means settling the case.

- Estimate how much money a settlement is worth to you, given the fact that a settlement eliminates the time and aggravation of going to court. Try putting a dollar value on your time and then multiplying by the number of hours you estimate a court fight will take. Also, based on the facts of your case, take into consideration the chances that you might lose or get less than you ask for.

> **TIP**
>
> **If you settle, sign a written agreement, pronto.** If you talk things out with your opponent, write down your agreement as soon as possible. Oral settlement agreements, especially between people who have little confidence in one another, are often not worth the breath used to express them. And writing down an agreement gives each party a chance to see whether they really have arrived at a complete understanding. Often one or more details must still be hashed out. (See "Get Your Settlement in Writing (a Release)," below, for more on how to reduce a compromise agreement to writing.)

RESOURCE
Learn more about negotiating. To brush up on your negotiating skills, try reading *Getting to Yes: Negotiating Agreement Without Giving In*, by Bruce Patton, Roger Fisher, and William Ury (Penguin), or *Getting Past No: Negotiating in Difficult Situations*, by William Ury (Bantam). *Neighbor Law: Fences, Trees, Boundaries & Noise*, by Emily Doskow and Lina Guillen (Nolo), has excellent advice on negotiating neighborhood quarrels.

Mediation

If you and the opposing party can't seem to resolve matters one on one, mediation is the next best settlement technique. Mediation is a procedure in which the disputants voluntarily meet with a neutral third party who helps them discuss the issues and arrive at their own solution. For small claims disputes, mediation is available right in the courthouse in many counties. In others, it's provided by community-based mediation programs.

Why Mediate?

Many people ask why they should waste any time at all mediating with an opponent who they believe is unreasonable. When the parties to a small claims court case voluntarily agree to mediate, the majority of disputes are settled. Settlement is especially likely when, deep down, one or both parties realize they have an interest in arriving at a solution that's at least minimally acceptable to the other party. This is particularly common in disputes between neighbors or businesspeople who live or work in the same geographical area and who really don't want the dispute to fester.

Studies have shown that people who agreed to have their cases mediated were more likely to be satisfied with the outcome of the case than litigants who went to trial. One reason for this is that people who arrive at a mediated settlement are more likely to pay up than are people who have a judgment imposed on them after losing a contested trial.

Is entering into mediation always a good idea? No. If you are determined to get the total amount you are asking for, and you will have no ongoing relationship with the other party (for example, your dispute is with a large corporation or government agency), bypassing mediation and going directly to court makes more sense.

Arbitration

In addition to mediation, a few states also offer binding arbitration before a volunteer lawyer as an alternative to having a case heard in small claims court. Typically, the arbitrator and the parties sit down at a table and discuss the case. If the parties don't arrive at their own solution, the arbitrator renders a decision just as a judge would. One advantage of arbitration over going before a small claims judge or a commissioner is that, in some areas, it's faster to meet with the arbitrator.

A possible disadvantage of arbitration, however, is that the arbitrator is likely to be a volunteer lawyer, who is likely to be less knowledgeable than a judge about the broad range of laws that can apply to consumers and small businesses.

Nonbinding Arbitration. In some areas, a procedure called nonbinding arbitration is available. This is much like mediation, in the sense that both parties must agree to any settlement. The only difference is that, unlike a mediator, who doesn't make a formal recommendation, the arbitrator will recommend—but not compel—a solution. Especially if it's more easily available than mediation, it's often a good idea to try nonbinding arbitration; the arbitrator's recommendation can be a pretty good indication of what will happen if the case ends up going to court.

How Does Mediation Work?

A small claims mediation session typically lasts between 30 minutes and three hours. Although many mediators are ex-attorneys or even ex-judges, they have no power to impose a decision on you. The result is that mediation

sessions tend to be much more relaxed than court proceedings, and they often result in compromises that both parties are better able to live with.

You can't force the other party into mediating—both of you must agree to engage in the process. However, many states now "strongly encourage" small claims litigants to mediate before they head into the courtroom, including telling them that the judge may look more favorably upon parties who willingly try to mediate. Your small claims court appointment may even be scheduled to include an extra block of time before the hearing so that you and the other party can meet with the mediator. Your discussions during the mediation session are confidential—if the mediation fails, the judge won't be told what went on.

Although it makes sense to approach mediation with an open mind and be ready to agree to a reasonable compromise, nothing requires you to agree on anything at this stage. It's your right to have your case presented to a judge if you wish. You can even call off the mediation in the middle, which is particularly appropriate if, despite your spirit of compromise, the other party refuses to realize that he or she is in the wrong or will only settle for an amount you can't possibly accept. Also watch out for result-oriented mediators who make you feel like you have to give up a large chunk of your claim just to reach a settlement. Being reasonable doesn't mean giving away the farm.

Assuming you do want to mediate, how can you get a reluctant opponent to the table? Often you can get help from your local court-sponsored or community mediation program. Typically, as soon as you notify a mediation program that you have a dispute and would like to try mediation, an employee or volunteer with the mediation program will contact the other party or parties and try to arrange a mediation session.

If you and the other party agree on a mediated settlement, it will normally be recorded by the mediator on a form called a "Mediated Agreement," or something similar. The agreement, signed by both parties, will spell out the terms of the settlement and the deadlines for payments or other actions. If the mediation occurs after the plaintiff has already filed a small claims case, some counties will add the agreement into the court record in a sealed envelope.

Should Defendants Mediate?

Suppose now that you are a defendant in a small claims case or have received a letter threatening a lawsuit. Should you ask for mediation? The answer is almost always a resounding yes, assuming you have a defense to all or part of the plaintiff's claim or believe the plaintiff is asking for too much money even though it's a decent case. Mediation will give you a great opportunity to present your side of the dispute and try to arrive at an acceptable compromise. It can also allow you to bring up other issues that may be poisoning your relationship with the plaintiff but would not be considered relevant in court. Finally, even if you don't settle, you'll likely learn more about the plaintiff's case and you'll be in a better position to defend yourself at trial.

RESOURCE

Preparing for mediation. People who are well prepared to engage in mediation are likely to achieve far better results than those who take a more casual approach. The best source of information on how to mediate successfully is *Mediate, Don't Litigate: Strategies for Successful Mediation*, by Peter Lovenheim, available as a downloadable eBook at www.nolo.com. If you read it before you mediate, you will almost certainly achieve better results than would have been possible otherwise.

Assuming both parties honor the agreement you reached in mediation, that's the end of the case—no court judgment is ever entered by the judge or reported to a credit agency. Some states will automatically set a second court date in case the agreement isn't honored. If your agreement is honored, however, then you can either advise the court to cancel the second date or simply not show up.

If your opponent doesn't honor his or her obligations under the mediated agreement by the deadline, you must go back to court and obtain a judgment. That's easy in the states where a second court date was scheduled automatically. In other states, you will need to request a new court date or simply request a judgment.

TIP

In case the mediated settlement agreement is broken, protect your right to ask for the full amount. Most disputes that are successfully mediated result in a settlement, as would occur where A sues B for $2,000 and agrees to accept $1,200. But if B fails to pay within the time allowed by the written mediation agreement, A may want a judgment for the full $2,000. After all, A no longer has an incentive to compromise if B isn't willing to end the dispute without a day in court. Add a sentence or two to your mediated agreement stating that if the other party doesn't meet the settlement obligations, you reserve the right to make your full, original claim in court.

Formal Demand Letters

If your efforts to talk out your problems fail and you decide not to propose or agree to mediation, your next step is to send your adversary a letter. Many courts require you to make a formal demand for payment. But even where writing a formal demand letter isn't legally required, there are two reasons why doing so makes great sense. First, in as many as one-third of all disputes, your demand letter will serve as a catalyst to settlement. Second, even if no settlement results, setting out your case in a formal letter affords you an excellent opportunity to lay your case before the judge in a carefully organized way. Or, put another way, it allows you to "manufacture" evidence that you will likely be permitted to use in court if your case isn't settled.

> EXAMPLE: Sunita purchases a designer dress on eBay from Maya. When it arrives, she realizes that the dress was meant to come with a jacket and is too skimpy to be worn without it. Maya refuses to take the dress back. She hangs up the phone whenever she hears Sunita's voice on the line. Sunita writes a demand letter outlining all of this and sends it via certified mail. Maya doesn't respond. In court, Maya feigns complete surprise, claiming, "I had no idea you had a problem with the dress—why didn't you say something before?" Sunita's demand letter, with its complete account of events, can now be used as evidence to back up Sunita's account of the dispute—and it will make Maya look less believable on the whole.

> CAUTION
> **You can be sued without first being sent a formal letter stating that a lawsuit is imminent.** Some people believe they can't be sued until they receive a formal letter asking for payment and saying that a lawsuit will be filed if it isn't forthcoming. This is not necessarily true. A simple past-due notice form from a creditor, stating that if the account isn't paid promptly court action will be pursued, is usually sufficient. In addition, a judge has the power to conclude that an oral demand for payment is adequate.

Composing Your Demand Letter

When writing your demand letter, here are some pointers to keep in mind:

Type your letter. If you don't have a computer or typewriter, try to get access to one. Many public libraries have computers that you can use for free or a minimal charge.

Concisely review the main facts of the dispute. At first it may seem a bit odd to outline these details; after all, your opponent knows the story. But remember—if you end up in court, the letter will be read by a judge, and you want the judge to understand what happened. Now is a good chance to make a record not only of the initial dispute, but of any subsequent phone conversations, unanswered calls, or inappropriate conduct by the defendant.

Be polite. Absolutely avoid personally attacking your adversary (even one who deserves it). The more you attack, the more you invite the other side to respond in a similarly angry vein.

Write with your goal in mind. The letter should encourage your opponent to make a businesslike analysis of the dispute and raise such questions as:

- What are my risks of losing?
- How much time will a defense take?
- Do I want the dispute to be decided in public?

Ask for exactly what you want. For example, if you want $2,000, don't beat around the bush—ask for it (or possibly a little more to allow some negotiating room). Explain how you arrived at this figure. And be sure to set a deadline. One week (two weeks at the outside) is usually best; anything longer and your opponent has less motivation to deal with you right away. Supply the actual date, to remove any doubt.

Conclude by stating you will promptly pursue your legal remedies if your demand is not met. Remind the defendant that a court judgment could adversely affect his or her credit rating.

Make and keep copies. Make a copy of each letter before you send it, and keep a copy of the post office receipts (use certified mail, return receipt requested). Keep all correspondence from your adversary, also.

Use certified mail. Send the demand letter via certified mail with a return receipt requested. If you do end up in small claims court, you can use the return receipt to counter any claim that your opponent didn't receive the demand letter.

A Real Small Claims Case

Now let's consider a real small claims case. The facts (with a little editorial license) are simple: Jennifer moved into Peter's house in August, agreeing to pay $550 per month in rent. The house had four bedrooms, each occupied by one person. The kitchen and other common areas were shared. Things went well enough until one chilly evening in October, when Jennifer turned on the heat. Peter was right behind her to turn it off, explaining that heat inflamed his allergies.

As the days passed and fall deepened, heat became more and more of an issue, until one cold, late November night Jennifer returned home from her waitress job to find her room "about the same temperature as the inside of an icicle." She started packing and moved out the next morning. She refused to pay Peter any additional rent, claiming that she was within her rights to terminate her month-to-month tenancy without giving notice because the house was uninhabitable. It took Peter one month to find a suitable tenant and to have that person move in. Therefore, he lost rent in the amount of $550.

After calling Jennifer several times and asking her to pay the $550, only to have her slam down the phone in disgust, Peter wrote her the following letter:

61 Spring Street

Detroit, MI 12344

January 1, 20xx

Jennifer Tenant

111 Lake Street

Detroit, MI 12344

Dear Jennifer:

You are a real idiot. Actually, you're worse than that: you're malicious—walking out on me before Christmas and leaving me with no tenant when you know that I needed the money to pay my child support. You know that I promised to get you an electric room heater. Don't think I don't know that the real reason you moved out was to live with your boyfriend.

Please send me the $550 I lost because it took me a month to rerent the place. If you don't, I will sue you.

In aggravation,

Peter Landperson

Peter Landperson

To which Jennifer replied:

111 Lake Street

Detroit, MI 12344

January 4, 20xx

Peter Landperson

61 Spring Street

Detroit, MI 12344

Dear Mr. Landperson:

You nearly froze me to death, you cheap bastard. I am surprised it only took a month to rent that iceberg of a room—you must have found a rich polar bear (ha ha). People like you should be locked up.

I hope you choke on an ice cube.

Jennifer Tenant

Jennifer Tenant

Both Peter and Jennifer made the same mistake. Instead of being businesslike, each deliberately set out to annoy the other, reducing any chance of compromise. In addition, they each assumed that they were writing only to the other, forgetting that the judge would be privy to their sentiments. Thus, both lost a valuable chance to present the judge with a coherent summary of the facts as they saw them. As evidence in a subsequent court proceeding, both letters were worthless.

Now let's interrupt these proceedings and give Peter and Jennifer another chance to write sensible letters.

After having a friend review his draft letter to former tenant Jennifer (where he called her an idiot and malicious), Peter wrote this more sensible letter:

Jennifer Tenant
61 Spring Street
Detroit, MI 12344
January 1, 20xx

Jennifer Tenant
111 Lake Street
Detroit, MI 12344

Dear Jennifer:

As you will recall, you moved into my house at 61 Spring Street on August 1, 20xx, agreeing to pay me $550 per month rent on the first of each month. On November 29, you suddenly moved out, having given me no advance notice whatsoever.

I realize you were unhappy that the house was on the cool side, but I don't believe this was a serious problem, as the temperature was at all times over 60 degrees and I had agreed to get you an electric heater by December.

I was unable to get a tenant to replace you (although I tried every way I could and asked you for help) until January 1, 20xx. As a result, I am short $550 rent. If necessary, I will take this dispute to court. I hope that this isn't necessary and that we can arrive at a sensible compromise.

I am also willing to try to mediate this dispute, if you agree. I have tried to call you with no success. Perhaps you can give me a call in the next week to talk this over.

Sincerely,

Peter Landperson

Peter Landperson

To which our now enlightened Jennifer promptly replied:

January 4, 20xx
111 Lake Street
Detroit, MI 12344

Peter Landperson
61 Spring Street
Detroit, MI 12344

Dear Peter:

I just received your letter and am sorry to say that I don't agree either with the facts as you have presented them, or with your demand for back rent.

When I moved in August 1, 20xx, you never told me that you had an allergy and that there would be a problem keeping the house at a normal temperature. I would not have moved in had you informed me of this.

From early October through November, I asked that you provide heat. You didn't. Finally, it became unbearable to return from work to a cold house, which was often below 60 degrees. It is true that I moved out suddenly, but I felt that I was within my rights under Michigan law, which clearly allows tenants to sue landlords for constructive eviction when the landlord fails to provide a necessity such as heat. In fact, you are lucky that I am not suing you for damages for constructive eviction.

Since you mentioned the nonexistent electric heater in your letter, let me respond to that. You first promised to get the heater over a month before I moved out and never did. Also, as I pointed out to you on several occasions, the heater was not a complete solution to the problem, as it would have heated only my room and not the kitchen, living room, or dining areas. You repeatedly told me that it would be impossible to heat these areas.

Peter, I sincerely regret the fact that you feel wronged, but I believe that I have been very fair with you. I am sure that you would have been able to rerent the room promptly if the house had been warm. I don't believe that any compromise is possible, so mediation does not make sense. If you wish to go to court, I'll be there with several witnesses who will support my position.

Sincerely,

Jennifer Tenant

Jennifer Tenant

As you can see, while the second two letters are less fun to read, they are far more informative. In this instance, the goal of reaching an acceptable compromise or agreeing to mediation was not met, but both parties have prepared a good outline of their positions for the judge. Of course, in court, both Peter and Jennifer will testify and present witnesses and possibly other evidence that will tell much the same story as is set out in the letters. However, court proceedings are often rushed and confused, and it's nice to have a written statement for the judge to fall back on. Be sure the judge is given a copy of your demand letter when your case is presented. The judge won't be able to guess that you have it; you will have to state that you have it and hand it to the clerk. (For more about how to conduct yourself in court, see Chapters 13–15.)

Sample Demand Letters

Below are letters a consumer might write to an auto repair shop after being victimized by a shoddy repair job and to a contractor who botched a remodeling contract.

Sample Demand Letter: Car Repair

June 16, 20xx

Tucker's Fix-It-Quick Garage
9938 Main Street
Houston, TX 12333

Dear Mr. Tucker,

On May 21, 20xx, I took my car to your garage for servicing. Shortly after picking it up the next day, the engine caught fire because of your failure to properly connect the fuel line to the fuel injector. Fortunately, I was able to douse the fire without injury.

As a direct result of the engine fire, I paid the ABC garage $1,281 for necessary repair work. I enclose a copy of their invoice.

In addition, I was without the use of my car for three days and had to rent a car to get to work. I enclose a copy of an invoice showing the rental cost of $145.

In a recent phone conversation, you claimed that the fire wasn't the result of your negligence and would have happened anyway. And you said that even if it was your fault, I should have brought my car back to your garage so you could have fixed it at a lower cost.

As to the first issue, Peter Klein of the ABC Garage is prepared to testify in court that the fire occurred because the fuel line was not properly connected to the fuel injector, the exact part of the car you were working on.

Second, I had no obligation to return the car to you for further repair. I had the damage you caused repaired at a commercially reasonable price and am prepared to prove this by presenting several higher estimates by other garages.

Please send me a check or money order for $1,426 on or before July 15. If I don't receive payment by that date, I'll promptly file this case in small claims court. And assuming I receive a judgment, which will be part of the public record available to credit agencies, I will promptly follow all legal avenues to collect it. You may reach me during the day at 444-555-2857 or in the evenings until 10 p.m. at 444-555-8967.

Sincerely,

Marsha Rizzoli
Marsha Rizzoli

Sample Demand Letter: Home Contractor

June 20, 20xx

Jane Brown

Beyond Repair Construction

10 Delaney Avenue

Seattle, WA 12355

Dear Ms. Brown:

Your firm recently did replacement tile work and other remodeling on my downstairs bathroom at 142 West Pine Street, here in Seattle. As per our written agreement, I paid you $4,175 upon completion of the job on May 17, 20xx.

Only two weeks later, on June 1, I noticed that the tile in the north portion of the shower had sunk almost half an inch, with the result that our shower floor was uneven and water pooled in the downhill corner before eventually going down the drain.

In our telephone conversations, you variously claimed that the problem:

- was in my imagination
- was my fault, because the floor was uneven to begin with, or
- was too minor to bother with.

Sorry, but I paid for a first-class remodeling job, and I expect to receive it. Please contact me within ten days to arrange to pay me $1,200 (the cost of redoing the work per the enclosed estimate from ABC Tile) or to arrange to redo the work yourself. If I don't hear from you by June 15, 20xx I will promptly file in small claims court.

Sincerely,

Ben Price

Ben Price

Get Your Settlement in Writing (a Release)

If you and the other party agree to a settlement, either on your own or with the help of a mediator, it's important to promptly write it down. When a mediator is involved, preparing a written agreement is usually the last step in the mediation process. If you and your opponent negotiate your own settlement, you'll need to cooperate to reduce it to writing. Lawyers call an agreement to settle a dispute a "release," because in exchange for some act (often the payment of money), one person gives up (or releases) his or her claim against another. For instance, if the paint on John's building is damaged when Sandra, a neighboring property owner, spray-paints her building on a windy day, John might agree to release Sandra from liability (that is, not sue Sandra) if she agrees to pay $2,000 to have the damaged area of John's building repainted.

A written release is valid if it is signed by both parties; is fair, in the sense that neither party was tricked into signing on the basis of a misrepresentation; and provides each party with some benefit (if you pay me $500, I won't sue you and I'll keep my dog out of your yard). If either party later violates the terms of the settlement, the other can file a lawsuit and receive a court judgment for appropriate damages.

It's important to understand that settlement agreements are powerful legal documents. If you completely release someone who damaged your car for $500, only to later find out that the damage was more extensive, you'll be stuck with the $500 unless you can convincingly claim that the other party was guilty of misrepresentation or fraud in getting you to sign the settlement agreement. Of course, in most situations, where the details of a dispute are all well known, a settlement can be comfortably signed with the knowledge that the dispute will finally be laid to rest.

Below we provide a sample release ("Sample General Release") adopted from Nolo's book, *101 Law Forms for Personal Use,* by the Editors of Nolo. This general release is used to settle a dispute over a contract, debt, or minor personal injury when only one party is alleged to have suffered damages or been injured.

Get the Court's Stamp of Approval

Assuming a small claims case has actually been filed, you may have a choice as to whether your agreement is presented to a judge and made part of a court order or is simply written as a binding contract between you and the other party. Especially if it's less trouble (sometimes getting a court order involves an extra trip to court), you may be tempted to accept a contract and not bother with a court order. Generally, I recommend against this unless you are sure the other party really will honor the agreement. A court order (judgment) is far easier to enforce than a contract. Especially if you suspect that the other side may not do what they promise, it is definitely worth a little extra effort to have your settlement contract incorporated into a judgment of a court. (This obviously won't be possible if the dispute is settled before a small claims lawsuit is even filed.)

RESOURCE

Where to get other types of release forms. The Nolo book *101 Law Forms for Personal Use* contains a number of specialized releases adapted to auto accidents, property damage, and personal injuries. It also contains mutual release forms for use when both parties are giving up claims. In addition, release forms are often available from office supply stores that carry legal documents and from lawyers' form books, available at law libraries.

No matter where you get your release, it should contain the following information:

- The names and addresses of the party being released (the potential defendant) and the party granting the release (the potential plaintiff).
- A brief description of the "what," "when," and "where" of the dispute or issue to which the release pertains. (The release below provides several blank lines for you to briefly describe the events giving rise to the need for the release.)

- A statement of what the person giving up a claim is getting in return. As mentioned, for a release to be a valid and enforceable contract, the person signing the release (releasor) must receive something of benefit (called "consideration" by lawyers) in exchange for agreeing to give up the right to sue. The release below provides a space for this "consideration" to be described. Typically, it is money. If so, simply enter the amount. If it is an agreement by the releasee to perform or not perform some act (for example, stop his dog from barking at night), describe the act.

- A statement that the release applies to all claims arising from the dispute or issue, both those known at the time the release is signed and those that may come along later. This provision is very common in releases; without it they wouldn't be worth much.

- A statement that the release binds all persons who might otherwise have a legal right to file a claim on behalf of the releasor (for example, the releasor's spouse or heirs). Although I have included this provision in my releases for caution's sake, it is rare that it will ever prove relevant. In fact, such persons are usually bound by the release anyway.

- The date the release is signed.

- The signatures of the parties. Legally, only the person granting a release needs to sign it, but we think it is a better practice for both parties to do so—after all, this important document contains statements that affect both of their rights. In the case of mutual releases, which occur when both parties give up a claim against the other, both must sign.

TIP
Use witnesses. There is no legal requirement for a release to be witnessed, but if you don't completely trust the other person and think he or she may later claim "it's not my signature," a witness can be a good idea. If a release involves a lot of money or a potentially large claim, you may want to bolster the chances of it being upheld (should it ever be challenged later) by signing it in front of a witness or two who can later testify, if the issue arises, that the other party was under no duress and appeared to know what he or she was doing. If your release involves a small claim, it is not necessary to do this.

Last Minute Agreements

Occasionally, disputes are settled while you are waiting for your case to be heard. Even on the day you go to court, it is proper to ask the other person to step into the hall for a moment to talk the matter over. If you can agree on a last-minute compromise, wait until the courtroom clerk calls your case by name and then tell the judge the amount you have agreed upon and whether the amount is to be paid all at once, or over time. Typically, the judge will order that the case be dismissed if one person pays the other the agreed-upon amount on the spot, or, if payment is to be made later, the judge will enter a judgment for the amount that you have agreed on.

Another possibility is that you and your opponent will agree to a last-minute attempt to mediate. If so, you will want to explain this to the judge, who in turn will normally delay ("continue," in legalese) your case until the mediation session takes place. If mediation works and your case settles, you and the other party should jointly notify the court clerk. Again, unless the agreed-upon amount is immediately paid, the debtor will normally want to return to court and have the settlement amount made part of an official court order (judgment).

Sample General Release

1. [*person signing release and agreeing not to sue*], Releasor, voluntarily and knowingly executes this release with the express intention of eliminating and canceling Releasee's liabilities and obligations as described below.

2. Releasor hereby releases [*person being released*], Releasee, from all claims, known or unknown, that have arisen or may arise from the following occurrence: [*description of events giving rise to release, including location and date if appropriate—see box for sample language*].

Sample Language:
 a. "Repair work incompletely done to Releasor's boat at the Fixmeup Shipyards on 5/6/20xx."
 b. "Agreement by Releasee made during the week of June 6, 20xx, to deliver and install custom built cabinets at Releasor's address no later than July 6, 20xx, which Releasee failed to keep."
 c. "A tree growing on Releasee's property at 1011 Oak Street fell into Releasor's backyard at 1013 Oak Street on August 7, 20xx. It damaged Releasor's fence, which had to be replaced. The tree itself had to be removed."

3. Releasor understands that, as to claims that are known to the parties when the release is signed, any statutory provisions that would otherwise apply to limit this general release are hereby waived. Releasor also understands that this release extends to claims arising out of this incident that are not known by Releasor at the time this release is signed.

4. In exchange for granting this release Releasor has received the following payment or other consideration: [*amount of money, or description of something else of value that person signing release received from other party—see box for sample language*].

Sample Language:
 a. "$150 cash."
 b. "A used RCA television set."
 c. "An agreement by [*Releasee's name*] to desist from further activities as described in Clause 3 of this release."
 d. "An agreement by [*Releasee's name*] to repair Releasor's Apple MacBook computer by January, 20xx."

Sample General Release (continued)

5. By signing this release Releasor additionally intends to bind his or her spouse, heirs, legal representatives, assigns, and anyone else claiming under him or her. Releasor has not assigned any claim covered by this release to any other party. Releasor also intends that this release apply to the heirs, personal representatives, assigns, insurers, and successors of Releasee as well as to the Releasee.

This release was executed on _____ , 20____ , at [*city and state*]

_____ _____
Releasor's signature Date

_____ _____
Releasor's name (print) County of residence

Releasor's address

_____ _____
Releasor's spouse's signature Date

_____ _____
Releasor's spouse's name (print) County of residence

_____ _____
Releasee's signature Date

_____ _____
Releasee's name (print) County of residence

Releasee's address

_____ _____
Releasee's spouse's signature Date

_____ _____
Releasee's spouse's name (print) County of residence

_____ _____
Witness's signature Date

_____ _____
Witness's name (print) County of residence

Witness's address

_____ _____
Witness's signature Date

_____ _____
Witness's name (print) County of residence

Witness's address

Who Can Sue?

ho can sue in small claims court? The answer is easy. You can— as long as you:

- are 18 years of age or an emancipated minor
- have not been declared mentally incompetent in a judicial proceeding, and
- are suing on your own claim.

CAUTION

Special requirements for some plaintiffs. Some states do not let unlicensed contractors and other businesspeople who work without required licenses to bring suit on claims related to their business. Prisoners are allowed to sue in some states but not in others. In states where they can sue, their cases often must be presented in writing. (In a few states, prisoners can name an adult representative to appear on their behalf.) Check your state's small claims rules before bringing suit.

What If You Want to Sue but Can't Appear in Court?

People who will find it difficult or impossible to show up in small claims court to present their case often ask whether there is another way to proceed. For people in certain categories—prisoners, business owners, landlords, and certain military personnel stationed out of state—the answer may be yes (check your state's rules for details). Even if you don't fit into an approved category, a small claims judge has the discretion to hear your case through a nonlawyer representative if you convince the judge that for some good reason, such as bad health or advanced age, you need assistance and the person you send to court is familiar with what happened. To see whether this procedure will work in your situation, talk to your county's small claims court adviser.

Married Couples

What if you and your spouse co-own a car that is vandalized by your neighbor's teenager? What if you and your spouse are both listed as payees

on a bad check? These are called "joint claims" and you and your spouse can and should sue together. If you are a married couple with a joint claim, you should list both your names as plaintiffs. It is usually okay for one spouse to appear at the hearing on behalf of both spouses as long as:

- the claim is joint
- the represented spouse has given written consent, which you should bring to court, and
- the court determines the interests of justice would be served.

Employees May Appear on Behalf of a Business

States used to require the owner of a business to show up in small claims court personally. This discouraged the owners of many small unincorporated businesses from using small claims court. For example, a dentist who wished to sue on an overdue bill would have had to show up in court.

These days, a number of states are more understanding of business time pressures. If a business (incorporated or unincorporated) wishes to sue on an unpaid bill, it can often send an employee to court to testify about the debt as it is reflected in the written records of the business. For instance, in many states, a landlord suing for unpaid rent can send a property manager to court to establish the fact that the rent was unpaid (but see cautions about bringing eviction cases in small claims court in Chapter 20). For a business owner to invoke this time-saving procedure, the employee sent to court must be familiar with the company's books and able to testify about how the debt was entered in them.

Make sure that anyone who goes to small claims court on behalf of your business has firsthand knowledge about the dispute. For example, if your rug store is suing a customer who refuses to pay because a carpet was improperly installed, you will probably lose if you send to court only your bookkeeper, who knows nothing about what happened on the particular job. In this situation, some judges may postpone the case for a few days to allow the business owner to show up with the carpet installer and present testimony about the quality of the repair, but don't count on it—try to send the appropriate person the first time.

Sole Proprietorships

If you own a small business and are the sole proprietor, you will list both your name and the name of your business on your court papers. Generally, a sole proprietor must appear personally at the court hearing.

> ⊘ CAUTION
>
> **Does your business use a fictitious name?** Most states require companies that use a fictitious name (such as Tasty Donut Shop) to file a declaration stating that you have properly executed, filed, and published a fictitious business name statement as required by your state's law. Check with the small claims clerk.

Business Partnerships

If you are filing a claim on behalf of a partnership, you should sue on behalf of the individual partners and the partnership itself. When it comes to appearing in court, most states allow either a partner or a regular employee to do so.

Corporations

If you are filing a claim on behalf of a corporation, whether profit or nonprofit, list the corporation itself as the plaintiff. In most states, the corporation may be represented at the hearing by either:

- an officer or director of the corporation, or
- an employee who is authorized to file claims on behalf of the corporation by the corporation's board of directors. If a nonofficer of a corporation signs the forms, the court clerk may want to see some documentation that the person suing is properly authorized.

Check your state laws for any special rules about corporations as plaintiffs.

Limited Liability Companies

List the limited liability company (LLC) as the plaintiff. Most states allow any member to appear in court but check your local rules.

Nonprofits and Unincorporated Associations

If you are suing on behalf of a nonprofit corporation or an unincorporated association, the plaintiff's claim should list the name of the corporation or association and the name of an officer or director who will appear in court (such as, "ABC Canine Happiness Society, by Philip Pup, Executive Director"). An officer may represent the nonprofit or unincorporated association at the hearing.

Motor Vehicle Claims

When a claim arises out of damage to a motor vehicle, the registered owner(s) of the vehicle must file in small claims court. So, if you are driving someone else's car and get hit by a third party, you can't sue for damage done to the car. The registered owner must file the lawsuit. However, if you are injured in the accident, you can sue the driver of the other car.

Government Agencies

If you are suing on behalf of a government agency such as a public library, city tax assessor's office, or county hospital, you should list the organization's official name as the plaintiff. When you file the papers, you must show the court clerk proper authorization to sue.

Special Rules for Prisoners and Military Personnel

In some states, prisoners are not allowed to bring small claims lawsuits. Other states have special procedures for prisoners who want to sue in small claims court. In California, for example, a prisoner who wants to sue in small claims court must file papers by mail and then either submit testimony in the form of written declarations or have another person appear on his or her behalf in court (Cal. Civ. Proc. Code § 116.540(f)).

In some states, military personnel who have been transferred out of state are also allowed to bring small claims court cases without having to appear in court personally. Check your state rules for information on how to do this.

Suits by Minors

If you are under 18 years old, your parent or legal guardian must sue for you. The exception is that, in some states, emancipated minors can sue on their own. When your parents or guardians sue on your behalf, they must fill out a form asking to have one of them appointed your guardian ad litem and have the form signed by the judge. "Guardian ad litem" means "guardian for the purposes of the lawsuit." Ask the court clerk for the rules in your state.

Class Actions (Group Lawsuits)

In small claims court there is no such thing as a true class action lawsuit, where a number of people in a similar situation ask a court's permission to join together in one lawsuit against the same defendant. However, as many community and advocacy groups have discovered, if a large number of people with a particular grievance (pollution, noise, drug sales) sue the same defendant at the same time in small claims courts, something remarkably like a class action is created.

This technique was pioneered in the early 1980s by a group of determined homeowners who lived near the San Francisco airport. Several times, the group won more than 100 small claims court judgments against the City of San Francisco, based on excessive noise. They hired expert witnesses, did research, ran training workshops, and paid for legal advice when needed, as part of a coordinated effort to efficiently present their cases. The City of San Francisco tried to fend off these cases by arguing that the homeowners were, in effect, involved in a class action lawsuit and such suits are not permitted in small claims court. A California court of appeals disagreed, saying, "Numerous 'mass' actions against the City alleging that noise from the City airport constituted a continuing nuisance were neither too 'complex' nor had such 'broad social policy import' that they were outside the jurisdiction of Small Claims Court …." *(City and County of San Francisco v. Small Claims Div., San Mateo Co.,* 190 Cal.Rptr. 340 (1983).)

A similar strategy has been widely used in many cities to shut down drug houses. Neighbors organize to sue landlords who rent to drug-selling tenants, claiming the legal theory of nuisance (use of property that unreasonably interferes with the rights of others—Chapter 2). In these cases the neighbors claimed the nuisance was the emotional and mental distress that accompanied living near a drug house. Typically, each neighbor sues for the maximum amount. Thus, 30 neighbors who coordinate their small claims filings can, together, bring what amounts to a $225,000 case. A number of drug house cases have resulted in large judgments, and problems that had dragged on for months or years were quickly cleaned up.

Successful mass small claims lawsuits based on legal nuisance have also been brought against polluting refineries and factories.

JUDGE'S TIP
Group lawsuits can lend credibility and weight to a "neighborhood quarrel." One of the purposes of the small claims court is to provide a neighborhood forum to resolve group lawsuits that might otherwise clog up the higher courts. If neighbors can band together to address problems of barking dogs, rock bands, drug houses, and so on, each individual's case will be that much more credible to the judge.

TIP
Select a small committee to coordinate your lawsuits. When a good-sized group of plaintiffs all sue the same defendant based on the same grievance, it's wise to coordinate strategy. This typically involves creating an informal plaintiffs' organization to organize intergroup communications, find witnesses and, if needed, expert witnesses (see Chapter 14), conduct a training session for everyone who will testify in court, discuss settlement offers, and, if requested, meet with the judge to plan how to efficiently and effectively present your multiple cases in court.

CAUTION
Losing defendants have the right to a new trial on appeal. People who sue and beat corporations, governmental entities, and other defendants with deep pockets in small claims court are likely to be faced with a tougher battle on appeal. That's because all losing small claims defendants have the right to appeal to superior court, where both sides have the right to be represented by a lawyer. (See Chapter 23.)

Participation by Attorneys and Bill Collectors

In the majority of states, you are permitted to be represented by an attorney in small claims court. In some states, attorneys are allowed only if the judge consents, and in other states attorneys are required if the party is a corporation. Some states don't allow representation by attorneys at all. (See the appendix for your state's rules.)

Even in states that don't allow lawyers in small claims court, it is still perfectly legal to get an attorney's advice about your small claims case.

Many states forbid the use of small claims court by "assignees" (a fancy term that usually refers to collection agencies). In other words, in these states you cannot hire someone to sue for an unpaid debt. But the majority of states still allow suits by collection agencies. Check with your small claims court clerk for information.

TIP

Attorneys can always bring suits on their own behalf. Even in states that don't allow attorneys to represent someone else in small claims court, attorneys are allowed to sue on or defend their own claims.

Suing Different Kinds of Defendants

Y ou are allowed to sue just about any defendant—person, sole proprietorship, partnership, corporation, LLC, or government entity—in small claims court. Under certain circumstances, you can even sue out-of-staters. Indeed, figuring out where to sue (see Chapter 9) is often more difficult than figuring out whom to sue.

One Person

If you are suing an individual, simply name the person on the form, using the most complete name that you know for that person. If the person calls himself J.R. Smith and you don't know what the J.R. stands for, simply sue him as J.R. Smith. However, if with a little effort you can find out that J stands for James, it's better to sue him as James R. Smith.

> **TIP**
> **What to do if a person uses several names.** Lots of people use two or more names. Thus Jason Graboskawitz may also use J.T. Grab. When in doubt, list the name the person uses most often for business purposes first, followed by the words "also known as" (or "a.k.a.") and any other names. Thus you might sue Jason Graboskawitz, a.k.a. J.T. Grab.

Two or More People

If you are suing more than one person on a claim arising from the same incident or contract, list the complete names of all defendants. Then you must "serve" (deliver copies of court papers to) each of them to bring them properly before the court. (See Chapter 11.) Listing both names is also required when the defendants are married: List the defendants as John Randolph Smith and Jane Smith, husband and wife (or "spouses" if the partners are in a same-sex marriage). Or, if you don't know the name of one spouse: John Randolph Smith and Mrs. John Randolph Smith, husband and wife.

EXAMPLE: J.R. and June Smith, who are married, borrow $1,200 from you to start an avocado pit polishing business. Unfortunately, in the middle of the polishing, the seeds begin to sprout. J.R. and June get so furious that they refuse to repay you. If you wish to sue them and get a judgment, you should list them as James R. Smith and June Smith—not Mr. and Mrs. Smith. But now suppose that J.R. borrowed $1,200 for the avocado pit business in January, June borrowed $1,000 to fix her motorcycle a month later, and neither loan was repaid. In this situation, you would sue each in separate small claims actions.

TIP

Two defendants are better than one, and three are better than two. If two or more people are responsible for your loss (for example, if three tenants damaged your apartment), sue them all. This will enable you to get judgments against several people. You'll be glad you did when you try to collect—if one defendant turns out to be an artful dodger, you can go after the others. (For more information on collecting your judgment, see Chapter 24.)

Individually Owned Businesses

List the name of the owner and the name of the business (Ralph C. Jones, individually and doing business as [d.b.a.] Jones's Texaco). But never just assume that the name of the business is really the same as the name of the owner. For all you know, Jim's Garage may be owned by Pablo Garcia Motors, Inc. (On suing a corporation, see below.) If you get a judgment against Jim's Garage and there is no Jim, it will be worthless unless you take steps to have the judgment changed to reflect the correct name. This can take extra time and trouble. Far better to be sure you sue the right person in the first place.

A few states have liberalized their rules and do not penalize plaintiffs who incorrectly state the business defendant's name. New York allows a plaintiff to sue a defendant under any name used in conducting business if it is impossible to find out the defendant's true name. California allows a plaintiff to correct a defendant's name at the time of the hearing and, in some cases, after judgment, if the defendant is a business person using a fictitious name.

How to Find Out Who Owns a Business

Many states require that all people who do business using a name other than their own file a fictitious business name statement with the county clerk in the county or counties in which the business operates. This is public information that you can get from the county clerk. Another way to figure out who owns a business is to check with the business tax and license office in the city where the business is located. (If the business is not located in an incorporated city, try the county.) The tax and license office will have a list of the owners of all businesses paying taxes in the city. They should be able to tell you, for example, that the Garden of Exotic Delights is owned by Rufus Clod. Once you find this out, you sue Rufus Clod, individually and d.b.a. The Garden of Exotic Delights.

If for some reason the tax and license office or the county clerk can't help, you may want to check with the state. Millions of people, from exterminators to embalmers, must register with one or another office in their state. So, if your beef is with a teacher, architect, smog control device installer, holder of a beer or wine license, or member of another profession that must register, you will very likely be able to learn who and where the person or business is with a phone call, an Internet search, or a letter. Check for the name of the profession in the phone book under the state government listings, or search your state's official website for the name of the profession. When you find an agency that looks like it should have jurisdiction over the type of business you wish to sue, call its public information number and explain your problem. It may take a little persistence, but eventually you should get the help you need.

Partnerships

All partners in a general partnership business are individually liable for all the acts of the business. You should list the names of all the business partners, even if your dispute is only with one (Patricia Sun and Farah Moon, d.b.a. Sacramento Gardens). Check with the local business tax and license office or recorder's office to find out who owns a particular partnership.

EXAMPLE: You go to a local cleaners with your new sky blue suit. They put too much cleaning fluid on it, which results in a small gray cloud that settles on the right rear shoulder. After trying unsuccessfully to get the cleaners to take responsibility for improving the weather on the back of your suit, you start thinking about a different kind of suit. When you start filling out your court papers, you realize that you know only that the store says "Perfection Cleaners" on the front, and that the guy who has been so unpleasant to you is named Bob. You call the city business tax and license people and they tell you that Perfection Cleaners is owned by Robert Johnson and Sal De Benno. You should sue both and also list the name of the business (Robert Johnson and Sal De Benno, d.b.a. Perfection Cleaners).

> CAUTION
> **Special procedures to sue limited partnerships.** Limited partnerships usually consist of one or more general partners who are subject to being sued, and a number of limited partners who, as investors, normally can't be sued. So if you are suing a limited partnership, list the name of the partnership itself and the general partner or partners. Do not list the limited partners. Limited partnerships must register with the secretary of state. For information on who to sue and serve with papers, contact the secretary of state.

Corporations and Limited Liability Companies (LLCs)

Corporations and limited liability companies (LLCs) are legal people. This means that you can sue, and enforce a judgment against, the business entity itself. You should not sue the owners, officers, or managers of the corporation or LLC as individuals, unless you have a personal claim against them that is separate from their role in the corporation or LLC. That's because in most situations, the real people who own or operate the corporation or LLC aren't themselves legally liable to pay the corporation's or LLC's debts (unless there was fraud or a personal guaranty). This concept is called personal limited liability and is a big reason many people choose to incorporate or form an LLC in the first place.

Be sure to list the full name of the corporation or LLC when you file suit (John's Liquors, Inc., a Corporation, or John's Liquors, LLC). Here again, the name on the door or on the stationery may not be the organization's real name, as corporations and LLCs sometimes use fictitious names. To be sure, check with the city or county business license office where the corporation or LLC is headquartered. Information is also usually available from either the secretary of state or the corporations commissioner's office for your state.

You may sue a corporation or LLC in your state if it does business there, even if its headquarters are in another state.

Motor Vehicle Accident Cases

Special rules apply when it comes to motor vehicle accidents. In most states, if your claim arises from an accident with an automobile, motorcycle, truck, or RV, you should name both the driver of the vehicle and the registered owner as defendants. This is because the vehicle's owner may be liable even if that person wasn't driving. Most of the time, you will obtain this information at the time of the accident. If the police make an accident report, it will contain this information. You can get a copy of any police report from the police department for a modest fee. If there was no police report—and assuming you have the license number of the offending vehicle—contact the Department of Motor Vehicles. Tell them you want to find out the name and address of the vehicle's owner for purposes of filing and serving a lawsuit based on a motor vehicle accident. This is a legitimate reason in most states, and you will get the information you need. However, in some states, you may need to complete some forms or jump through some other hoops to learn the owner's name, and the owner of the car may be notified of your request.

Remember, when you sue more than one person (in this case the driver and the owner, if they are different), serve papers on both. When a business owns a vehicle, sue both the driver and the owners of the business. If a minor child is driving the car, find out the parents' names and, if possible, whether they gave their child permission to drive. (See "How to Sue Minors," below.)

EXAMPLE: You are involved in a car accident, and the driver of the other car is a young woman who first identifies herself as "Suzie Q" and then tells the police that her name is Suzanne Quigley. When you try to talk to Suzie about paying to replace your smashed headlight, she blows you off. You request a copy of the accident report from the police and find out that Suzanne is 17 and was driving a car owned by her parents, whose names are George and Mary Quigley. You strike out when you ask Suzanne's parents to pay for the damage but find out she was driving the car with their permission. When you sue, you list the defendants as follows: Suzanne Quigley, also known as Suzie Q, a minor; and George Quigley and Mary Quigley, husband and wife and parents of defendant Suzanne Quigley and co-owners of the motor vehicle.

How to Sue Minors

It is very difficult to succeed when you sue a minor for breach of contract, because minors can disavow (back out of) any contract they sign as long as they do it before they turn 18. The only exception is if the contract was for a necessity of life—for example, food—in which case the minor's parents are probably responsible. You can sue emancipated minors, that is, people under 18 who are legally treated as adults. This includes minors who are on active duty in the armed services, are married, or have been emancipated (freed from parental control) by court order.

What about damage caused by minors? Although it is legal to sue minors for injuring you or damaging your property, it's rarely worthwhile, because most are broke and therefore can't pay the judgment. (There are exceptions, of course.) However, if you do wish to sue someone under 18, do it like this: "John Jeffrey, a minor, and William Jeffrey, his father."

But what about suing the offending kid's parents? Normally, a parent is not legally responsible to pay for damages negligently caused by his or her children. However, there are some exceptions to this rule. If the parent had a duty to watch the child and failed to do so, you might have a cause of action against the parents for negligent supervision. For instance, if you're injured after an unruly toddler knocks you down in the mall, the facts might show that the parents weren't correctly watching (and restraining) the child.

Also, in virtually all states, if a child is guilty of "malicious or willful misconduct," a parent may be liable up to a certain dollar amount per act for all property damage ($10,000 in some states; often a lot more if a gun is involved) and sometimes for personal injuries. Parents may also be liable for damage done by their minor children in auto accidents, if they authorized the child to drive. (Check the index to your state's laws under "Minors," "Children," or "Parent and Child" for the rules in your state.)

> **EXAMPLE 1:** John Johnson, age 17, trips over his shoelace while delivering your newspaper and crashes through your glass door. Can you recover from John's parents? Probably not, as John is not guilty of "willful misconduct."

> **EXAMPLE 2:** John shoots out the same glass door with a slingshot after you have repeatedly asked his parents to disarm him. Can you recover from the parents? Probably.

How to Sue Government Agencies

Many states have special rules and procedures that must be followed before a suit can be brought against a state or local government agency. Often, you have to act very quickly or you lose your right to sue. Your local small claims court might have information on the procedures you must follow and time limits you must meet. Check your state's small claims court website (see the appendix) or call your local small claims court. If you don't find the information you need, contact the government agency.

Claims Against a City

Typically, before you can sue a city because your car was illegally towed or a city employee damaged your property or injured you, or the city did anything else to you involving personal injury or property damage, you must file a claim with the city and have it denied. To do this, get a claim form from the local city clerk. For cases involving personal injury or damage to property, your claim usually must be filed within six months of the date of the incident. For breach of contract claims or real property damage claims, you usually have one year to file.

Often, the city attorney will be in charge of reviewing your claim and making a recommendation to the city council. Sometimes the recommendation will be to pay you, but often it will be to deny the claim. After the city acts, you usually have a certain time period (six months is typical) to file your small claims case. Save a copy of your denial letter from the city; the small claims court will want to see it.

Claims Against a County, District, or State

The rules for suits against counties and districts (for example, school districts) and the state are usually the same as the rules for claims against a city. You'll need to file a complaint against the governing entity before you can go to small claims court. Get the complaint form and file it promptly (within six months for personal injury or property damage and one year for breach of contract or damage to real property). If your claim is denied, you usually have six months to file in small claims court.

> CAUTION
> **No lawsuits against the U.S. government in small claims court.** You can't bring a small claims suit against the federal government, a federal agency, or even against a federal employee for actions relating to his or her employment. The federal government may not be sued in any state court without its consent. Suits against the federal government normally must be filed in federal district court.

A Deceased Person's Estate

You can still file a lawsuit or collect a judgment even if the defendant has died. You will direct your efforts at the deceased person's estate—that is, the property the person left behind. Act promptly; if you don't, your claim may be barred by law.

Unless the defendant arranged for everything in the estate to pass outside of probate (by using a living trust or other probate-avoidance device), there will probably be a probate court proceeding. It's conducted by the estate's "personal representative"—the executor named in the deceased person's will or, if there is no will, an administrator appointed by the court. Often, the surviving spouse or an adult child is the personal representative.

A personal representative who knows that you were owed money is required to send you a notification of the death. The notice will advise you to make a claim by a certain deadline, set by law. You will probably have at least two to four months in which to file your claim in the probate proceeding.

If you don't get a notice of the death, you can still submit a claim. Find out whether or not there's a probate proceeding (and if so, who the personal representative is) by checking probate records in the county where the defendant lived at the time of death. If you miss the deadline, a late claim may be allowed up to one year from the date of death.

You make an official claim by submitting a regular bill or by using a court document called a creditor's claim. Submit your claim directly to the probate court and serve a copy on the personal representative. If you file a formal claim and the personal representative rejects it, you can file suit against the estate.

What if there's no probate proceeding? In that case, your best bet is to present your claim to the deceased person's spouse, child, or close relative. If it is denied or ignored, you have the right to file suit against anyone who inherits from the deceased. Do it as soon as possible.

Where Can You Sue?

Small claims courts are local. This makes sense, because the dollar amounts involved aren't large enough to justify people traveling great distances to go to court. A small claims court judicial district is the same as a county. The next county will have its own similar, but separate, small claims court. Normally, your dispute will be with a person or business located nearby. If so, all you really need to know is that you can sue in the county in which the defendant lives or, if a business is involved, where its main place of business is located.

Occasionally, however, the person or business you want to sue resides at a considerable distance from where you live. How you should proceed in this situation depends primarily on whether the defendant is located in your state or a different state.

Out-of-State Defendants

Skip ahead to "Businesses," below, if you're planning to sue a business. Otherwise, read on.

Individuals

The basic rule is that state courts—including small claims courts—only have the power (lawyers call this jurisdiction) to hear cases involving individuals who live in or are present in the state. If you want to sue someone who lives in another state and doesn't travel to your state, you will have to sue in the state where the person lives, not in the state where you live. Often you can file papers by mail, but normally you'll need to show up in person on court day. (Some states allow people on active duty in the military and occasionally others to present their case entirely in writing.)

There are, however, circumstances under which you can use your state's small claims court to sue an out-of-state resident:

- Out-of-state residents can successfully be sued in-state if you manage to serve them with court papers while they're physically within your state's borders *and* if the dispute arose in your state. For example, you live in Florida and a nonresident injures you or damages your

property while he or she is in Florida, or a contract with a nonresident was negotiated, performed, or violated in Florida. (On serving court papers, see Chapter 11.)

- A nonresident who has a vehicle accident in your state may be sued in your state's small claims court no matter where that person lives. Similarly, a nonresident owner of a vehicle may be sued no matter where the person lives if his or her car was being driven in your state by another person and was involved in an accident. Contact your small claims court clerk for details.

- The out-of-state owner of real property (including owners of apartments and other rental housing) located in your state may be sued here on claims relating to that property.

Businesses

When it comes to suing a business in small claims court, you may sue any business that is organized (incorporated or established as an LLC) in your state.

In addition, you may bring suit against any business—whether incorporated or not—if one of the following conditions is true:

- the business was responsible for injuring you or damaging your property in your state *and* you can find a way to serve your court papers on the business in your state (see Chapter 11 on serving court papers)

- the business breaches a contract with you that was negotiated or was to be performed in your state *and* you can find a way to serve your court papers on the business in your state (see Chapter 11 on serving court papers)

- the business has an office, warehouse, retail establishment, restaurant, or other physical facility here, even if that business is headquartered or organized elsewhere, or

- the business does regular business in your state by selling products or services, employing a sales rep who calls on you personally or by phone to solicit business, sending you a catalog to solicit your business, or placing advertising in your state's media.

TIP

The short story about suing out-of-state businesses. What it comes down to is that most large national businesses can be sued in any state, but smaller businesses that are headquartered in another state, do no business in your state, and have no physical presence in your state can be sued only in the states where they operate.

EXAMPLE 1: While on vacation in Florida, you slip and fall in the ticket office of a small locally owned commuter airline that operates only in Florida. When you return home to Maine, you file suit against the airline for your injuries in small claims court. The judge will toss out your case, because Maine courts do not have the power (jurisdiction) to hear a case involving a defendant that doesn't operate, advertise, or solicit business in Maine. The only place you can sue the little airline is in Florida.

EXAMPLE 2: You're at home in Maine and planning your vacation to Florida, and you slip and fall in the ticket office of a national airline that has its headquarters in Florida. This time, you can sue the airline for your injuries in small claims court. The fact that the airline does business in Maine gives this state's courts the power to hear your case, even though the airline has its headquarters elsewhere.

EXAMPLE 3: You own a small graphic design company in Maine and negotiate a contract over the phone and via email with a clothing designer in New York to design business cards and signs for a new store that the clothing designer plans to open in Maine. You complete the work on time but the designer refuses to pay you. Can you sue the designer in Maine's small claims court? Yes. It's arguable whether the contract was negotiated in Maine, but it's a fact that you performed the work in Maine. Thus, you can sue the designer in Maine small claims court *if* you can serve your court papers on the designer within Maine's borders.

Defendants in Your State

If the person or business you want to sue resides or does business in your state, you have to decide which small claims court should hear your suit.

Of all the aspects of small claims court that differ from state to state, the rules on where to sue seem to be the most variable. Some states let you sue only in the district or county where the defendant resides. Others also allow

you to sue where an accident occurred, a contract was broken or originally signed, merchandise was purchased, a corporation does business, and so on.

You'll need to refer to the rules for your local small claims court to determine where to sue (look at your state's listing in the appendix). The first thing you will want to look at is what type of political subdivisions (judicial district, precinct, city, county) your state uses to define the geographical boundaries of its small claims courts. Next, you will want to carefully study your local rules in order to understand the criteria used to define which district a particular lawsuit should be brought in (for example, suits can always be brought where a defendant lives). If this information is not set out in the information sheet, call the clerk of the court and ask. Often you may be eligible to sue in more than one judicial district (for example, where a defendant lives or where a traffic accident occurred). If you have a choice, you'll obviously want to pick the court that is most convenient for you.

TIP

In a few states you can sue for larger amounts in some areas. In some states, such as New York, Pennsylvania, and Tennessee, you can sue for higher amounts in certain counties. Obviously, if yours is a larger claim, you'll want to see whether you are eligible to sue in one of these locations. (The rules for all states are set out in the appendix.)

General Rules on Where You Can Sue

Depending on the specific rules of your state, you can generally sue in any one of the following political subdivisions:

- the judicial district in which the defendant resides or has a place of business at the time you file your lawsuit
- the judicial district in which the contract underlying your lawsuit was supposed to be carried out
- the judicial district in which the injury underlying your lawsuit occurred, or
- the judicial district in which the rental property is located (for landlord-tenant security deposit disputes or evictions).

Now let's consider some typical rules about where you can sue within a state.

Where the Defendant Lives or Does Business

Because most small claims disputes are local, most plaintiffs follow the simplest provisions of the rules about where you can sue. They sue individual defendants in the judicial district where they live and business defendants (corporations, LLCs, or unincorporated businesses) in the judicial district where they do business.

> **EXAMPLE:** Downhill Skier lives in City County, but also owns a mountain cabin in Snowy County, where he spends several months a year. Late one snowy afternoon, Downhill drives his new SUV from the ski slopes to his nearby cabin. Turning into his driveway, he executes a bad slalom skid right into Woodsey Carpenter's elderly but much-loved pickup. Where can Woodsey properly sue? Obviously, Woodsey can sue in City County where Downhill has his permanent address, and he can probably also sue in Snowy County where Downhill's cabin is located, on the theory that Downhill also lives there. In many states, Woodsey is also eligible to sue Downhill in Snowy County because small claims cases may be filed where the damage occurred.

Where the Contract Was Signed

Most states assume that the place where a written contract is signed is also where it will be carried out. Therefore, you can usually sue where the contract was signed, if a problem develops.

Arizona, California, Indiana, and a few other states are more thorough. (See the appendix.) In these states, a suit can be brought either where the contract was signed or where the contract was to be performed. This is good common sense, as the law assumes that, if people enter into a contract to perform something at a certain location, it is probably reasonably convenient to both. If, for example, Downhill gets a telephone installed in his mountain cabin, or has the fender on his SUV fixed by a Snowy County mechanic, or has a cesspool put in at his cabin, or agrees to sit (and pay) for a portrait in

Snowy County, he can be sued in Snowy County if he fails to keep his part of the bargain. Of course, as we learned above, Downhill can also be sued in City County, where he resides permanently.

> **EXAMPLE:** John Gravenstein lives in Sonoma County, California, where he owns an apple orchard. He signs a contract to buy spare parts from Acme Mechanical Apple Picker Co., an international corporation with offices in San Francisco, New York, Paris, and Guatemala City. John signs the contract in Sonoma County. The parts are sent to John from San Francisco via UPS. They turn out to be defective. After trying and failing to reach a settlement with Acme, John wants to know if he can sue them in Sonoma County. Yes. Even though Acme doesn't have a business office in Sonoma County and they performed no action there in connection with their agreement to sell John the spare parts, the contract was signed there.

TIP
If you have a choice of judicial districts, pick the most convenient one. As you should now understand, there may be two, three, or more judicial districts in which you can properly file your case. In this situation, simply choose the one that serves you best. As long as that district is proper, you have no obligation to pick one the defendant prefers.

Unfortunately, it isn't always easy to determine the location where a contract was entered into—particularly when the people who made the contract did so from different locations. If you enter a contract over the phone or online, for example, there could be an argument that the contract was entered into either where you are or where the other party is. Rather than trying to learn and apply all the intricacies of contract law, your best bet is probably to sue in the place most convenient to you, claiming that the contract was made there. On the other hand, if someone sues you at the wrong end of the state and you believe there is a good argument that the contract was formed where you live (that is, where you accepted the other party's offer), write to the court as soon as you have been served and ask that the case be dismissed. (See "If You Are Sued in the Wrong Court," below.)

Where the Injury Occurred

Most states allow you to sue in the judicial district where the act or omission underlying the lawsuit occurred (see the appendix). "Act or omission" is a shorthand term that lumps together things that lead to lawsuits like automobile accidents, warranty disputes, and landlord-tenant disputes, for the purpose of deciding where you're allowed to sue. This means that if you are in a car accident, a dog bites you, a tree falls on your head, or a neighbor floods your cactus garden, you can sue in the judicial district where the event or injury occurred, even if this is a different district from the one in which the defendant resides.

> **EXAMPLE:** Addison is returning to his home in Indianapolis from Bloomington, Indiana, following an Indiana University basketball game. At the same time, Lenore is rushing to Bloomington from her home in Brown County, Indiana, more than 40 miles west of Bloomington. Lenore runs a red light and demolishes Addison's Toyota near the Indiana University gym in downtown Bloomington, which is in Monroe County. After parking his car and taking a bus home, Addison tries to figure out where he can sue Lenore if they can't work out a fair settlement. Unfortunately for him, he can't sue in Indianapolis, as Lenore doesn't reside there and the accident didn't happen there. Addison would have to sue either in Monroe County, where his property was damaged, or in Brown County, where Lenore lives. Luckily for Addison, Monroe County is just an hour from Indianapolis.

If You Are Sued in the Wrong Court

The sometimes complicated rules as to where you can sue and be sued mean that occasionally people and businesses are sued in the wrong court. If you are served with court papers that list an improper judicial district for the hearing, you have two choices.

1. Show up and go ahead with the case. Although the court has independent authority to transfer a case to a correct court, the judge is likely to go ahead with your trial if both parties show up ready to proceed. Doing this may be a good choice if the court you are sued in is reasonably convenient.

2. Challenge the location in which the case is filed (called "challenging venue"). You can challenge venue by:
 - promptly writing a letter to the court explaining the reasons why you believe the case has been filed in the wrong place, and sending a copy of the letter to all other parties (this would essentially be equivalent to a "motion to change venue"), or
 - showing up on the court date and challenging the location in person (some judges consider your appearance a waiver of venue, so be sure to check with your court before taking this approach).

If a court determines that the suit has been filed in the wrong court, it will either dismiss the case or transfer it to a proper court. A dismissal shouldn't be a problem as long as the plaintiff sued reasonably promptly after the loss occurred, because the plaintiff still has plenty of time to refile, with no worries that too much time will have passed. (See Chapter 5 for information about statutes of limitations.) If the defendant challenges venue with a letter but the court rules that, in fact, the suit was brought in the correct court, then the judge will probably delay the hearing for a few days to give the defendant time to make arrangements to appear.

Sample Letter by Defendant Challenging Venue

2100 Coast Drive
Beachtown, FL 12344
December 12, 20xx

Small Claims Court
600 Washington
Tallahassee, FL 12344

Re: *Upton vs. Downey*
 # 987 321

Dear Judge:

I am the defendant in this case. Because I have been sued in the wrong court and will be highly inconvenienced if I have to defend myself there, I request that you please dismiss this court action.

My request is based on the fact I live in Beachtown, FL, and the car accident that gave rise to this case occurred in Orange County. The fact that plaintiff later moved to Tallahassee and chose to file suit in your court does not amount to a valid legal reason to have it heard there.

Sincerely,

Fred Downey
Fred Downey

Filing Fees, Court Papers, and Court Dates

How Much Does It Cost?

Fees for filing a case in small claims court are very moderate—usually not much more than $75. In some states, people with very low incomes can ask to have court filing fees waived. Normally, a defendant doesn't have to pay anything unless the defendant files a claim against the plaintiff (often called a counterclaim). There is usually an additional fee for serving papers on the opposing party, unless you are in a state that allows personal service to be carried out by a nonprofessional process server and you have a friend who will do it for you without charge. (See Chapter 11.) Most states allow service by certified or registered mail, which doesn't cost much. In a few situations, you may have to hire a professional process server. How much this costs will depend partly on how hard it is to find the person you need to serve. You can get your filing fees and service costs added to the court judgment if you win. (See Chapter 15.)

Filing Your Lawsuit

Now let's look at how you obtain and fill out the papers you need to start your lawsuit. To get started, check your state's small claims court information website. You should be able to get the information and forms you need to begin your lawsuit online (see Appendix A for your state's website). If you get the forms from your state's website, you will also need to check whether the county or court where you plan to file has additional forms or requirements for filing a small claims court action (some do). You can also visit or call the small claims court where you plan to file your lawsuit.

To start your case, you will have to file a complaint or claim. This form is often called a plaintiff's statement, general claim, or plaintiff's claim. Most states have forms and free self-help information on their small claims court website. You can also get the forms from the court where you will be filing your lawsuit. If you do it this way, you will likely receive a package with all the forms you need and instructions for filling out the forms and filing your papers.

In most cases, you will need to provide the following information to complete your complaint or claim:

- your full name, address, and telephone number
- the correct name and address of the person or persons you are suing (including whether this is an individual, partnership, sole proprietor, limited liability company, or corporation)
- the amount of your claim
- the reason the defendant owes you money, and
- whether you have any other claims against that person or other small claims cases.

Other information may be required as well. Follow the instructions on your forms and if you still have questions, ask your local small claims court clerk for help. In most states, small claims clerks are required to help people fill out these forms.

CAUTION

Be sure you name everything properly. Chapter 7 has details about the correct way to list yourself or your business as the plaintiff. In Chapter 8, we discuss how to properly name the defendant.

You will need to check the rules of the court where you are filing your case and follow those procedures for filing your papers and paying your filing fee. In most jurisdictions, you can file your papers in person or by mail. You'll need to file the original signed document and required number of copies with the court. Some courts allow electronic filing (eFiling) for small claims cases, either by the plaintiff directly or through an approved online service provider; eFiling is becoming more widely used for small claims and is even required in some jurisdictions. Be sure to check and follow the rules for the court where you plan to file your case.

You will also need to pay the court a filing fee. If you can't afford the fee, you may be able to have it waived. Check with your local court for rules on waiving this fee.

In most small claims courts, you don't need to provide written evidence until you get to court. Some small claims courts, however—such as those in Washington, DC—require that certain types of evidence (such as copies of unpaid bills, contracts, or other documents on which the claim is based) be provided at the time you file your first papers.

Whether or not your state's rules require written documentation of certain types of claims, it is wise to spend a little time thinking about how you will prove your case. I discuss this in detail in the later chapters of this book. You should read ahead and figure out exactly what proof you will need and how you will present it before you file your first court papers. Being right is one thing—proving it is another.

The Defendant's Forms

In most states, a defendant doesn't have to file any papers to defend a case in small claims court unless the defendant wants the case transferred to formal court. However, in a few states, a defendant must respond in writing. (See the appendix for your state's rules.) In the majority of states, defendants simply show up for the hearing on the date and at the time indicated on the papers served on them, ready to tell their side of the story. (If you need to get the hearing delayed, see "Your Court Date," below.) It is proper, and advisable, for a defendant to call or write the plaintiff and see whether a fair settlement can be reached without going to court, or to propose mediation. (See Chapter 6.)

Sometimes a party you planned to sue sues you first (for example, over a traffic accident where you each believe the other is at fault). As long as your grievance stems from the same incident, you can file a defendant's claim (sometimes called a counterclaim) for up to the small claims court maximum and have it heard by a judge at the same time that the plaintiff's claim against you is considered. However, if you believe that the plaintiff owes you money as the result of a different injury or breach of contract, you may have to file your own separate case.

In all states you must file any defendant's claim (counterclaim) in writing within a certain time period after being served with the plaintiff's claim (usually ten to 30 days). When you file a defendant's claim, you become a plaintiff as far as this claim is concerned. In those states where only the defendant can appeal, this means that if you lose your defendant's claim, you can't appeal that part of the case. Of course, even in these states, if you lose on the original plaintiff's claim, you can normally appeal that portion of the judgment. Appeal rules vary from state to state and can be complicated. (See Chapter 23 and the appendix.)

In most states, if a defendant's claim is for more than the small claims maximum, the case will be transferred to a formal court. Some states allow transfers only at the discretion of a judge, who may inquire whether the defendant's claim is made in good faith. Check your court rules and your state's listing in Appendix A. A defendant who does not want to cope with the procedures of formal court may be wise to scale down the claim to fit under the small claims limit. (See Chapter 4.)

> **CAUTION**
> **A defendant may be required to file a defendant's claim or lose the right to do so.** A defendant who has a claim against a plaintiff arising out of the incident underlying the plaintiff's lawsuit will almost always want to promptly file it. Some states require defendants to file a counterclaim as part of the plaintiff's lawsuit; others allow defendants to file their own lawsuit later. If this is an issue for you, check your state's rules.

Jury Trials

Jury trials are not available in small claims court in most states. Plaintiffs know this when they file and can usually opt for a different court if they want trial by jury. Defendants, of course, don't have this up-front choice. To compensate, some states allow a defendant who wants a jury trial to transfer a case to a formal court no matter how small the claim. Others allow transfer only when the defendant's claim exceeds the small claims court maximum. Normally, a defendant must request a jury trial (or a transfer to a court where a jury is permitted) promptly after being served with court papers. And jury fees (often ranging from $100 to $500) must typically be paid in advance. Fees are normally recoverable if you win. Asking for a jury trial also tends to delay proceedings, and some people make the request for this reason. Check your state's rules on jury trials in small claims court.

Your Court Date

One of the great advantages of small claims court is that disputes are heard quickly. This is important. Many people avoid lawyers and the regular courts

primarily because they can take what seems like forever. In small claims court, you should get a court date in a relatively short time frame.

It is sometimes impossible for a plaintiff or defendant to be present on the date the court sets for the hearing. If this happens, you should contact the court immediately and ask that the case be rescheduled. Ask the clerk of the court or check your local court rules for any specific requirements for rescheduling a case. Oftentimes, you'll be required to make your request in writing and explain why you need a delay. Here's a sample of a letter requesting a postponement. Be sure to also send a copy to the other party at the same time you give the letter to the court.

Sample Letter Requesting Postponement

37 Birdwalk Boulevard
Trenton, NJ

January 15, 20xx

Clerk
Small Claims Court
Trenton, NJ

Re: Small Claims No. 374-628

Dear Clerk:

I have been served with a complaint (No. 374-628) by John's Laundry, Inc. The date set for a hearing, February 15, falls on the day of my son's graduation from Nursing School in Oscaloosa, Oklahoma, which my husband and I plan to attend.

I called John's Laundry and asked to have the case delayed one week. They did not return my call.

I feel that I have a good defense to this suit. Please delay this case until any date after February 22, except March 13, which is my day for a medical checkup.

Thank you,

Sally Wren

Sally Wren

cc: John's Laundry

Before making your request to the court, you can try to contact the other party in the case to see if you can agree to a mutually acceptable time for a new court date. If you both agree to reschedule, you could give the court a joint request for postponement signed by both parties. Here's a sample (but check your local rules for any specific requirements in your jurisdiction).

Sample Joint Request for Postponement

11 South Street
Denver, CO.

January 10, 20xx

Clerk of the Small Claims Court
Denver, CO

Re: SC 4117 (*Rodriguez v. McNally*)

Mr. Rodriguez and I agree to request that you postpone this case to a date after March 1, 20xx. If possible, we would prefer that it not be scheduled on March 27 or 28.

John McNally
John McNally

John Rodriguez
John Rodriguez

What if an emergency occurs just a few days before a scheduled hearing? The court still has the power to reschedule your case if the judge is convinced that circumstances warrant it (for example, a key witness has left town to attend a funeral). Contact the court clerk immediately, explain the problem, and ask for guidance.

 RELATED TOPIC

What if your opponent doesn't show up? For detailed instructions on how to proceed if your opponent (whether you're the plaintiff or defendant) doesn't show up to the court hearing, see Chapter 15.

Serving Your Papers

After the plaintiff files a claim with the small claims clerk, he or she must deliver a copy of the claim to each defendant. This is called service of process, and no lawsuit is complete without it. The reason you must serve the other side is obvious: Defendants in a case need to know about any claims against them and must be notified of the day, time, and place that they can show up to defend themselves. In addition, any defendant who files a defendant's claim against a plaintiff must serve copies of that claim on all plaintiffs in the case. Service of process rules also apply if you need to deliver a subpoena to a witness. (See Chapter 14.)

> CAUTION
>
> **Check to be sure your papers were served.** Never show up in court on the day of the court hearing on the assumption that your certified mail service has been accomplished. If the defendant didn't sign for the paper, you will be wasting your time. Call the court clerk a couple of days in advance and verify that the service of process has been completed. This means the certified letter has been signed for by the defendant, not by someone else at the address.

Who Must Be Served

All defendants on the plaintiff's claim or all plaintiffs on the defendant's claim must be served. It is not enough to serve one defendant or plaintiff and assume that that person will tell the others. This is true even if the parties are married, live together, or do business together.

> CAUTION
>
> **If you don't serve a party, the judge will postpone the hearing or dismiss your case against that party.** If you sue only one person and don't serve that person according to the rules, then the judge will probably postpone the hearing until after you're able to serve that person. If you sue more than one person and serve only one properly, the judge cannot enter a judgment against those people you didn't serve and will dismiss your action against those parties. Some states will allow you to refile your claim against those parties if you wish.

Where Can Papers Be Served?

Normally, papers must be served in the state where you filed your lawsuit. Thus, you can't sue someone in a Massachusetts court and serve papers on them in Oklahoma. An exception involves suits having to do with motor vehicle accidents or lawsuits against out-of-state owners of real estate located in-state. Many states allow out-of-state service on this type of claim. Your small claims court clerk will show you how this is handled in your state.

Assuming the person you want to sue resides or does business in your state, you can serve papers anyplace in the state. (See Chapter 9.)

Serving an Individual

There are several ways to serve papers on individual defendants. (See "Serving a Business," below, for information on serving a business.) All depend on your knowing where the defendant is. If you can't find the defendant personally and do not know where the person lives or works, you won't be able to complete service, and it probably makes little sense to file a lawsuit.

Serving Someone With a Post Office Box

If you know nothing more than the individual defendant's post office box, you'll need to get a street address in order to serve the person. To do this, you must give the post office a written statement saying that you need the address solely to serve legal papers in a pending lawsuit. (See "Sample Request to Post Office for Boxholder's Address," below.) This should work, but if it doesn't, refer the post office employee to the Post Office's Administrative Support Manual § 352.44e(2). There is no fee for the Post Office providing this information. (39 CFR § 265.6(d)(4)(ii).)

Sample Request to Post Office for Boxholder's Address

June 1, 20xx

Postmaster
Minneapolis, MN 12333

REQUEST FOR BOXHOLDER INFORMATION NEEDED FOR SERVICE OF
LEGAL PROCESS

Please furnish the name and street address of the following post office
box holder:

> Don Defendant
> P.O. Box 0000
> Minneapolis, MN 12333

1. Capacity of requester (e.g., process server, attorney, party representing self):
 Party representing self.

2. Statute or regulation that empowers me to serve process (not required when
 requester is an attorney or a party acting pro se—except a corporation acting
 pro se must cite statute): I am a party representing myself.

3. The names of all known parties to the litigation: Peggy Plaintiff and
 Don Defendant.

4. The court in which the case has been or will be heard: Hennepin County
 Small Claims Court, City Hall, Room 306, Minneapolis, MN 55415.

5. The docket or other identifying number if one has been issued:
 Case Number 000000.

6. The capacity in which this individual is to be served (e.g., defendant or
 witness): Defendant.

WARNING: THE SUBMISSION OF FALSE INFORMATION TO OBTAIN AND USE
BOXHOLDER INFORMATION FOR ANY PURPOSE OTHER THAN THE SERVICE
OF LEGAL PROCESS IN CONNECTION WITH ACTUAL OR PROSPECTIVE
LITIGATION COULD RESULT IN CRIMINAL PENALTIES INCLUDING A FINE OF
UP TO $10,000 OR IMPRISONMENT OF NOT MORE THAN 5 YEARS, OR BOTH
(TITLE 18 U.S.C. SECTION 1001).

Sample Request to Post Office for Boxholder's Address (continued)

I certify that the above information is true and that the address information is needed and will be used solely for service of legal process in conjunction with actual or prospective litigation.

Peggy Plaintiff

Peggy Plaintiff

123 Maiden Lane

Minneapolis, MN 12333

Personal Service

Personal service means that someone hands the defendant the relevant papers. You have various options regarding who performs this task. Of course, if you use someone who doesn't personally know the defendant, the server will need to be particularly careful to serve the right person. These are your options for who can serve the defendant.

- **Sheriff, marshal, or constable.** All states allow personal service to be made by law officers, although not all officers will serve civil subpoenas. Using this method is often valuable for its sobering effect. The fee can be added to your judgment if you win.

- **Private process servers.** Many states also allow service by private process servers, whom you will find listed in the yellow pages. Fees charged are usually based on how long the service takes. See your state's listing in the appendix to find out whether your state allows service by private process servers.

- **Service by disinterested adult.** Some states (see the appendix) allow service by any person who is at least 18 years old, except the person bringing the suit. Any person means just that—a relative or a friend is fine. However, states often require that this person be approved by the court.

How to Find a Good Process Server

Unfortunately, sheriff's offices in some states are getting out of the process-serving business. This means that you may have to hire a private person or company. Some of these are truly fly-by-night—they've figured out that process serving is a quick way to make a buck. You may even see them cruising around the courthouse looking for business. To make sure you're dealing with a business that backs up its promises, do a little research first. One indicator of trustworthiness is how long the process server has been in business—ask to see a business license or look in the phone book for process servers who list the date their business was founded. You can also ask the small claims court clerk for a list of registered process servers. If you know any lawyers, you can ask them for a recommendation.

CAUTION

A mailbox isn't personal enough. No matter who serves the papers, if personal service is used, the claim and a summons must be handed to the defendant. You can't simply leave the paper at the defendant's job or home or in the mailbox. If the process server locates the right person, but the person refuses to take the paper, acts hostile, or attempts to run away, the process server should simply put the paper down and leave. Valid service has been accomplished. The process server should never try to use force to get a defendant to take any papers.

Serving Someone in the Military

It is proper to serve someone who is on active duty in the armed forces. If the person shows up, fine. If not, however, you have a problem. Although you can usually get a default judgment against a properly served defendant who fails to show up, this is not true if the person you are suing is in the military (other than the reserves).

Default judgments cannot normally be taken against people on active duty in the armed forces, because Congress has given our military personnel special protections. To get a default judgment, you will probably have to file a statement under penalty of perjury that the defendant is not in the military. This declaration is available from the clerk. Clerks almost always accept a Declaration of Nonmilitary Service signed by the plaintiff, as long as the plaintiff reasonably believes that the defendant is not on active duty. This constitutes a lenient interpretation of the law by clerks, but no one seems to be complaining.

Certified Mail

In the majority of states, you can serve papers by sending them to the defendant via certified mail with a return receipt requested. In some states, service by certified (or registered) mail is one among several ways you may serve papers. Other states require you to try service by certified mail first, before any other method of service. (See Appendix A.) Normally, the court clerk does the mailing for you and charges a small fee. This is recoverable

if you win. (See Chapter 15.) The mail method is both cheap and easy, but in most states the defendant must sign for the letter for this type of service to be effective. (In a few states, service is accomplished even if a certified letter is rejected by the defendant.) Most businesses and many individuals routinely sign to accept their mail. However, some people never do, knowing instinctively, or perhaps from past experience, that nothing good ever comes by certified mail. The consensus in an informal survey of court clerks is that about 50% of court papers served by certified mail are accepted. If you try using the mail to serve your papers and fail, and you end up having to pay a process server, tell the judge about it as part of your presentation and chances are your costs will be added to the judgment.

Regular First-Class Mail

A minority of states allow papers to be served by first-class mail. The states differ, however, on what you must do if the defendant doesn't answer your complaint within the time limit. New York, for example, presumes that the defendant received the papers unless the envelope comes back as "undeliverable." Check with your court clerk to see if this method is available in your area.

Substituted Service (or "Nail and Mail")

It can be difficult to serve certain individuals. Some have developed their skill at avoiding process servers into a high art. In some states, avoiding service no longer works, as there is now a procedure that allows "substituted service" if you make "reasonable efforts" to serve a defendant and fail. Often the slang for this type of service is "nail and mail," because in several states, if you are unable to serve the defendant personally, you do not have to leave the claim with a live person. Instead, you can simply tack one copy to the defendant's door and mail the second copy.

In a typical state, substituted service works like this:

1. Small claims papers may be served by an adult who is not named in the lawsuit by leaving a copy at the person's dwelling place in the presence of a competent member of the household who is at least age 18 (and who must be told what the papers are about) or at the person's

workplace during normal business hours with the person in charge (who must be told what the papers are about).

2. On the same day, a copy of the papers must also be mailed to the defendant by first-class mail.

Service is complete ten days after mailing. Be sure that all steps, including mailing the extra copy, are carried out by an adult who is not named in the lawsuit.

Serving a Business

When you sue a business, the same methods of service discussed above can be used. However, if you use the personal service or certified mail service methods, you'll need to know how the business is legally organized in order to determine whom you must serve. (See "Who Should Be Served," below.) And if you know only a business defendant's post office box, you'll normally want to get its street address. (See "Serving Someone With a Post Office Box," above.)

Whom to Serve When Suing a Business

When suing a business, you need to serve your court papers on the owner, a partner, the president, vice-president, secretary, treasurer, or the business's agent for service of process. How do you find out who this person is?

One simple approach is to call the business and ask who, and where, they are. If they won't tell you, the city or county tax and license people where the business is located should be able to do so. (See Chapter 8.) For a corporation, limited partnership, or LLC organized in your state, you should be able to get this information from your secretary of state's office.

Who Should Be Served?

No matter which method of service you choose, who you must serve depends on how the business is organized.

Sole proprietorship. Serve the owner.

Partnership. Serve at least one partner.

Limited partnership. Serve the partner who runs the business (the general partner) or the agent for service of process.

Corporation (profit or nonprofit). Serve an officer (president, vice president, secretary, or treasurer) or the agent for service of process.

Limited liability company. Serve an officer (president, vice president, secretary, or treasurer) or the agent for service of process.

Substituted or Personal Service

If you need to serve papers on a business with a local office, store, or other physical location, personal service or substituted service is best if your state allows this type of service. (See the appendix.) Have a process server or "disinterested adult" attempt to deliver the papers personally to the proper person at the business address. If the person is unavailable, the process server should leave the papers at the defendant's business during usual business hours with the person in charge (this is the first step in "substituted service"). Then, mail a copy of the summons and complaint, via certified mail, to the person to be served at the same address.

Certified Mail Service

Service via certified mail is probably your best bet if the business doesn't have a local office, store, or other physical location and if your state allows this type of service. (See the appendix.) To serve a business via certified mail, ask the court clerk to send the court papers to the proper person and address and pay the small fee. You can serve:

- the proper person as listed in "Who Should Be Served?" above, or
- the business's registered agent for service of process, if the business has its only address outside of your state.

How to Serve a Government Agency

As discussed in Chapter 8, before you can sue a city, county, or other government agency you must first file an administrative (in-house) claim

against that agency within a specified number of days after the incident that gave rise to your claim. (The fact that you have done this must be stated in your plaintiff's claim.) After your claim is denied—or if it is ignored—you can go ahead and sue in small claims court. To serve your papers, call the governmental body in question and ask who should be served. Then proceed, following the rules set out in "Serving an Individual," above.

Time Limits for Serving a Claim

The plaintiff in a small claims case is responsible for making sure that the defendant receives copies of the lawsuit before the hearing date. Every state has its own rule about the deadline by which the defendant must be served; some states require as few as five days before the hearing, whereas others require as many as 30 days. Check with your small claims court clerk for the rules in your state.

If the defendant is served fewer than the required number of days before the trial date, he or she can either go ahead with the trial anyway or request a postponement. If you're the defendant and it's impossible for you to show up in person to ask for a delay, call the court clerk. Point out that you weren't served in the proper time and that you want the case postponed. The clerk should see to it that a default judgment is not entered against you. (See Chapter 10.) But just to be sure, get the clerk's name and take thorough notes about your conversation.

To count the days to see whether service has been accomplished in the correct time, do not count the day the service is made, but do count the day of the court appearance. Also count weekends and holidays, unless the last day falls on a weekend or holiday. If so, the period extends to the next day that is not a holiday.

> **EXAMPLE:** Jack serves Julie on July 12 in Los Angeles, California, with court papers listing a July 22 court date. California's rules require Jack to serve Julie with the court papers at least 15 days before the hearing. July 13 is a Sunday. To figure out the days, you do not count July 12, the day of service, but you do count July 13, 14, 15, 16, 17, 18, 19, 20, 21, and 22, for a total of ten days. Ten days is not enough time before the hearing date. Julie can either request a postponement because she wasn't served according to the rules, or she can choose to go ahead with the hearing.

If you are unable to serve the defendant within the proper time, simply ask the court clerk for a new court date and try again.

Proof of Service—Letting the Court Know

If you have asked the court clerk to serve your papers by certified mail, you need do nothing else. The court clerk sends out the certified mail for you, and the signed post office receipt comes back directly to the clerk if service is accomplished. It's as simple as that.

However, a court has no way of knowing whether or not papers have been successfully filed by personal service, substituted service, or first-class mail unless you tell them. So, you are required to do so. Notification is accomplished by filing a form known as a Proof of Service with the court clerk after the service has been made. (See "Sample Proof of Service," below.) The Proof of Service form must be signed by the person actually making the service. A Proof of Service is used both by the plaintiff and by the defendant if the defendant files a defendant's claim. It must be returned to the clerk's office.

Serving a Defendant's Claim

A defendant's claim is the form filed by a defendant who wishes to sue the plaintiff for money damages. A defendant's claim should be filed with the clerk and served on the plaintiff within the proper number of days before the hearing. Days are counted in the same way as discussed above.

If you are a defendant who has filed a claim and you are unable to serve the plaintiff, simply show up on the court hearing date with your papers and serve the plaintiff in the hallway (not in the courtroom). Then explain to the judge why it was impossible to locate the plaintiff earlier. The judge will normally delay the case for a few days, unless both you and the plaintiff agree to proceed with your claim that day. Either way, the judge should accept your defendant's claim as having been validly served.

Serving Subpoenas

In Chapter 14, we discuss subpoenaing witnesses and documents. The rules as to who can do the serving are the same as those set forth in "Serving an Individual," above, with one important difference: Any person, including the person bringing the suit, can serve the subpoena. In addition, in many states, the person making the service must be ready to pay the person subpoenaed a witness fee on the spot if it is requested. This is often a flat fee (normally $40–$100), plus a mileage fee based on the distance to the courthouse. If you hire a sheriff or marshal to do the service, he or she will ask you to pay this fee, plus the service fee, in advance. In many states, if the witness doesn't ask for the fee, it will be returned to you. (See Chapter 14 for details.)

A witness must be served with a subpoena far enough in advance of the court hearing date to give the witness "reasonable time" to prepare for and travel to the hearing.

Costs of Service

Professional process servers commonly charge from $30–$100 per service, depending on how far they must travel. You can usually get these costs of service added to your judgment if you win, but be sure to remind the judge to do this when you conclude your court presentation. However, a few courts will not give the successful party an award to cover a process server's costs unless the person first tried to have the papers served by the cheaper certified mail approach. Other courts prefer that you don't use the mail approach at all; they feel that it wastes time because too often the mail isn't accepted. Ask the small claims clerk or small claims adviser in your district how the court prefers that you accomplish service and how much the judge will allow as a service of process fee.

Sample Proof of Service

SC-104 Proof of Service	*Clerk stamps date here when form is filed.*

Use this form to serve a **person,** a **business,** or a **public entity.** To learn more about proof of service, read *What Is "Proof of Service"?,* Form SC-104B. To learn more about how to serve a business or entity, read *How to Serve a Business or Public Entity,* Form SC-104C.

To serve a **business,** you must serve **one** of the following people:
- Owner (for a sole proprietorship)
- Partner (for a partnership) or general partner (for a limited partnership)
- Any officer or general manager (corporation or association)
- Any person authorized for service by the business (corporation, association, general partnership, limited partnership)
- Any person authorized for service with the Secretary of State (corporation, association, limited liability company [LLC], limited liability partnership [LLP], limited partnership)

To serve a **public entity,** you must first file a claim with that entity, then serve **one** of the following people:
- Clerk (of a city or county)
- Chief officer or director (of a public agency)
- Any person authorized for service by the entity

Fill in court name and street address:
Superior Court of California, County of
Alameda
600 Washington Street
3rd Floor
Oakland, CA 94607

Fill in case number, case name, hearing date, day, time, and department below:

Case Number:
002006

Case Name:
Printer v. Acme Illusions, Inc.

Hearing Date: 6/15/20xx

Time: 9:00 a.m. **Dept.:** 304

(1) a. If you are serving a **person,** write the person's name below:

 b. If you are serving a **business** or **entity,** write the name of the business or entity, the person authorized for service, and that person's job title:

Acme Illusions, Inc. Waldo Fergus, President
<u>Business or Agency Name</u>

<u>Person Authorized for Service Job Title</u>

(2) **Instructions to Server:**
You must be at least 18 years old and **not be named in this case.** Follow these steps:
- Give a copy of all the documents checked in **(3)** to the person in **(1),** *or*
- Give a copy of all the documents checked in **(3)** to one of the following people:
 - a. A competent adult (at least 18) living with, and at the home of the person in **(1),** *or*
 - b. An adult (at least 18) who seems to be in charge at the usual workplace of the person in **(1),** *or*
 - c. An adult (at least 18) who seems to be in charge where the person in **(1)** usually receives mail (but not a U.S. Post Office box), if there is no known physical address for the person in **(1)**.
 and mail a copy of the documents left with one of the adults in a, b, or c above to the person in **(1)**.

THEN
- Complete and sign this form, and
- Give or mail your completed form to the person who asked you to serve these court papers, *in time for the form to be filed with the court at least 5 days before the hearing.*

(3) **I served the person in (1) a copy of the documents checked below:**

a. ☒ SC-100, *Plaintiff's Claim and ORDER to Go to Small Claims Court*

b. ☐ SC-120, *Defendant's Claim and ORDER to Go to Small Claims Court*

c. ☐ Order for examination *(This form must be personally served. Check the form that was served):*
> **Note:** *The court can issue a civil arrest warrant if the served party does not come to court **only** if the order for examination was personally served by a registered process server, sheriff, marshal, or someone appointed by the court.*
>
> (1) ☐ SC-134, *Application and Order to Produce Statement of Assets and to Appear for Examination*
>
> (2) ☐ AT-138/EJ-125, *Application and Order for Appearance and Examination*

d. ☐ Other *(specify):* _____

Judicial Council of California, www.courtinfo.ca.gov
Revised January 1, 2009, Optional Form
Code of Civil Procedure, §§ 116.340, 415.10, 415.20

Proof of Service
(Small Claims)

SC-104, Page 1 of 2 →

Sample Proof of Service (page 2)

Case name: Printer v. Acme Illusions, Inc.

Case Number:

002006

(4) **Fill out "a" or "b" below:**

a. ☐ **Personal Service:** I personally gave copies of the documents checked in ③ to the person in ①:

On *(date):* _____ At *(time):* _____ ☐ a.m. ☐ p.m.

At this address: _____

City: _____ State:_____ Zip: _____

b. ☒ **Substituted Service:** I personally gave copies of the documents checked in ③ *(a, b, or d)* to *(check one):*

☐ A competent adult (at least 18) at the **home** of, and living with the person in① , or

☐ An adult who seems to be in charge where the person in① usually **works**, or

☒ An adult who seems to be in charge where the person in① usually **receives mail**, or has a private post office box (not a U.S. Post Office box), if there is no known physical address for the person in①.

I told that adult, "Please give these court papers to (name of person in①)."

I did this on *(date):* May 10, 20xx At *(time):* 10:15 ☒ a.m. ☐ p.m.

At this address: _____ 100 Primrose Path _____

City: _____ Oakland _____ State: CA ____ Zip: ___ 94602 ____

Name or description of the person I gave the papers to: Donna Doolittle

After serving the court papers, I put copies of the documents listed in ③ in an envelope, sealed the envelope, and put first-class prepaid postage on it. I addressed the envelope to the person in ① at the address where I left the copies.

I mailed the envelope on *(date):* 5/11/20xx from *(city, state):* Fremont, CA

by leaving it *(check one):*

a. ☒ At a U.S. Postal Service mail drop, or

b. ☐ At an office or business mail drop where I know the mail is picked up every day and deposited with the U.S. Postal Service, or

c. ☐ With someone else I asked to mail the documents to the person in ①, and I have attached that person's completed Form SC-104A.

(5) **Server's Information**

Name: ___ Margaret Middleman _____ Phone: ___ 510-703-2220 _____

Address: 23 Treelined Way _____

City: Fremont _____ State: CA ____ Zip: 94536 _____

Fee for service: $ ___ -0- _____

If you are a registered process server:

County of registration: _____ Registration number: _____

(6) I declare under penalty of perjury under California state law that I am at least 18 years old and not named in this case and that the information above is true and correct.

Date: 5/11/20xx _____

___ Margaret Middleman _____ ▶ *Margaret Middleman*

Type or print server's name *Server signs here after serving*

Proof of Service
(Small Claims)

The Defendant's Options

Thhis chapter is devoted to the concerns of small claims defendants. A lot of this material has been discussed already from the plaintiff's perspective. This chapter gives an overview of a small claims case from the point of view of the defendant—the person being sued.

> CAUTION
>
> **A response may be required.** In some states, the defendant is required to make a written response to the plaintiff's claim to avoid having a default judgment entered. The deadline for submitting the response differs from state to state. Check the appendix for your state's rules.

If You Are Not Properly Served

You may conclude that you were not properly served with the plaintiff's court papers. Perhaps the plaintiff's claim was left with your neighbors, or maybe you weren't given the correct number of days in which to respond. Because there are one or more procedural defects in the plaintiff's case, you may be tempted to not show up in court. This would be a mistake. The judge may be unaware of or overlook the problem and issue a default judgment against you; that is, a decision in favor of the plaintiff. If this happens, you will have to go to the trouble of requesting that the default judgment be vacated.

When the plaintiff fails to have court papers properly served on you or makes some other procedural error, your best course of action is to contact the court in writing, explain the problem, and ask that the case be dismissed. If the court can't or won't help, show up on the day in question and make your request in person. If the problem involves a failure to serve papers on you properly, chances are the plaintiff will re-serve you at this time, but at least the case should be delayed to give you a chance to prepare your defense.

If You Are Sued in the Wrong Court

If you think the plaintiff has filed suit in the wrong small claims court or, in legal lingo, "in the wrong venue," you can challenge the court's right to hear the case (challenge the venue).

As discussed in Chapter 9, you can do this in two ways. First, you can go to court on the day your case is scheduled and request that the case be dismissed. If the judge disagrees with you, he or she will simply go ahead and hear the case. However, if the judge agrees that the location is improper, your case will either be dismissed or transferred to a court in the appropriate judicial district.

Your second, and probably easier, option is to write to the court, explaining why you think the claim was brought in the wrong place. Send a copy of your letter to each of the other parties. If the judge agrees that the suit was brought in the wrong place, the case will be dismissed. If the judge disagrees, he or she will postpone the hearing to give you an opportunity to appear. You will receive notification of the court's decision by mail.

> **TIP**
>
> **Out-of-state defendants should ask for a dismissal.** As discussed in Chapter 9, if you don't live—or do business—in the state in which you are sued, the small claims court normally doesn't have power ("jurisdiction") to enter a valid judgment against you, unless court papers are served on you while you happen to be in the state. Exceptions to this rule exist for out-of-staters sued because of a dispute involving their real property located in the state or because of a traffic accident that occurred in the state. If you are an out-of-state resident and receive small claims papers via the mail, promptly write a letter to the court explaining that you do not believe you are subject to the court's jurisdiction. Send a copy of your letter to each of the other parties. Stay in touch with the court until you are sure the case has been dismissed.

If the Statute of Limitations Has Expired

Plaintiffs do not have an indefinite period of time in which to sue someone for a perceived wrong. If the plaintiff is suing you about an event that happened in the hazy past, check Chapter 5 to see whether the plaintiff has missed the deadline (statute of limitations) for suing. The statutes of limitations are different for different types of lawsuits but are never less than one year from the date of the incident. The main exception to this rule is if the plaintiff is suing a government agency, in which case the plaintiff must file an administrative claim form with the government within a shorter period of time.

Try to Compromise

If you feel that perhaps the plaintiff is partly right but that you are being sued for too much, your best bet is to try to work out a compromise settlement. One good approach is to call or write the plaintiff and make a settlement offer. How much to offer depends on the relative merits of your case as compared to the plaintiff's, and whether the plaintiff is asking for a reasonable or inflated amount. Assuming the plaintiff has a pretty strong legal position (you probably are legally liable) and is asking the court for an amount that's reasonable, a good starting point is to make an initial offer to pay about half of the request. Remember, even with a strong case, the plaintiff may be motivated to accept your offer if for no other reason than to save the time and trouble it takes to prepare for and appear in court. More likely, your initial offer will set in motion a little dance of offer and counteroffer, ending with the plaintiff accepting a compromise—maybe between 65% and 80% of the original demand. Obviously, if the plaintiff is asking for way too much, or you are not sure that a judge would find that you are liable in the first place, you'll want to offer less or fight the case. Any settlement you make should be set down in writing. (See Chapter 6 for more on how to negotiate.)

> ⓘ CAUTION
> **Don't rely on being judgment-proof.** Some defendants who have no money are tempted not to show up and defend a case in small claims court because they figure that, even if they lose, the plaintiff can't collect. If you have a decent defense, this is not a good idea. Judgments are good for anywhere from five to 20 years, depending on the state (see Chapter 24) and can be renewed, if necessary. Hopefully, you'll get a job or otherwise put a few dollars together sometime in the future and, if so, you probably won't want them immediately taken away to satisfy a small claims judgment that you believe shouldn't have been entered in the first place. So defend yourself while you can. One possible exception to this "always fight back if you have a decent case" advice is if you plan to declare Chapter 7 bankruptcy. Bankruptcy wipes out most debts, including small claims judgments. However, keep in mind that if possible, it's usually in your best interest to file for bankruptcy before the case goes to trial and a judgment is entered against you.

 RELATED TOPIC
More information on personal bankruptcy. See *How to File for Chapter 7 Bankruptcy*, by Cara O'Neill and Albin Renauer (Nolo).

Try to Mediate

Engaging in mediation is frequently beneficial to the defendant, because mediation tends to encourage a settlement for a lower amount than the plaintiff has demanded. In addition, mediation gives the defendant a chance to raise issues that would not be considered relevant by a small claims court judge. For example, in a dispute between neighbors, local businesspeople, or relatives, mediation affords an opportunity for both legal and emotional concerns to be raised and dealt with. (See Chapter 6 for more on mediation.)

TIP
Ask the small claims clerk for help setting up mediation. Mediation of small claims cases works in various ways in different states. In many it can take place in the courthouse itself and is encouraged by the small claims court. In others, it's available at a nearby community mediation project. Ask the small claims court clerk or check your small claims court website to find out where mediation is available in your area. Then, if necessary, contact the mediation project and enlist their help in bringing the plaintiff to the table.

If You Have No Defense

Now let's assume that you were properly served with the plaintiff's papers in a proper court before the deadline, you have no valid defense to the merits of the case, and neither you nor the plaintiff want to compromise. Perhaps you borrowed money under the terms of a written contract and haven't been able to pay it back. Because you know you'll lose, you may conclude that it makes little sense to defend yourself in court. Your decision not to show up will very likely result in a default judgment against you. This judgment will most probably be for the dollar amount demanded by the plaintiff, plus the amount of the filing fee and any reasonable costs to serve the papers on you. (In Chapter 15 you can read about default judgments and how you can probably get one vacated if you act immediately.)

> ⊙ TIP
> **Even if you owe 100% of the plaintiff's demand, it never hurts to make an offer.** Especially if you have the money, why not offer to pay 75%–90% of what the plaintiff requests. To save the trouble of going to court—or for some other reason you may never guess—the plaintiff may accept, even though it is almost certain that the person would win a judgment for the whole amount by going to court.

Paying in Installments

If you do not dispute the amount of the plaintiff's claim but you want to make payments in installments rather than all at once, your best bet is to show up on the day your case is scheduled and explain your situation to the judge. Tell the judge how much you can afford to pay each month. The judge has the discretion to allow you to pay the judgment in installments.

Explain why it would be difficult or impossible to pay any judgment all at once. For example, if you are on a fixed income, have recently been unemployed and have a lot of debts, or have a low or moderate income and a large family, just state these facts. (See Chapter 23 for more on paying a judgment in installments.)

If You, Not the Plaintiff, Were Wronged—File a Defendant's Claim

Finally, some defendants will not only want to dispute the plaintiff's claim but will also want to sue the plaintiff back. Perhaps you are outraged that the plaintiff sued first, because you are the person who was wronged. To assert your own claim against the plaintiff, promptly file a defendant's claim (sometimes called a counterclaim) for up to the dollar limit for your state's small claims court. (See the appendix.) If you want to sue for a greater amount, ask the small claims clerk how to transfer the case to a higher court.

Transferring Your Case to a Higher Court

Depending on state law and the facts of your case, you may be able to have your case transferred out of small claims court to a higher court. This may be called municipal, superior, district, county, justice, circuit, city, or civil court. Whatever the name used in your state, this court will allow lawyers and require far more paperwork than is required in small claims court.

Transfer rules vary greatly from one state to the next. Some states allow any defendant to transfer any case, while others allow it only if the defendant files his or her own claim (a counterclaim) for an amount greater than the small claims limit or makes a request for a jury trial. Still other states allow a case to be transferred only with the discretionary approval of a judge. And some states don't allow transfers at all.

If you are interested in transferring your case, look at the brief summary for your state in the appendix to see if it's possible. Then, you absolutely need to consult your state's rules. But first it makes sense to ask yourself why you would want to transfer a case out of small claims court. My answer is that it is rarely a good idea. Because small claims court is cheaper, more user-friendly, and far less time-consuming than formal court, you'll usually want to defend your case right there, unless, of course, you want to file a defendant's claim (counterclaim) for an amount significantly over the small claims limit. Here are some other situations in which it might make sense to transfer your case:

- To get a jury trial (in states where transfer for this reason is allowed). In my view, nonlawyers are almost always better off trying a case before a judge under relaxed small claims rules than submitting to the extra level of formality a jury trial adds to the already fussy rules of formal court. But some people disagree, believing that there is no justice without a jury.

- Because you know how to navigate in formal court far better than the plaintiff—or are willing to hire a lawyer to represent you. Yes, this approach may be a tad cynical, but given the opportunistic nature of many plaintiffs, why not take full advantage of every possible edge you have?

Fight Back

Suppose now you feel you don't owe the plaintiff a dime and you want to actively fight the case filed against you. To do this, file a response to the plaintiff's claim if required (see the appendix), then show up in court on the date stated in the papers served on you, ready to present your side of the story.

> **RELATED TOPIC**
> **Defendant's claim.** For more on what to do if you wish to sue the plaintiff, see Chapters 10 and 11.

Assuming your case stays in small claims court, both your claim and the plaintiff's will be heard together. You should prepare and present your case just as you would if you had filed first—that is, understand the legal basics that underlie your case, make a practical and convincing oral presentation, and back it up with as much hard evidence as you can find.

Before you even think about the merits of the plaintiff's case, your first job is to check to be sure the plaintiff has brought it within the time allowed by the statute of limitations. (See Chapter 5.) If not, tell the judge at the beginning of your presentation and request that the plaintiff's case be dismissed.

To successfully present your defense, you'll want to be prepared to make a well-organized, convincing oral statement, backed up with as much evidence as possible. Good case presentation strategies, including how to present witnesses, estimates, diagrams, and other evidence, are discussed in Chapters 13–22 and apply both to defendants and plaintiffs. If the plaintiff has asked for too much money, you'll also want to be sure you tell the judge exactly why it is too much. (See Chapter 4.)

Take apart your opponent's case. To do this, you will normally want to focus on any facts that show you are not legally liable. Reread Chapter 2 to see what the plaintiff must prove for all the common types of small claims cases and see whether you can disprove any key points. If after doing this you conclude the plaintiff arguably does have a winning case, next consider whether he or she has asked for the right dollar amount. Obviously, if you can convince a judge that you only owe a couple of hundred, not several thousand, dollars, you will have won a substantial victory. (On calculating damages, see Chapter 4.)

EXAMPLE 1: The plaintiff sues you for a breach of contract. You reread Chapter 2 to understand what the plaintiff must prove to win the case. Then, assuming the facts support your position, you might present evidence that no contract existed in the first place or that, even if a contract did exist, the plaintiff violated its terms so thoroughly that you were justified in considering it void. And even if you have to admit that you broke a valid contract, you might claim the plaintiff is asking for far too much money.

EXAMPLE 2: You are sued by someone claiming your negligent conduct resulted in his property being damaged (as would be the case in a fender bender). To successfully defend, you want to convince the court that you were not negligent (careless), or, if you were, that the plaintiff was more negligent. And even if the judge decides that the accident was your fault, you might want to claim that the plaintiff paid far more than was necessary to have the car fixed.

Gather evidence. As emphasized in Chapters 13 and 14, the key to winning (or not losing) in small claims court is very often to convince the judge that your version of the facts is correct. To do this, you'll normally need to back up your oral presentation with convincing evidence. One good approach is to present the testimony of an eyewitness (if you are lucky enough to have one) or an expert witness who agrees with your position (for example, a mechanic who can explain how the plaintiff damaged your engine). In addition, you will want to show the judge any available documentary evidence such as letters, photos, and opinions of experts—or sometimes even damaged property—that back up your version of events. For example, if you are a computer repair person sued by someone who claims you ruined his or her computer, you may want to get a written opinion from another repair shop that the current problem with the computer has nothing to do with the defect you fixed. In addition, it would make sense to present any advertisements or trade pricing data that tend to show that the plaintiff is placing an inflated value on the ruined but very old computer. And don't forget that you can also bring along physical evidence. Suppose, for example, you are sued for nonpayment on a handmade ceramic tea service that you commissioned from the plaintiff. If you can bring that teapot into court and show the judge that it doesn't pour properly, your defense may be in the bag.

Be prepared to make a convincing courtroom presentation. The plaintiff gets to talk first. Patiently and quietly wait until it's your turn. When the plaintiff is done, be prepared to make a short and logical presentation of why the plaintiff should receive little or nothing. Once you have your arguments thought out, it is an extremely good idea to practice exactly what you plan to say in front of a friend or family member until it is perfect. One trick to getting and keeping the judge's attention is not to repeat uncontested facts presented by the plaintiff; instead, immediately focus on why the plaintiff's case is misguided.

EXAMPLE: Tom, the landlord, listens patiently as Evie, the tenant, spends five minutes presenting a rambling, sometimes incorrect history of their landlord-tenant relationship as an introduction to her main point that she should have gotten her security deposit back because she left the rental unit clean and undamaged. When it's finally Tom's turn, he ignores Evie's inconsequential mistakes. Instead, he focuses on the exact point of the dispute by saying, "Your Honor, the key to my defense is that the plaintiff left the rental at 127 Spring Street in a dirty and damaged condition. I have pictures to demonstrate this and a reliable witness to back it up. But first I would like to briefly list the three worst problems."

Getting Ready for Court

Once you've filed papers with the small claims clerk and properly served the other party, the preliminaries are over and you are ready for the main event—your day in court.

Chances are good that, like most of us, your idea of what a court proceeding is like comes mostly from Hollywood. If so, put aside everything you think you have learned by watching the media and just be yourself. To succeed in small claims court, you don't need fancy clothes, words, or attitudes. Just use plain English to tell the judge what happened and why you are right.

This aside, most people who present or defend small claims cases do pretty well. But it's also true that only a few make outstanding presentations. It's fair to ask, what set this elite group apart? That's right—practice and preparation. The people who do best are those who prepare carefully enough that they are able to make a clear, concise presentation, backed up by the orderly introduction of convincing evidence.

The rest of this chapter and Chapters 14 and 15 contain basic information about how small claims court works and how to prepare.

JUDGE'S TIP

Watch small claims court in action before your own hearing. If you're nervous about your court date or if you want to get a taste of how the court might approach your type of dispute, feel free to visit the court while it is in session and observe how the judges handle and then rule on the cases that are presented to them. You may even see an example of your type of case.

TIP

Need an interpreter? If you do not speak English, you may bring a friend or relative to translate for you in small claims court. If you don't have a personal contact who can serve as interpreter, contact your small claims court to see if there are interpreters available to translate the court proceedings. If no court interpreter is available, there are nonprofit and other organizations that offer interpreter services to low-income persons free of charge. Be sure to contact the appropriate organization well in advance of your court date to ask for help.

Using a Private Lawyer

Many states allow lawyers to represent clients in small claims court, although some states do not. Even in states that allow lawyers, however, the amount of money at stake often doesn't justify paying a lawyer's legal fees. It may be cost-effective, though, to hire a lawyer to give you advice only. If you are worried about some legal aspect of your case and can't get an answer from the court clerk or by doing your own research (see Chapter 25), it might make sense to discuss the problem with a lawyer. It should not cost more than $150–$250 for a short consultation. Make sure you negotiate the fee in advance.

JUDGE'S TIP

It's perfectly proper to get assistance from a lawyer. A lawyer can be extremely helpful in preparing your case, especially if it's complicated. For help finding a lawyer, check Nolo's Lawyer Directory at www.nolo.com/lawyers. It offers comprehensive profiles of the lawyers who advertise there, including area of expertise (such as personal injury or landlord-tenant law). For advice on hiring and working with a lawyer, including what to ask a prospective attorney, see the article "Tips on Hiring and Working with Lawyers" at www.nolo.com/legal-encyclopedia/lawyers-lawfirms/tips.html.

Consider Mediation—Again

As discussed in considerable detail in Chapter 6, free or low-cost mediation services are available in many communities. Normally the choice of whether to mediate is yours. However, the courts in some judicial districts may require it or so strongly encourage the parties to mediate that it seems like it's required. Ask any small claims clerk for information on how to contact local mediation programs.

Mediation programs are designed to help people settle their own disputes—not to impose a decision, as is done in small claims court. Especially if you will inevitably have a continuing relationship with the person with whom you have a dispute—as is the case with a neighbor, family member, or many business relationships—trying to achieve a compromise settlement is almost always wiser than fighting it out in court.

Even if your opponent previously has been reluctant to engage in mediation, you can again raise this possibility with the judge just before your case is heard by telling the judge you are still willing to mediate. The judge, who has the power to postpone the case to allow the parties to try to settle it, may attempt to talk the other party into giving mediation a try. As part of doing so, the judge will probably point out that if the case is settled, the amount of the judgment will not appear on the loser's credit record.

Be Prepared

Once you are pretty sure your case can't be settled and you will need to go to court, your best approach is to practice presenting it. Line up an objective, tough-minded friend and run through your entire case just as you plan to on court day. Ask your friend for suggestions, not compliments. For example, your friend may tell you that you need a witness or written documentation, a better grasp of the legal technicalities involved, or a better-organized presentation. Take this advice to heart and make all possible improvements. Then, practice again.

The four key phrases to remember as you prepare and practice your courtroom presentation are:

- **Be polite** to the judge, your opponent, the clerk, and the bailiff.
- **Bring evidence** from witnesses or documents to supplement your own verbal statement of the facts.
- **Organize your presentation** to include only necessary facts in a logical way.
- **Keep it short.** Remember that the person who is deciding your case has heard thousands of similar stories and will get bored or annoyed if you are needlessly repetitive.

Finally, don't let the robe and other trappings of judicial office obscure the fact that you are dealing with a human being who, like anyone else, is far more likely to be sympathetic to your point of view if you can show that you occupy the moral high ground (for example, you are honest, kind, and pay your debts) and that your opponent is the bad guy (tricky, hard-hearted, and fails to keep promises).

Getting to the Courthouse

Before you locate the right courtroom, you obviously have to get to the right building. Sometimes doing this can be tricky, because small claims courts are often not in the main courthouse. Like a half-forgotten relative, many are housed wherever the city or county has an empty room. In short, don't assume that you know where your small claims court is unless you've been there before or have asked the court clerk for specific directions. Plaintiffs have already had to find the clerk's office to file their papers, so they probably know where the courtroom is, but defendants should check this out in advance. Be sure, too, that your witnesses know exactly where and when to show up. And do plan to be a few minutes early—people who rush in flustered and late start with a strike against them.

Small claims cases are most often scheduled either at 9 a.m or early in the afternoon. Usually a number of cases are set for the same time and heard in turn. In other words, your case may be scheduled for 9 a.m. but may not actually start until about 10 a.m. Arrive a few minutes before 9 a.m. and use any wait time to watch other cases before your own begins. In larger cities, Saturday or evening sessions may also be held. If it is not convenient for you to go to court during business hours and night court is an option, request that your case be scheduled at one of these other sessions.

The Courtroom

Most small claims proceedings are conducted in standard courtrooms also used for regular trials.

> **CAUTION**
> **Leave sharp metal objects at home.** This may seem like common sense, but remember that all visitors to courthouses must pass through metal detectors, and if you have scissors, metal knitting needles, a knife, or any other weaponlike object with you, it will be confiscated or held for you by security.

Courtroom Etiquette 101

From watching television, most of us know that lawyers often dress in expensive, formidable-looking suits. No such formal dress is required for your appearance in small claims court. Although it's polite to dress in a neat and professional manner, it's not required, and if you are coming directly to court from your work as a housepainter, for example, the judge will probably understand and excuse your paint-splattered appearance.

It is also polite—but not required—for parties and witnesses to stand when they address the judge. The respectful and recommended way to address the judge directly is "Your Honor." If you need to refer to the judge in the third person, say "Her Honor" (for example, speaking to the bailiff, "Please give Her Honor these documents").

Other suggestions for showing respect to the court and the other litigants come from Commissioner Douglas G. Carnahan:

- Don't walk in the "well" of the courtroom, which is the area between the lawyers' table and the judge's bench. This is a security zone, and the bailiff will prevent you from entering it, sometimes rather aggressively.
- Turn off your cell phones before you enter the courtroom.
- Keep courtroom chitchat to a minimum. Many judges find it distracting.
- Even while you are waiting for your case to be called, an attentive, pleasant demeanor will make a good impression on the judge. This means pay attention, don't check emails on your iPhone, don't chew gum, and don't listen to your iPod.

Most judges still sit on an elevated platform (called "the bench") and wear black robes. In addition to the judge, a clerk and a bailiff will normally be present. They usually sit at tables immediately in front of or next to the judge. The clerk's job is to keep the judge supplied with necessary files and papers and to make sure that proceedings flow smoothly. The bailiff is there to keep order in the courtroom if tempers get out of hand.

Courtrooms are divided about two-thirds of the way toward the front by a fence (known to lawyers as the "bar"). The public must stay on the opposite side of the bar from the judge, clerk, bailiff, and parties, unless asked to

come forward. This invitation occurs when the clerk calls your case by name (*Smith vs. Jones* or *Abercrombie vs. Lee*). At this point you and any witnesses will normally be asked to step to the front of the room and sit at a table (known as the "counsel table"). You will then face the judge with your back to the spectator section of the courtroom. In a few courtrooms, judges try to hurry things along by asking everyone to stand while their case is being heard. The idea seems to be that if people can't sit down, they will present their cases faster.

In small claims courts, you must swear (or affirm, if you wish) to tell the truth. Often this oath is administered before the first case is heard, to everyone who will testify at that entire session. However, occasionally the oath will be administered to participants separately as each case is called.

In the great majority of small claims courts, you, your opponent, and your witnesses will present the entire case from the counsel table. This means that neither you nor your witnesses sit in the witness box next to the judge.

 JUDGE'S TIP
Be nice to the clerk and the bailiff. The clerk organizes the paperwork, and the bailiff keeps order, although sometimes each person shares some of the other's work. Don't antagonize them; they will often report their (positive or negative) impressions to the judge.

The Judge or Commissioner

The person who hears your case may be a regular court judge who also presides over many other types of cases. But, increasingly, full-time commissioners and referees are being hired to handle small claims cases. Commissioners are attorneys trained to preside over small claims cases but who are paid lower salaries and benefits than are paid to judges (a bit like colleges hiring nontenured instructors instead of full professors). By and large, commissioners and referees—who usually hear small claims cases on a daily basis—do a very competent job, sometimes better than judges, who have other duties and occasionally act as if they are too important to hear such small disputes.

Temporary Judges (Judges Pro Tem)

In addition to commissioners and regular judges, volunteer lawyers are also routinely appointed when a judge or commissioner is ill or on vacation. The legal slang for a temporary judge is "judge pro tem." If your case comes up on a day when only a pro tem judge is present, you will be given a choice as to whether you want to go ahead or have your case rescheduled on a day when a regular judge or commissioner will be present.

Especially if your case is contested and you feel it involves fairly complicated legal issues, you may not want to accept a pro tem judge. Pro tem judges are not paid, and often do not have as much practical experience in the legal areas that are commonly heard in small claims court. They receive some training, but usually don't have the experience or training that a regular judge or commissioner has. Although some are excellent, you may not want to take a gamble by accepting one. It is your choice, so make sure you think it through.

CAUTION

Pay attention to any forms you are asked to sign about the judge for your case. In some courtrooms, before court begins for the day, a clerk will ask you to sign a form accepting a particular judge, without clearly explaining that the judge is a local lawyer serving on a temporary (pro tem) basis and that you have the right to say no. Whenever you are asked to approve a judge, that means the person is a substitute for the real judge, and you have the right to say no.

CAUTION

You can't appeal from an arbitrator's decision in New York. To save time, residents of the Empire State are often encouraged to have their cases heard by a volunteer lawyer arbitrator instead of a small claims court judge. But beware of this alternative. In addition to getting a less experienced decision maker, there is no right to appeal from an arbitrator's decision, as there is from the decision of a regular small claims judge.

Disqualifying a Prejudiced Judge

What if your case will be heard by a regular judge or commissioner whom you don't like, either because you know the person or because you have been put off by the way the person has handled other cases? For example, you might live in a small town or city and be convinced a particular judge, whose reputation you know, is likely to be hard on you (for example, you are a landlord and the judge is known to be pro-tenant). Laws exist in nearly all states that allow you to "disqualify" a regular judge simply on your honest belief that the judge is "prejudiced" against you. No one will ask you to prove it. To disqualify a judge, in some states you can simply say, when your case is called (after you've been "sworn in"), something like this: "Your Honor, I believe you are prejudiced against my interest, and I request a trial before another judge." In other states, you need to put your disqualification request in writing and file it in advance. If you think you may want to take advantage of a disqualification procedure, check with the small claims clerk before your court date to be sure you understand the rules.

Especially for cases where a lot is at stake—for example, a group of people file nuisance cases based on drug dealing or noise (see Chapter 20)—it often makes sense to do some research on the judge who is likely to be assigned your case. Start by asking the small claims court clerk for a list of the judges who may be assigned to your case. One good way to check them out is to have someone in your group (or perhaps a friend or relative) who has the necessary contacts talk to several local lawyers who have practiced before the listed judges. Many lawyers will readily share their opinions, especially if they consider a particular judge to be unfair or incompetent. If you discover reliable information about a particular judge that makes you doubt that person's ability to be fair, be prepared to challenge the judge.

JUDGE'S TIP

If you're going to reject a temporary or regular judge, you must do it before the judge does anything with your case. You cannot "test" a judge's opinion about the case, decide you don't like it, then try to reject him or her. This is not only ineffective but also rude.

JUDGE'S TIP

You don't have to say why you believe a judge is prejudiced. After you state your challenge, the judge may have you take the oath again and ask you to repeat your challenge. You aren't expected to say why you challenged the judge, just that you believe he is prejudiced against you or your cause. —Judge (Ret.) Roderic Duncan

Your Courtroom Strategy

Normally, the plaintiff will be asked to present his or her case first and introduce any witnesses, who will also get a chance to have their say. When the plaintiff is done, it will be the defendant's turn to speak and present witnesses. Both sides should have any papers or other evidence that backs up their story carefully organized to present to the judge. This can include bills, receipts, estimates, photographs, contracts, letters to or from your opponent, and other types of documentation or physical evidence. At the appropriate place in your presentation, tell the judge you have evidence you want to present, and then hand it to the clerk, who in turn will give it to the judge. Appropriate documentation can be a huge aid to winning your case.

TIP

Copies of documents. You should bring at least three copies of each document you plan to show the judge: one for you, one for the judge, and one for your opponent. You can highlight or otherwise make notes on your copies to remind yourself why the particular document is important.

As you plan your courtroom strategy, give thought to your opponent. What sort of presentation will the person make? And even more important, how can you best counter any arguments? Figuring out how to cope with your opponent's best points is not only an effective way to flesh out your case, but it can be a good way to turn the negative energy you probably feel (frustration, annoyance, anger) into something creative.

Always be polite when presenting or defending your case. If you are hostile or sarcastic, you run the considerable risk of losing the respect of the judge. Never interrupt your opponent when he or she is speaking—you

will get your chance. When you do, lay out the key facts that support your position directly to the judge; don't get into an argument with the other side. It's the judge you need to convince, not your opponent.

Organize Your Testimony and Evidence

It's essential that you organize what you have to say and the physical evidence you wish to show the judge. Do this by dividing your testimony into a list of the main points you want to make. Under each heading, note any items of physical or documentary evidence you wish to show the judge. If your evidence consists of a number of items, make sure that you put them in order and can find each item quickly.

Let's assume you are the plaintiff in a case that is based on a hotel's failure to return your deposit when you canceled a wedding reception three months before the event was to be held. Your list of key points—and the evidence to back them up—might look like this:

- Valley View Hotel refused to return my $500 deposit when I canceled my wedding reception.
- This was true even though I canceled 83 days before the event.
- The contract I signed with the hotel allowed a full refund if cancellation occurred more than 60 days before the event. (Show contract to the judge.)
- When I canceled, Valley View told me (and claims they sent me a letter stating) that their cancellation policy had been changed the previous month to require 90 days' notice in order to get a refund.
- I never received a letter and had no idea of the policy change until I canceled and asked for my money back.
- Even if Valley View did send me a letter, the change should not affect my contract, which was signed before the policy change. The key point here is, because I never signed a new contract, the existing contract was still valid.
- In any event, the hotel has a duty to try and rerent the banquet room to minimize (mitigate) any damages they suffered. And they had plenty of time (83 days) to do so.
- Ninety days is an unreasonably long cancellation policy.

- Here is a list of the cancellation policies of five other hotels in the area, all of which allow a full refund on much shorter notice than 83 days. (Give list to the judge.)

Because Valley View goes second, their representative can't know in advance what the plaintiff will say and what evidence it will present. It follows that Valley View will need to adopt a little more flexible approach. Still, chances are that Valley View reps have talked to the plaintiff or exchanged letters, so they probably have a pretty good idea of what to expect. Accordingly, Valley View's list might look something like this.

- True, we didn't refund the $500. The reason was we turned down two other receptions for that same day before the plaintiff canceled. Because we ended up with no other function, we lost at least $500.
- Although it is true that the written contract allowed cancellation prior to 60 days before the event, plaintiff was notified that this policy had been changed to 90 days before the contract was signed in two ways:
 - A sign on the reservations desk where the plaintiff sat to sign the contract. (Show sign to judge.)
 - Testimony of Angie Ells, who booked the reservation. Angie will testify that she included a written notice of the change with the contract package. (Show judge a copy of the notice.)

💡 **TIP**

How to cope with the big lie. Although not an everyday occurrence, big lies definitely are told in small claims court and can sometimes strongly influence the judge in your opponent's favor if you aren't prepared to poke holes in them. If your adversary tells a whopper, your best approach is to wait calmly for your turn to speak and then say something like this: "Your Honor, almost everything defendant (or plaintiff) has said about __X__ is simply not true. Please let me prove this to you with facts." Then present your testimony and evidence—or if you have already shown the judge key evidence, remind the judge of how it demonstrates that your opponent's story is totally false. For example, if your former landlord who failed to return your security deposit swears you left the apartment filthy, you will totally destroy his or her credibility if you can show the judge photos that demonstrate how clean it really was. Fortunately, if you can demonstrate that your opponent has told one big lie, the judge will distrust and hopefully disbelieve the rest of what that person says.

Witnesses

t can be extremely helpful to have someone in court with you who knows the facts of your case firsthand and can support your point of view. In many types of cases, such as car accidents or disputes over whether or not a tenant left an apartment clean, witnesses are particularly valuable. However, in other fact situations, witnesses aren't as necessary. For example, if a friend borrowed $500 and didn't pay it back, you don't need a witness to prove that your now ex-friend's signature on the promissory note is genuine, unless you expect the person to claim that it was forged.

What Makes a Good Witness

A good witness should have firsthand or personal knowledge of the facts in dispute. This means the person saw something that helps establish your case (for example, the car accident, dog bite, or dirty apartment) or is an expert you have consulted about an important aspect of your case (for example, a car mechanic who testifies that your engine wasn't fixed properly). The judge will not be interested in the testimony of a person who is repeating secondhand or generalized information such as "I know Joe is a good, safe driver and would never have done anything reckless," or "I didn't see Joe's apartment before he moved out, but both Joe and his mother, who couldn't be here today, told me that they worked for two days cleaning it up."

Above all, a good witness is believable. This isn't always an easy quality to define. For example, a police officer may be a symbol of integrity to some people, but others will automatically discount much of what he or she says. But remember, it's the judge you are trying to convince, and judges tend to be fairly establishment folk. They make comfortable salaries, own their own homes, and generally tend to like the existing order of things, and most judges would be likely to believe a police officer.

In many types of cases, such as a car accident, you won't have much choice as to witnesses. You will be lucky to have one person who saw what happened. Often this will be a close friend or family member. There is no rule that says you can't have these people testify for you. Indeed, a person's spouse, roommate, or close friend can often give very convincing testimony. But given a choice, it is usually better to have a witness who is neither buddy nor kin. That's because a judge may discount the testimony of people to

whom you are close on the theory that they would naturally be biased in your favor.

> **TIP**
>
> **Try to dispel a judge's cynicism about friends or family who are witnesses.** Have a closely related witness bend over backward to treat the other side as fairly as possible. Thus, if your brother is your only witness to the fact that ABC Painting splashed paint on your boat, he might point out to the judge not only that he saw ABC employees screw up, but that it was a very windy day and the painter was understandably having a hard time keeping the paint on the dock where it belonged.

In some types of disputes, such as whether your house was properly painted or the work on the car engine was completed competently, you have an opportunity to plan ahead to locate witnesses. That's because the type of witness you need is usually not an eyewitness who saw the work in progress but instead an expert in the field who can convincingly explain what went wrong. Obviously this type of witness is only valuable if the person really does have good credentials and relevant knowledge so that a judge is likely to believe what he or she says. Thus, in a dispute over whether or not car repairs were properly done, it's preferable to bring a letter from a car mechanic with 20 years' experience who has completed a load of training courses rather than one from your neighbor "who knows a lot about cars."

As with your own presentation, the best way to be sure your witness really will be able to explain the key facts to the judge succinctly and concisely is to have the person practice his or her testimony in advance. As long as the person sticks to the truth, rehearsing the exact words to say in court is completely legal. I suggest meeting with your witness and a friend you have asked to act as a mock judge. Start by presenting your case to the pretend judge exactly as you plan to do it in court. Then ask your witness to stand and explain his or her version of what happened. Have your friend ask the witness questions about anything that's unclear in the presentation, as a judge would do.

If at first your witness is a little disorganized or unsure, work to develop a coherent presentation that covers all key points. When he or she says something that sounds good, write it down and practice it several times before your court date.

Selecting and Preparing Witnesses

- Educate your witness thoroughly about your legal and factual position and what your opponent is likely to say. In court, witnesses will be on their own, and you want to be sure that the story comes out right. It is completely legal to thoroughly discuss the case with your witness beforehand, as long as you do not coach or encourage the witness to lie or exaggerate.
- Never ask a witness to testify in court unless you know exactly what the person will say. This sounds basic, but people have lost cases because their witnesses got mixed up, and in one instance, the witness actually supported the other side.
- Never use a subpoena to require a witness to be present unless you make sure that it is okay with the witness, as might be the case if the person needs a good reason to take off a few hours from his or her job. (For more about subpoenas, see "How to Subpoena Witnesses," below.) Otherwise you may end up making the person mad enough to testify against you.
- Do not offer to pay an eyewitness to testify on your behalf (except for the small witness fee he or she is entitled to by law). If discovered, your payment will likely be seen as a bribe.
- On the other hand, it's proper and perfectly legal to pay an expert witness—say a car mechanic who has examined your engine—a reasonable fee for his or her time in court in addition to the time the person spent checking your car. As a cheaper and easier alternative, however, the experts can simply write a letter to the judge explaining their findings, which you can then present as part of your case.

For tips on selecting and preparing witnesses for specific types of cases, see Chapters 16–22.

How to Subpoena Witnesses

In small claims court, you should almost never use a subpoena to compel a witness to come to court and testify unless the witness has already agreed

to testify. This is because the very act of dragging someone into court who doesn't want to come may set that person against you.

However, there are unusual circumstances when you may need to subpoena a witness. For example, your witness may need proof that he or she is testifying for you in court on a specific day in order to get approval to miss work. Or, in rare cases, you may really need testimony from a reluctant witness, in which case you can compel the witness to show up by using a subpoena and informing the witness that the court may impose a fine for failure to appear.

In most states, you can require that a witness with firsthand knowledge of what happened be present if that person resides within a certain distance from the courthouse. (The distance varies from state to state. It is often about 150 miles, but in some states subpoenas reach only within county boundaries.)

Expert witnesses cannot be subpoenaed. For this reason they often submit their opinions in writing, a practice that is allowed in most courts.

Below is the standard California subpoena form. The one in your state should look quite similar. Normally, you need to prepare an original and two copies. Once prepared, take the subpoena form to the clerk, who will issue it. Service must be made personally, and you must return the proof of service, which is often on the back of the subpoena, to the clerk's office. (Rules for service are discussed in Chapter 11.)

A subpoenaed witness is usually entitled to a modest fee upon demand. You must pay your witness this fee ahead of time if the witness asks for it.

If you pay your witness transportation fees (as required by law), write a short receipt so that you can prove how much you paid when it comes time to ask the judge to reimburse you for the expense.

The judge has discretion as to whether or not to reimburse you for witness fees. Most judges are strict about this, making the loser pay the winner's witness fees only if they find that the subpoenaed witness was essential to the case. This means that if your case is so strong that you don't need a witness to appear in person but you subpoena one anyway, you may well have to pay the witness fee even though you won the case. (For more information on recovering costs associated with your small claims lawsuit, see Chapter 15.)

Sample Small Claims Subpoena

Name and Address of Court: **Small Claims Court, County of Alameda**
Berkeley-Albany Judicial District
2000 Center Street, Berkeley, CA 94704

SC-107

SMALL CLAIMS CASE NO. **(123456)**

PLAINTIFF/DEMANDANTE *(Name, address, and telephone number of each):*

Public Library
100 Allston Way
Berkeley, CA 94704

Telephone No.:

DEFENDANT/DEMANDADO *(Name, address, and telephone number of each):*

John O'Gara
100 Scenic Drive
Berkeley, CA 94702

Telephone No.:

Telephone No.:

☐ See attached sheet for additional plaintiffs and defendants.

Telephone No.:

SMALL CLAIMS SUBPOENA
FOR PERSONAL APPEARANCE AND PRODUCTION OF DOCUMENTS
AND THINGS AT TRIAL OR HEARING AND DECLARATION

THE PEOPLE OF THE STATE OF CALIFORNIA, TO *(name, address, and telephone number of witness, if known):*

Jane Doe

1. **YOU ARE ORDERED TO APPEAR AS A WITNESS in this case at the date, time, and place shown in the box below UNLESS your appearance is excused as indicated in box 4b below or you make an agreement with the person named in item 2 below.**

 a. Date: Time: ☐ Dept.: ☐ Div.: ☐ Room:
 b. Address:

2. **IF YOU HAVE ANY QUESTIONS ABOUT THE TIME OR DATE YOU ARE TO APPEAR, OR IF YOU WANT TO BE CERTAIN THAT YOUR PRESENCE IS REQUIRED, CONTACT THE FOLLOWING PERSON BEFORE THE DATE ON WHICH YOU ARE TO APPEAR:**

 a. Name of subpoenaing party: **John O'Gara** b. Telephone number: **510-555-1212**

3. **Witness Fees:** You are entitled to witness fees and mileage actually traveled both ways, as provided by law, if you request them at the time of service. You may request them before your scheduled appearance from the person named in item 2.

PRODUCTION OF DOCUMENTS AND THINGS

(Complete item 4 only if you want the witness to produce documents and things at the trial or hearing.)

4. YOU ARE *(item a or b must be checked)*:

 a. ☒ Ordered to appear in person and to produce the records described in the declaration on page two. The personal attendance of the custodian or other qualified witness and the production of the original records are required by this subpoena. The procedure authorized by Evidence Code sections 1560(b), 1561, and 1562 will not be deemed sufficient compliance with this subpoena.

 b. ☐ Not required to appear in person if you produce (i) the records described in the declaration on page two and (ii) a completed declaration of custodian of records in compliance with Evidence Code sections 1560, 1561, 1562, and 1271. (1) Place a copy of the records in an envelope (or other wrapper). Enclose the original declaration of the custodian with the records. Seal the envelope. (2) Attach a copy of this subpoena to the envelope or write on the envelope the case name and number; your name; and the date, time, and place from item 1 in the box above. (3) Place this first envelope in an outer envelope, seal it, and mail it to the clerk of the court at the address in item 1. (4) Mail a copy of your declaration to the attorney or party listed at the top of this form.

5. **IF YOU HAVE BEEN SERVED WITH THIS SUBPOENA AS A CUSTODIAN OF CONSUMER OR EMPLOYEE RECORDS UNDER CODE OF CIVIL PROCEDURE SECTION 1985.3 OR 1985.6 AND A MOTION TO QUASH OR AN OBJECTION HAS BEEN SERVED ON YOU, A COURT ORDER OR AGREEMENT OF THE PARTIES, WITNESSES, *AND* CONSUMER OR EMPLOYEE AFFECTED MUST BE OBTAINED BEFORE YOU ARE REQUIRED TO PRODUCE CONSUMER OR EMPLOYEE RECORDS.**

DISOBEDIENCE OF THIS SUBPOENA MAY BE PUNISHED AS CONTEMPT BY THIS COURT. YOU WILL ALSO BE LIABLE FOR THE SUM OF FIVE HUNDRED DOLLARS AND ALL DAMAGES RESULTING FROM YOUR FAILURE TO OBEY.

[SEAL] Date issued:

Clerk, by _____, Deputy

(See reverse for declaration in support of subpoena) **Page one of three**

Form Adopted for Mandatory Use
Judicial Council of California
SC-107 [Rev. January 1, 2000]

SMALL CLAIMS SUBPOENA
AND DECLARATION

Code of Civil Procedure,
§ 1985 et seq.

Sample Small Claims Subpoena (continued)

PLAINTIFF/PETITIONER: Public Library, 100 Allston Way, Berkeley	CASE NUMBER:
DEFENDANT/RESPONDENT: John O'Gara, 100 Scenic Dr., Berkeley	123456

**DECLARATION IN SUPPORT OF
SMALL CLAIMS SUBPOENA FOR PERSONAL APPEARANCE
AND PRODUCTION OF DOCUMENT AND THINGS AT TRIAL OR HEARING
(Code Civil Procedure sections 1985, 1987.5)**

1. I, the undersigned, declare I am the ☐ plaintiff [X] defendant ☐ judgment creditor
 ☐ other *(specify)*: in the above entitled action.

2. The witness has possession or control of the following documents or other things and shall produce them at the time and place specified on the *Small Claims Subpoena* on the first page of this form.

 a. [X] For trial or hearing *(specify the exact documents or other things to be produced by the witness)*:

 Book inventory information collected by the main branch of the public library during the calendar year 20xx.

 ☐ Continued on Attachment 2a.

 b. ☐ After trial to enforce a judgment *(specify the exact documents or other things to be produced by the party who is the judgment debtor or other witness possessing records relating to the judgment debtor)*:

 (1) ☐ Payroll receipts, stubs, and other records concerning employment of the party. Receipts, invoices, documents, and other papers or records concerning any and all accounts receivable of the party.

 (2) ☐ Bank account statements, canceled checks, and check registers from any and all bank accounts in which the party has an interest.

 (3) ☐ Savings account passbooks and statements, savings and loan account passbooks and statements, and credit union share account passbooks and statements of the party.

 (4) ☐ Stock certificates, bonds, money market certificates, and any other records, documents, or papers concerning all investments of the party.

 (5) ☐ California registration certificates and ownership certificates for all vehicles registered to the party.

 (6) ☐ Deeds to any and all real property owned or being purchased by the party.

 (7) ☐ Other *(specify)*:

3. Good cause exists for the production of the documents or other things described in paragraph 2 for the following reasons:

 My contention is that I returned the books for which the library is suing me. The inventory should back me up on this.

 ☐ Continued on Attachment 3.

4. These documents are material to the issues involved in this case for the following reasons:

 The location of the books at issue is central to this case.

 ☐ Continued on Attachment 4.

I declare under penalty of perjury under the laws of the State of California that the foregoing is true and correct.

Date: **May 20, 20xx**

John O'Gara ▶ *John O'Gara*
 (TYPE OR PRINT NAME) (SIGNATURE OF PARTY)

(See proof of service on page three)

| SC-107 [Rev. January 1, 2000] | **SMALL CLAIMS SUBPOENA
AND DECLARATION** | Page two of three |

How to Subpoena Police and Other Peace Officers

You normally use the standard subpoena form to subpoena a police officer, firefighter, or other peace officer to testify about anything observed or investigated in the course of duty. Fill the form out, take it to the court clerk for a seal and date stamp, then take it to the relevant police or fire department to comply with any of their additional procedures. (For example, the police department may require two copies of the subpoena instead of one.) Give the witnesses plenty of advance notice. You will have to pay the officer's salary for the time taken off work to appear. You must pay this in advance in the form of a deposit (usually about $200), payable to the agency employing the officer. The subpoena may be served on the officer personally or on the officer's superior.

Depending on the amount of the officer's time that is used, you may eventually get a refund of some of your deposit. Don't hold your breath, however. Many law enforcement offices are seemingly unaware that this is a deposit and not a flat fee, and have no procedure in place for issuing refunds.

How to Subpoena Documents

In addition to witnesses, you can also subpoena documents. This is rarely done in small claims court, but there are times when it may be helpful. An organization (such as a police department, phone company, hospital, or corporation) may have certain books, ledgers, papers, or other documents, including electronically stored information, that can help your case. Unless the organization volunteers to bring the documents to court for you (which is rare), you'll need to prepare a court order, called a "subpoena duces tecum," that directs the person in the organization who is in charge of the records to send them directly to the court. This subpoena is very similar to the standard subpoena form, except for the added space where you describe the papers or other documents you want. Keep in mind that successfully bringing documents before the court does not guarantee that the judge will admit them into evidence. The judge must be convinced that the records are relevant to your case.

To get a subpoena duces tecum issued, you normally follow a procedure along the following lines: Attach to the completed subpoena form an affidavit stating "under penalty of perjury" why you need the written material. Prepare three copies of all papers and, after you get the clerk to issue the subpoena, serve it on the witness using personal service, as described in Chapter 11. As with a regular subpoena, the witness is entitled to ask for a fee. The Proof of Service is on the back of the subpoena form; it must be filled out and returned to the clerk.

> **CAUTION**
> **Rules for subpoenas vary from state to state.** Technical rules on filing and serving papers, as well as paying witness fees, vary considerably from one state to the next. Make sure you know what will be required. Also, before subpoenaing documents, be sure to ask whether the other side will simply give you photocopies in advance.

A subpoena duces tecum must be directed to the person who is in charge of the documents, books, or records you want produced in court. It may take a few phone calls to find out who this is. Be sure you get this information accurately. If you list someone on the subpoena duces tecum who has nothing to do with the documents, you won't get them. When dealing with a large corporation, public utility, or municipal government, it is wise to list the person who is in overall charge of the department where the records are kept. Thus, if you want records having to do with library fines from a public library, or having to do with business license fees from the city tax and license department, you should not list the city manager or the mayor, but should list the head librarian or the director of the tax and license office.

> **EXAMPLE:** You are being sued by the city on behalf of the public library for $800 for eight rare books that they state you failed to return. You know you did return the books but can't seem to get that across to the library, which insists on treating you like a thief. You learn that each April the library takes a yearly inventory of all books on their shelves. You believe that if you can get access to that inventory, you may be able to figure out where the library misplaced the books, or at least show that a significant percentage of the library's other books are not accounted for, raising the implication that they, not you, lost the books.

Your first step is to ask the library to voluntarily open the inventory to you. If they refuse, you may well want to subpoena it. Here's how:

1. Complete the subpoena form.

2. Prepare a declaration under penalty of perjury. Briefly describe the documents you need and why they are necessary to prove issues involved in the case. If you want the custodian of the records to show up in person, give a reason. Don't argue the merits of your case.

3. Have a subpoena issued by the small claims clerk. Then deliver the subpoena to the head librarian, and don't forget to properly fill out the proof of service (see Chapter 11) and return it to the clerk.

TIP

Ask to examine documents prior to your court hearing. The documents you have subpoenaed will be mailed or presented to the court—not to you. You will probably want an opportunity to examine them and should request that from the judge, who may well let you look at them right there in the courtroom while other cases go ahead. Or, if necessary, the judge may postpone the case for a few days and arrange to have you examine the documents at the place of business where the records are normally kept.

Witness Testimony by Letter

In most small claims courts, there are no formal rules of evidence requiring a witness to testify in person (but be sure to check your local rules). It is often preferable to have a witness appear in court, but this isn't always possible, and a judge will accept written statements from both eyewitnesses ("I was there and saw the filthy apartment") and expert witnesses ("I examined the transmission and found that a rebuilt part was installed improperly"). If you do present the written statement of a witness, make sure the witness states the following facts:

For an eyewitness:

- who the witness is—name, age (or adult or minor status), county of residence, and relationship to the plaintiff or defendant
- the date of the event, and
- what that person saw, heard, smelled, felt, or tasted, and where and how it transpired.

For an expert witness:

- who the witness is—name and relationship to the plaintiff or defendant
- the witness's work and education credentials, which demonstrate that person's expertise in the field she or he is commenting on (if these are lengthy, it's a good idea to attach the person's résumé)
- what the witness did to be able to render his or her opinion ("I examined the paint on Mr. Jones's 35-foot Cabin Cruiser and subjected it to the following test…")
- when the witness did the work
- his or her conclusion ("The paint used was not suitable for salt water immersion")
- if possible, an estimate of the cost to redo the work properly, and
- any other facts that have a bearing on the dispute.

> TIP
> **Make sure you establish your expert's experience and training.** It's a good idea to attach to an expert's letter a separate list of the expert's credentials. If your expert has a résumé listing credentials, attach it to the letter in which the witness states his or her findings. The more distinguished your expert, the more likely the judge is to respect the opinion.

Sample Letter by Eyewitness

Victor Van Cleve
37 Ogden Court
Kansas City, KS 12333
September 30, 20xx

Presiding Judge
Small Claims Court
Kansas City, KS 12333
Re: *John Swift vs. Peter Petrakos*
Small Claims Case No. 11478
Your Honor:

On September 15, 20xx, at approximately 7:30 a.m, I was parked near the corner of South Dora and 7th Streets in Larchville. I was parked on South Dora, about three parking spaces south of the intersection. Just after 7:30 a.m., I witnessed an auto accident involving John Swift and Peter Petrakos.

I clearly saw Mr. Petrakos's yellow Toyota, which was heading north on South Dora, go through a red light and hit Mr. Swift's blue van, which was proceeding west on 7th, well inside the 25 MPH speed limit. I noticed that the traffic light facing Mr. Petrakos did not turn to green for ten seconds or so after the accident, so it is clear to me that Mr. Petrakos really did go through the light while it was fully red. In short, this was not a situation where Mr. Petrakos was just a tiny bit early getting into the intersection at a light change.

Sincerely,

Victor Van Cleve
Victor Van Cleve

Sample Letter by Expert Witness

Gail McClosky
47 Penrod Street
Helena, MT 12344
September 30, 20xx

Judge
Small Claims Court
Helena, MT 12344

Re: *James Dills vs. R & B Construction*
Small Claims Case No. 11478

Your Honor:

I am a fully licensed contractor with 20 years' experience here in Helena (Contractor's License 4021B). For the last ten years I've run my own five-person contracting company specializing in building enclosures and buildings to house horses and other large animals. I enclose a résumé outlining my specialized training and experience in this field.

On April 23, 20xx, I was asked by James Dills to inspect several new stalls he had contracted to be built in the main barn of his Lazy T Riding Stable by R&B Construction.

In my opinion these stalls are seriously below normal industry standards, for three reasons.

1. They are too small for the animals intended to be kept in them. [*Continue with details.*]

2. Walls and doors are built of plywood too thin to safely contain an agitated animal. [*Continue with details.*]

3. Construction is so rough and unfinished in several places as to pose a danger of injury to an animal intended to be kept there. [*Continue with details.*]

In conclusion, I believe the stalls are so poorly constructed they can't reasonably be upgraded to provide safe habitable housing for horses. Were they mine, I would rip them out and start over.

Sincerely,

Gail McClosky
Gail McClosky

Judges as Witnesses

A small claims judge has great discretion to climb down off the bench to check out an important fact. Asking a judge to check out a key fact in your case can be a valuable technique in some situations. For example, in disputes involving damaged clothing it is routine to bring the damaged or defective garment into court for the judge's examination. Indeed, it normally makes sense to bring physical evidence that meets these three criteria:

- showing it to the judge will help your case
- it will fit through the door, and
- bringing it into the courtroom is not dangerous or inappropriate, as would be the case with an animal, firearm, or extremely dirty or smelly items.

But what if your evidence is impossible to bring into the courtroom, such as a car with a poor paint job. Be creative and understand that judges have flexibility and discretion about how to handle their cases. For example, you could ask the judge to accompany you outside the building to the parking lot to examine the car. Many judges will agree do so if you make a convincing argument as to why it is necessary to understand the dispute (and especially if it won't take too long). For instance, in one case the judge was disturbed one morning when two eyewitnesses gave seriously contradictory testimony about a traffic accident. He questioned both in detail and then took the case under submission. That evening, he drove over to the relevant corner. Once there, it was clear that one of the witnesses couldn't possibly have seen the accident from the spot on which she claimed to be standing (in front of a particular restaurant). The judge decided the case in favor of the other party.

> ⓘ CAUTION
> **Don't waste a judge's time.** Never ask a judge to take time to leave court to view evidence if you can establish or prove the same point by other means, such as by presenting the testimony (or letter) of a witness or by showing the judge a photograph.

 JUDGE'S TIP
Small claims court judges may independently consult expert witnesses.
Many small claims judges keep lists of "experts" whom they consult from time to time regarding particular issues in medicine, dentistry, plumbing, auto repair—you name it. If a judge is going to do this, he or she should tell the parties so they have some idea where the decision is coming from. If you think the judge is considering such a step, don't be shy about asking if that is indeed the intention and what expert the judge has in mind. It would not be untoward, for instance, to ask the judge to state in the written judgment the source of any expert advice. The worst the judge can do is say no.

JUDGE'S TIP
A judge may go on a "walkabout." A colleague who was deciding a small claims neighborhood nuisance case went out and walked through the neighborhood in question, getting a stronger understanding of the problem than if he had remained in the courtroom. —Judge (Ret.) Roderic Duncan

Testimony by Telephone

A surprising number of small claims court judges will take testimony over the phone if a witness cannot be present because the person is ill, disabled, out of state, or can't take time off from work. While procedures vary, some courts will do this by setting up a conference call so that the opposing party has the opportunity to hear what is being said and to respond.

Don't assume that a particular judge will allow telephone testimony. If you think you'll need to have a witness testify by phone, explain your problem to the court clerk well in advance. If you get a negative response, don't give up—ask the judge when you get into the courtroom. Be sure you also present a letter from the witness stating what the person would testify to if he or she was present in court (for example, your opponent's car ran a red light and broadsided you) and explaining why it is impossible to be there. This letter should look like the first sample letter in "Witness Testimony by Letter," above, except the witness should add:

Mr. Swift has asked me to testify on his behalf, and normally I would be happy to do so. However, I will be in New York City on business during the months of October, November, and December 20xx and cannot be present.

I have asked Mr. Swift to let me know the day and approximate time of the court hearing and have told him that I will give him a phone number where I can be reached. If you think it desirable, I will be pleased to give my testimony by phone.

Your Day in Court

Thhis chapter focuses on how to present your case to the judge. We'll go over what typically happens when you appear before the judge so you have a good understanding of what to expect. We'll also cover some basic courtroom etiquette—the dos and don'ts—so you can make the most of your day in court.

If the Defendant Is a No-Show

If one party to a case doesn't appear in court on the proper day at the proper time, the case is normally decided in favor of the other. Before doing so, the judge will verify that the defendant was properly served with court papers and that neither party requested a postponement.

> **TIP**
> **Don't rely on a second chance.** In some states, if neither party appears, the judge may take the case "off calendar," meaning the case is delayed until a future date. Don't count on it, however. Make every effort to show up or notify the court clerk if you are unavoidably detained.

If the plaintiff appears but the defendant doesn't, the judge in most states normally will ask the plaintiff to state briefly the basic facts of the case and present any important written evidence, such as a copy of the written contract at issue. In the few states that require a defendant to file a written answer (see the appendix), the plaintiff should be able to find out before the court date whether the other side is planning to appear. If you ascertain ahead of time that the defendant is not going to appear, you will want to know what, if anything, you must do to get a default judgment.

> **JUDGE'S TIP**
> **Don't expect to win just because your opponent failed to appear.** The law requires that you give enough evidence to show that the defendant actually owes you money.

Because the defendant is not present to contradict anything you say, the judge usually will rule in your favor as long as you state the bare bones of a valid legal claim. The defendant has no right to appeal this judgment in

most states (see Chapter 23), unless the judge decides to reopen the case by vacating the default judgment.

If the defendant isn't present, a judge only wants to hear the basic facts necessary to support a judgment in your favor. You do not need to make an extended argument, because in the absence of your opponent the judge will assume your version of what happened is true.

> EXAMPLE: "Your Honor, I own the Racafrax Auto Repair Shop. On January 11, 20xx, I repaired defendant's 20xx Honda Prius. He paid me $500 and agreed to pay another $500 on March 1. He has not made the second payment. I have copies of the contract defendant signed and of several unpaid bills I sent him. I am asking for a judgment of $500 plus $55 for my court filing fee and the cost of having the papers served."

If you are the defendant in a case where a default judgment was entered against you and you have a good excuse for failing to appear at the hearing, you can ask the judge to retract the judgment. This is called "setting aside the judgment" or "vacating the judgment." Courts are not very sympathetic to setting aside or vacating a default judgment unless you can show that the original papers weren't properly served and that you didn't know about the hearing. In some states, this can happen if someone signs your name for a certified letter and then doesn't give it to you. In all states, it can occur when a dishonest process server doesn't serve you, but tells the court otherwise. As soon as you find out that a default judgment has been entered against you, call the court clerk. It doesn't make any difference if the hearing you missed was months before, as long as you move to set it aside immediately upon learning about it.

If a default judgment has been entered against you after you were properly served, you will face an uphill struggle to get it set aside. A few judges will accept excuses ("I forgot," "I was sick," "I got called out of town"). Generally, however, judges assume that you could have at least called, or had a friend call, no matter what the emergency, and they will not vacate the judgment except for an extremely good cause.

To set aside a default, go to the small claims court clerk's office and ask for the proper form, which will normally be titled something like Notice of Motion to Vacate Judgment.

Sometimes the defendant files a motion to vacate a default judgment after a writ of execution to collect the small claims judgment has already been entered for the plaintiff. In most states, under these circumstances, the writ of execution will be recalled (stayed) by the court until a decision on the motion to vacate the default judgment is made. If the writ of execution has already been served as part of an effort to collect, the defendant must file a motion to suspend the writ of execution (often called a Motion to Stay or Quash the Writ of Execution), pending the court's decision on whether or not to set aside the default judgment and reopen the case. For more information on how to do this, or to find out the exact rules for your state, consult your small claims court clerk.

In most states, you can't appeal a default judgment. Unless you get the default set aside, the judgment will be final.

How to Handle a Motion to Vacate Judgment

Some judges will vacate defaults on the basis of almost any hard luck story. Others, however, will refuse to vacate a default judgment unless the defendant makes a written request for a postponement before the hearing or can show that a real emergency caused him or her to miss the hearing. An example of such an emergency might be a death in the family or never having received the original court papers and therefore not knowing a hearing was scheduled.

Because the judge has discretion as to whether to vacate a default, it's impossible to predict what any particular judge will do. For this reason, defendants should make their motion to vacate the judgment as soon as they realize they missed the original hearing.

Plaintiffs, who benefit from a default judgment and understandably would prefer it to stand, should emphasize that they played by the rules and showed up on the original hearing date, whereas the defendant failed to do so and, assuming it's true, failed to request a postponement. If the plaintiff had witnesses ready to testify at the original hearing, and these people will have a hard time coming to court a second time, plaintiffs should also mention this (and perhaps submit written statements from the witnesses).

If the small claims judge grants the defendant's motion to vacate a default judgment, then one of two things will happen. If all parties are present and agree, the small claims judge may hear the original case without rescheduling it. If, however, the plaintiff is not present for the hearing on the defendant's motion to vacate judgment, or if the parties do not agree to hear the case then and there, the judge will reschedule the hearing and the clerk will mail written notice of the new hearing date to the parties.

If the small claims judge decides not to set aside the default, defendants in most states can appeal the judge's refusal (but not the decision in the case itself) to a higher court. (See Chapter 23 for more on appeals.)

If the higher court judge agrees with the small claims court judge, then the case is over and the plaintiff wins. If, however, the appeals court judge disagrees with the small claims court judge and vacates the default judgment, and if both parties are present and agree, the appeals court judge in most states can hear and decide the case immediately. If both parties aren't present or do not agree, then the appeals court judge will order the small claims court to schedule another hearing.

TIP
Always be ready to argue your side of the actual case. If the judge decides to grant the defendant's motion to vacate judgment, the judge will ask the parties whether they are prepared to argue the underlying case. Or, if the defendant appeals to superior court and the judgment is set aside there, the superior court judge has the authority to decide the underlying small claims court case. For that reason, both parties should always be prepared to argue the case whenever they have a hearing.

If the Plaintiff Is a No-Show

Occasionally, though less frequently, it is the plaintiff who fails to show up. In this situation, the judge normally will either dismiss the case or decide it based on the defendant's evidence, especially if the defendant filed a defendant's claim. The defendant usually will prefer to have the judge decide

the case, because if the case is simply dismissed (called a "dismissal without prejudice"), the plaintiff can refile it.

If a plaintiff does not show up at the hearing and did not request a postponement, it's likely the judge will dismiss the case. If the judge dismisses the case "without prejudice," this means the plaintiff can refile the case as long as the statute of limitations has not run out in the meantime. Normally, you have to refile quickly (many states have a 30-day limit).

However, if the judge dismisses the case "with prejudice," the plaintiff can't refile the case without first asking the judge to cancel (vacate or set aside) the dismissal. A judge is most likely to dismiss a case with prejudice if the defendant shows up in court and the plaintiff did not file a written request for postponement before the court date.

The judge is most likely to grant your motion to set aside the dismissal if both of the following are true:

- The plaintiff moves to have the judgment vacated promptly upon learning of his or her mistake. "Promptly" usually means within 30 days after the day the dismissal was entered and is thought by most judges to be a much shorter time.
- The plaintiff has a good explanation as to why he or she was unable to be present or call on the day the case was regularly scheduled. A judge might accept something like this: "I had a flu with a high fever and simply lost track of a couple of days. As soon as I felt better, which was two days after my case was dismissed, I came to the clerk's office to try to get the case rescheduled."

To get a dismissal vacated, ask the small claims court clerk for the rules and forms you should use.

If the judge enters a default judgment for the defendant, the plaintiff cannot appeal the judgment but may appeal the judge's decision to give the defendant a default judgment. Remember, the plaintiff is the one who initiated the case and established the hearing date, so no one is going to have a great deal of sympathy for the plaintiff's failure to show up, and the plaintiff's reason for not appearing must be a very good one and should be supported by written evidence. The procedure for vacating or setting aside a judgment is the same as the procedure discussed above for defendants.

Your Day in Court

The big moment has arrived. You're in the courtroom, all parties are present, and your case is called by the clerk. What happens now? First, the judge will ask everyone's name and who they are (plaintiff, defendant, or witness). Second, the judge will ask the plaintiff to briefly state his or her case. After the plaintiff and any witnesses for the plaintiff speak, the defendant will have a turn.

Tips for Both Parties

Before we focus on the plaintiff's and defendant's presentations, here are a few tips both parties should find helpful. These are not rules written on golden tablets, just suggestions.

- **Stand when you make your presentation to the judge.** Standing gives most people a sense of presence and confidence at a time when they may be a little nervous. It's fine to sit while your opponent is talking. If the judge interrupts your opponent's presentation to ask you a quick question that requires a short answer, there is no need to leap to your feet to answer it.
- **Be as brief as you can while still being sure to explain and document your case thoroughly.**
- **Start with the end of the story, not the beginning.** That is, describe your loss and how much you are asking for. Then go back and tell your story chronologically.
- **Don't read your statement.** Reading in court is almost always a bore. But you may find it helpful to make a few notes on a card to serve as a reminder in case you get nervous or forget something. If you decide to do this, list the headings of the various points you want to make in an outline form. Be sure your list is easy to read at a glance and that the topics are in the correct order. (See Chapter 13 for a sample list.)
- **During your or your witness's presentation, the judge is likely to interrupt to ask questions.** Never put the judge off by saying you'll get to the point later in your presentation. Far better to directly answer any questions. Just be sure that you and your witnesses eventually get a

chance to make all of your key points. If you feel rushed, say so. The judge will normally slow things down a little.

> **JUDGE'S TIP**
>
> **Really, don't interrupt.** When I presided over small claims cases, I would start each session by announcing, "Please do not interrupt the other side when they are speaking, no matter how outrageous you think any particular statement might be. I promise you'll have a turn to tell me your side of the case. I don't usually use a point system in deciding a case, but if you interrupt the other side while they are speaking and sing out with something like, 'That's a lie!,' I'd be tempted to subtract a point from any score I was keeping. And you never know, you might need that point later on." I'd smile at the audience, and they'd chuckle, but when the first person violated that rule, there'd be a big groan from the audience. —Judge (Ret.) Roderic Duncan

- **Try to present any portion of your case that is difficult to explain verbally in another way.** This often means bringing your damaged clothing or other exhibits, such as photographs or canceled checks, and presenting them to the judge in an organized way. Short videos can be helpful, but call in advance to see whether they are allowed and what technology is used to show them.
- **Don't act like a lawyer when asking your witnesses to testify.** Let your witnesses tell their story and only ask questions at the end if they've left out an important fact.
- **Use drawings if helpful.** If drawings will be helpful, as is almost always true in cases involving car accidents, be sure to ask the judge for permission to use the blackboard or dry erase board which should be available in the courtroom. You will want to draw clearly and legibly the first time, so it's wise to practice in advance or prepare a small version of the drawing ahead of time to copy from.
- **If you are the defendant, don't repeat facts already presented by the plaintiff that you don't dispute** (for example, that the two of you had a fender bender at a certain corner in a certain city at a certain time during certain weather conditions). Instead, focus on the facts of your principal disagreement (whether the light facing you was green or red, for example) and introduce evidence to prove that point.

- **Ask for a continuance if necessary.** The best laid plans can occasionally go haywire. Perhaps a key witness doesn't show up, or maybe, despite careful preparation, you overlook some aspect of the case that the judge feels is crucial. If this occurs, you may want to ask the judge to reschedule the case on another day so that you can prepare better. It is perfectly proper to make this sort of request. Whether or not it will be granted is up to the judge. If the judge feels that more evidence isn't likely to change the result, or that you are making the request as a stalling tactic, it will not be granted. If, despite the fact that you prepared conscientiously, there is a good reason for a delay, it will usually be allowed.

- **Recognize that a judge who is convinced that one side is morally in the right will bend over backward to find a legal reason to rule in that person's favor.** For example, if you lent a friend money in an emergency and he is now trying to wriggle out of his obligation based on a legal technicality (claims the loan was really a gift), make sure the judge understands the trouble your opponent's bad act has caused you (you can't afford to pay college tuition).

- **If you've done legal research and believe that a statute or court decision supports your position, call it to the attention of the judge as part of your oral presentation.** If possible, it's also a good idea to back this up with a brief written memo. (See "Sample Legal Research Memo," below.) Begin with the name and number of your case. Then list the official citation of the statute, ordinance, or court case you think helps your case and briefly explain why. (See Chapter 25 for an explanation of how to cite statutes and cases.) In court, give one copy of the memo to the clerk to hand to the judge and another to your opponent.

JUDGE'S TIP

Less can be more when you're testifying. If the judge asks you a question like, "Did you have a written lease with the landlord?" the better answer is either "Yes" or "No," as appropriate, not something like: "Well, Your Honor, before I answer that question I need to tell you the background of the case. I first met the landlord in 1967, and then …" You get the idea.

Sample Legal Research Memo

MEMO

August 10, 20xx

Lee vs. Yew
Small Claims #127654

To: Small Claims Judge
From: Robert Yew, Defendant
Re: California law on boundary trees

This case involves Mr. Lee, my next-door neighbor, suing me because he claims my Monterey Pine tree drops debris on his roof and yard. Although he is asking for a judgment of $500 for cleanup costs, what he really wants is for me to pay several thousand dollars to remove the 80-foot tree.

There is only one problem with Mr. Lee's argument—because the tree touches our boundary line, the tree is half his. That's because California law, as set forth in Civil Code Section 834, clearly states that "Trees whose trunks stand partly on the land of two or more coterminous owners, belong to them in common."

Mr. Lee will argue that the tree was planted 100% on my property by the person who owned my house before I bought it and that the tree is still 90% on my side of the property line. Both contentions are true, but as you can see under Civil Code Section 834, it makes no difference. As long as the tree touches the boundary line—which the photographs I have presented the court clearly prove—the tree belongs to both of us as co-owners (tenants in common). (*Anderson v. Weiland*, 12 Cal.2d 730 (1936).)

I have offered to try and mediate the dispute, but so far Mr. Lee says, "No." I hope he will change his mind.

Respectfully submitted,

Robert Yew

Robert Yew

> **TIP**
>
> **Practice your presentation early and often.** As emphasized throughout this book, it pays to practice making your oral presentation ahead of time. Have a tough-minded friend or family member play the part of judge, ask questions, and try to poke holes in your best points. Run through your presentation several times until you get it right.

From the Plaintiff's Side

If you are the plaintiff, you should clearly tell the judge what the dispute is about before you start describing the details of what happened.

If your case involves a car accident, you might start by saying:

"This case involves a car accident at Cedar and Rose Streets in which my car suffered $872 worth of damage when the defendant ran a red light and hit my front fender."

That introduction is much better than:

"It all started when I was driving down Rose Street after having a bagel with cream cheese for breakfast."

It's a rare case where the plaintiff's initial presentation should take longer than five minutes. As part of your statement, you should present and explain the relevance of any papers, photos, or other documentary evidence. You should hand these to the clerk, who will pass them on to the judge. You should also be sure to tell the judge if you have any witnesses to present.

Your witness will normally be given a chance to speak after you complete your presentation. The witness should be well prepared to state any key information in an organized way (for example, that he or she inspected the apartment immediately after you did your final cleanup and found it to be clean). Too often, when witnesses are asked to testify, they either leave out important points or are so disorganized that the force of their testimony is lost. (For information on preparing your witnesses, see Chapter 14.)

> **JUDGE'S TIP**
>
> **The judge will probably question your witnesses.** Don't count on being allowed to ask your witnesses questions or cross-examine the other party or their

witnesses. Most judges will want to do any questioning of witnesses that is going to take place. Hostile feelings often bubble forth if the parties are allowed to ask questions of opposing witnesses. If one of your witnesses forgets an important point, wait until the judge is about to excuse the witness and then politely suggest that the judge allow the witness to make a further statement, for example, "Your Honor, Ms. Peterson hasn't said anything about the color of the traffic light. Would it be possible for you to ask her to cover that subject?" If your opponent or one of her witnesses skirts an important issue, say something similar, like, "Your Honor, the defendant hasn't said anything about how many beers he drank that night. I would appreciate it if you would ask him to cover that subject." —Judge (Ret.) Roderic Duncan

From the Defendant's Side

Sooner or later it will finally be the defendant's turn. Defendants often get so angry at something the plaintiff has said that when they get to speak, they attack angrily. This is usually counterproductive. Far better to calmly and clearly present your side of the dispute to the judge. Start with the key point of contention and then fill in the details of what happened from your point of view. If the plaintiff has made significant false or misleading statements, these should definitely be pointed out. But to show the judge how calm and fair-minded you are, wait until after you have made your key points to calmly point out your opponent's misstatements.

> EXAMPLE: "Your Honor, it's true that the bumper of my truck hit the defendant's fender and pushed it in slightly. But the key thing I want you to understand is that this happened because the defendant's pickup entered the intersection before it was clear and therefore the accident was his fault. Here is what happened. I was driving south on Cedar and entered the intersection just as the light first turned yellow. I slowed briefly near the center line behind a car that was turning left and then continued across, at which point the defendant's car darted in front of me..."

Recovering Costs

Both plaintiff and defendant are entitled to ask that a judgment in their favor include any recoverable costs, such as for filing and serving court

papers or subpoenaing essential witnesses. Sometimes defendants have no costs, unless they subpoena a necessary witness. In most states, costs that are recoverable by the winner include:

- The plaintiff's court filing fee (defendants pay no fee to appear unless they file a defendant's claim).
- Service of process costs. A plaintiff must always pay this fee, which can vary from a few dollars where certified mail is used to considerably more if a professional process service is required. A defendant will normally only have to pay to serve papers if he or she files a defendant's claim (counterclaim).
- Subpoenaed witness fees, if approved by the judge. Both the plaintiff and defendant can incur this cost if a witness must be subpoenaed and claims a fee. Fees for subpoenaing witnesses and documents are likely to be approved only if the judge believes the presence of the witness in court was necessary to prove the case.
- The cost of obtaining necessary documents, such as verification of car ownership. (Both plaintiffs and defendants can have these costs.)

If you forget to get your costs added to the judgment in court and want to go to the trouble, ask the small claims clerk what to do. Usually you can file a written request for costs within a few days of the judgment. For information on recovering costs incurred after judgment when your opponent won't voluntarily pay the judgment, see "Property Liens" in Chapter 24.

CAUTION
Some costs are not recoverable. You can't recover for such personal expenses as taking time off from work to prepare for or attend court, paying a babysitter, parking your car, or making photocopies of evidence.

A Sample Contested Case

Now let's look at how a contested case might be presented from both the plaintiff's and defendant's perspectives.

Clerk: *"The next case is John Andrews v. Robertson Realty. Will everyone please come forward?"* (Four people come forward and sit at the table facing the judge.)

Judge: *"Good morning. Which one of you is Mr. Andrews? Okay, will you begin, Mr. Andrews?"*

John Andrews: (stands) *"This is a case about my failure to get a $700 cleaning deposit returned, Your Honor. I rented a house from Robertson Realty at 1611 Spruce Street in Rockford in March 20xx on a month-to-month tenancy. On January 10, 20xx, I sent Mr. Robertson a written notice that I was planning to move on March 10. In fact, I moved out on March 8 and left the place extremely clean. I know it was clean because I spent eight hours, a lot of them on my hands and knees, cleaning it. In addition, all of my rent was properly paid. A few days after I moved out, I asked Mr. Robertson to return my $700 deposit. He wrote me a letter stating that the place was dirty and he was keeping my deposit.*

"I have with me a copy of a letter I wrote to Mr. Robertson on March 15 setting out my position in more detail. I also have some photographs that my friend, Carol Spann, who is here as a witness, took on the day I moved out. I believe the pictures show pretty clearly that I did a thorough cleanup." (John Andrews hands the letter and pictures to the clerk, who hands them to the judge.)

"Your Honor, I am asking not only for the $700 deposit, but also for $1,400 in punitive damages, which the law of this state allows a tenant when a landlord improperly refuses to return a deposit."

Judge: *"Mr. Andrews, will you introduce your witness?"*

Andrews: *"Yes, this is Carol Spann. She helped me clean up and move on March 7 and 8."*

Judge: (looking at the pictures) *"Ms. Spann, were you in the house the day John Andrews moved out?"*

Carol Spann: (standing) *"Yes, your Honor, I was—and the day before, too. I helped clean up, and I can say that we did a good job. Not only did we do the normal washing and scrubbing, but we waxed the kitchen floor, cleaned the bathroom tile, and shampooed the rugs."*

Judge: (turning to Mr. Robertson) *"Okay, now it's your turn to tell me why the deposit wasn't returned."*

Harry Robertson: (standing) *"I don't know how they could have cleaned the place up, your Honor, because it was filthy when I inspected it on March 9. Let me give you a few specifics. There was mildew and mold around the bathtub, the windows were filthy, the refrigerator hadn't been defrosted, and there was dog—how shall I say it—dog manure in the basement. Your Honor, I have brought*

along Clem Houndstooth as a witness. Mr. Houndstooth is the tenant who moved in three days after Mr. Andrews moved out. Incidentally, your Honor, the place was so dirty that I only charged Mr. Houndstooth a $200 cleaning deposit, because he agreed to clean it up himself."

Judge: (looking at Clem Houndstooth) *"Do you wish to say something?"*

Clem Houndstooth: (standing) *"Yes, I do. Mr. Robertson asked me to come down and back him up and I am glad to do it because I put in two full days cleaning that place up. I like a clean house, your Honor, not a halfway clean, halfway dirty house. I just don't think that a house is clean if the oven is full of gunk, there is mold in the bathroom, and the insides of the cupboards are grimy. All these conditions existed at 1611 Spruce Street when I moved in. I just don't believe that anyone could think that that place was clean."*

Judge: *"Mr. Andrews, do you have anything to add?"*

John Andrews: (standing up) *"Yes, I sure do. First, as to the mildew problem. The house is 40 years old, and there is some dampness in the wall of the bathroom. Maybe there is a leaky pipe someplace behind the tile. I cleaned it a number of times, but it always came back. I talked to Mr. Fisk in Mr. Robertson's office about the problem about a month after I moved in, and he told me that I would have to do the best I could because they couldn't afford to tear the wall apart. As to the cupboards and stove, they are both old. The cabinets haven't been painted in ten years, so, of course, they aren't perfect, and that old stove was a lot dirtier when I moved in than it is now, because I can tell you I personally worked on it with oven cleaner for over an hour."*

Judge: *"What about the refrigerator, Mr. Andrews? Was that defrosted?"*

John Andrews: *"No, your Honor, it wasn't, but it had been defrosted about three weeks before I moved out, and I thought that it was good enough the way it was."*

Judge: *"Okay, if no one else has anything to add, I want to return your pictures and letters. You will receive my decision by mail in a few days."*

The case presented is based closely on a real small claims case. Here is how the judge decided the case.

"This is a typical case in which both sides have some right on their side. What is clean to one person may be dirty to another. Based on what I heard, I would have to guess that the old tenant made a fairly conscientious effort to clean up and probably left the place about as clean as it was when he moved in, but that the new tenant, Houndstooth, had much higher

standards and convinced the landlord that it was filthy. The landlord may not have needed too much convincing since he probably would just as well keep the deposit. But I did hear enough to convince me that Andrews, the old tenant, didn't do a perfect job cleaning up. My decision will be that Andrews gets a judgment for the return of $450 of the $700 deposit, with no punitive damages. I believe that $250 is more than enough to compensate the landlord for any damages he suffered as a result of the house 'being a little dirty.'"

I then asked the judge if he felt that the case was well presented. He replied substantially as follows:

"Better than average. I think I got a pretty good idea of what the problems were. The witnesses were helpful and the pictures gave me a pretty good idea that the place wasn't a total mess. Both sides could have done better, however. Andrews could have presented a witness to testify to the condition of the house when he moved in if, in fact, it was truly a lot dirtier than when he left. Another witness to testify to the fact that the house was clean when he moved out would have been good, too. His friend, Carol Spann, seemed to be a very close friend, and I wasn't sure that she was objective when it came to judging whether or not the place was clean. The landlord, Robertson, could also have done better. He could have presented a more disinterested witness, although I must say that Houndstooth's testimony was pretty convincing. Also he could have had pictures documenting the dirty conditions and an estimate from a cleaning company for how much they would have charged to clean the place up. Without going to too much trouble, I think both sides could have probably done somewhat better with more thorough preparation."

Motor Vehicle Repair Cases

magine that you go to the auto repair shop to pick up your trusty old steed after a complete engine overhaul. The bill, which you agreed to pay in advance, is $1,225. This always seemed a little steep, but the mechanic talked you into it by claiming he would do a great job and that the overhauled engine should last another 50,000 miles. At any rate, you write a check and drive out of the garage in something approaching a cheerful mood. As you head up the first hill, you start to hear a funny noise. You drive back to the garage in a sour mood. Not only are you out $1,225, but your car runs worse than it did when you brought it in.

After a bit of foot stomping, you get someone to say that they will look over the car. The next day you call the garage. Nothing has been done. You yell at the garage owner and then call your bank to stop payment on the check, but it already has been cashed. The next day the garage owner tells you the problem is in a part of the engine they didn't work on. "Give us another $500 and we can surely solve this new problem." You pick up your mechanical friend and drive it home—very slowly. You are furious and decide to pursue every legal remedy, no matter what the trouble. How do you start? First, park your car, take a shower, and maybe sleep on it for a night. Nothing gets decided well when you're mad. Then, read this chapter and decide whether you want to take action.

Do You Have a Case?

Following the approach presented throughout this book, ask yourself these two key questions:

- Have you suffered a loss?
- Can you prove the defendant's negligence caused your loss?

The first question is easy. Your car works worse than it did before you paid a lot of money to have it fixed. Clearly, you have suffered a loss.

The second question is tougher. The car now works less well than before you had it fixed, and you are convinced that a lousy repair job caused your problem. But in this type of case, it's likely the garage owner will claim the work was done properly and that the car simply needs more work. For all the judge knows, this may even be true. In short, to win this type of case it's

your job to prove that the repair work was not up to a reasonable standard of competence. Doing so will make your case; failing to do so will break it.

Collect Available Evidence

Gather all the relevant evidence, pronto. In this situation, this means getting your used parts (it's a good idea to do this any time you have major work done). If the garage will not give them to you, ask again by letter, keeping a copy for your file. If you get the parts, fine—if you don't, you have evidence that the garage is badly run or has something to hide.

Have Your Car Checked by an Expert

Before you drive many miles after the disputed work is done, have your car checked by an experienced mechanic. Sometimes it is possible to get a free estimate from a repair shop. In this situation, however, you are probably better off paying someone to look at the engine thoroughly, with the understanding that if the need arises, the mechanic will testify on your behalf in small claims court—or at the very least, will write a letter stating what's wrong with the engine. A few states require that you present three written estimates in small claims court. Whether this is required or not in your state, it's a good idea to have them.

Try to Settle

By now you should have a pretty good idea what the first garage did wrong. Call and ask them to redo the job or refund part or all of your money. Often the repair shop will agree to do additional work to avoid a hassle. If they agree to take the car back, insist on a written agreement detailing what they will do and how long it will take. Also, talk to the mechanic who will actually work on the car to be sure you both have the same understanding about what needs to be done. You may be a little paranoid about taking your car back to the garage that just screwed it up. Nevertheless, unless they have proven themselves outrageously incompetent, this is probably your best approach because it's usually easier to get work redone than it is to get a big refund. Also, if you sue and the garage owner shows up in court and says he offered to work on the car again but you refused, it may weaken your case.

Write a Demand Letter

If the garage isn't cooperative, it's time to write a formal demand letter. Remember our discussion in Chapter 6. Your letter should be short, polite, and written with an eye to a judge reading it. (See sample letter, below.)

> ◯ **TIP**
> **Be sure to emphasize any promise made by the garage.** Most small independent garages don't make a written warranty or guarantee on their work. However, if you were given any promises in writing, mention them in your letter. Also, if you were promised things orally about the quality of the work the garage planned to do and you relied on these statements as part of your decision to authorize the repairs, make sure the letter describes this express oral warranty. (See Chapter 2.)

File Your Court Papers

If you still get no satisfactory response from the garage, file your papers at the small claims court clerk's office in the county where the garage is located.

Prepare for Court

If you want the judge to understand your case, you must understand it yourself. Sounds simple, doesn't it?

Arguing a case in small claims court without being able to explain the problem clearly will likely end in a bad loss. To be able to convince a judge that the mechanic failed to properly repair your car will likely require you to do some homework. After all, the people from the garage will likely show up in court with a terrific-sounding story about the wonderful job they did with pistons, bearings, and camshaft.

In many cases, a 15-minute conversation with a knowledgeable mechanic might be all you really need to understand what the first mechanic did wrong. (Also, your local library might have car manuals with diagrams.) In court, you want to be armed with knowledge so you have no trouble explaining to the judge that the mechanic did a substandard job.

Sample Car Repair Demand Letter

Haig Mackey
15 Orange Street
Hamden, CT 12344
October 1, 20xx

Happy Days Motors
100 Speedway
New Haven, CT 12333

Dear People:

On August 13, 20xx, I brought my 2005 Ford to your garage. You agreed to do a complete engine rebuild job for $2,000. You told me, "Your car will be running like a watch when we're through with it." The car worked well when I brought it in, but was a little short on power. Two days later, when I picked up my car, it barely moved at all. The engine made such a clanging noise that I've been afraid to drive it.

I have repeatedly asked you to fix the car or to refund my money. You have refused.

I've had two mechanics check out my car since you worked on it. Both agree you did your work improperly and even installed some used parts instead of new ones, which you did not tell me. The work you did on the engine rings was particularly poorly done.

After receiving no response from you, I had the work redone at a cost of $1,500. My car now works well. Please refund my $2,000. Should you fail to do so within ten days, I will promptly file complaints with the local Better Business Bureau and take this dispute to small claims court. I hope to hear from you promptly.

Sincerely,

Haig Mackey
Haig Mackey

cc: Connecticut Dept. of Consumer Affairs
 Bureau of Automotive Repair
 Hartford, CT 12333

TIP

Remember, the judge is probably not a mechanic. It's important to pay attention to the human being to whom you are presenting your case. It's no secret that many, if not most, small claims judges don't understand the insides of cars any better than you do. So be prepared to make a convincing presentation to a person who nods his or her head but doesn't really understand the difference between the drive shaft and the axle.

Appearing in Court

When you show up in court, be sure that you are well organized. Bring all the letters you have written or received about your car problem, any written warranty, photographs if they are helpful, and your used parts if they aid in making your case. If you have a witness to oral statements made by the garage, be sure to bring that person with you to court. Or if that's impossible, ask the person to write a letter explaining what he or she heard. Also, be sure to present any letter(s) written by an independent expert(s) who has arranged to examine your car. Even one cogent letter from an experienced mechanic, explaining how the repair job was botched, when combined with your own informed presentation, can make you a winner.

If you are well prepared you should win the sort of case outlined here without difficulty. Judges drive cars and have to get them fixed; they tend to be sympathetic with this type of consumer complaint. Simply present your story (see Chapter 15), your documentation, and your witnesses. If you feel that your opponent is snowing the judge with a lot of technical lingo, get things back on track by asking that all jargon be explained in ordinary English. This will be a relief to everyone in the courtroom except your opponent.

TIP

A good drawing can help. In cases involving machinery, people can give effective testimony by presenting a large drawing illustrating the mistake or problem. This approach is most effective when your expert appears in court and authoritatively points to the drawing to detail the problem.

Motor Vehicle Purchase Cases

O ccasionally, someone buys a vehicle and drives it a short way, only to have it fall apart. And too frequently the seller of the defective vehicle won't stand behind the product. What can you do if you are the victim of this kind of rip-off? There are major differences in how you should approach your problem depending on whether you purchased a new or used vehicle, so let's look at each situation separately.

New Vehicles

It can be especially frustrating to buy a new car and have it break down much sooner than it should. Most states have a law (the "lemon law") that requires the car dealer or manufacturer to give you a new car or a refund if your new car breaks down during the first 18 months or first 18,000 miles of the car's warranty period, whichever ends sooner. Unfortunately, because most new vehicles cost more than the small claims maximum, it is unlikely that you will be able to bring a small claims lawsuit against a car dealer or manufacturer for violating the lemon law.

RESOURCE

Making lemonade out of your lemon. For more information on lemon laws, see the following websites:

- www.autopedia.com (includes individual summaries of each state's lemon laws)
- www.autosafety.org (includes information on defects common to particular car models).

What if your car breaks down just outside the warranty period? Luckily, you may still have a winnable case: When a relatively new car falls apart for no good reason, many small claims court judges bend over backward to look for a legal way to give you protection over and above the actual written warranty that comes with the vehicle. For example, you still may be able to recover some money under one of the following approaches:

Prove that the defects arose while your car was still under warranty. Often a newish car that suffers serious mechanical problems soon after the warranty period runs out suffered similar problems during the warranty period. If so, you will want to argue that the dealer made inadequate repairs in the first instance and should still be responsible for the subsequent problems.

TIP

Document your attempts to have your car repaired. Make sure the judge knows about all the trips you have made to the dealer's repair shop. One way to establish this is by presenting copies of work orders you signed. If you don't have these or other records, request copies from the dealer (see Chapter 14 for instructions on subpoenaing documents), or sit down with a calendar and reconstruct the dates you brought your car in for repair. In court, give the copies or your list to the judge. If you have only your list, explain that it's your best estimate. The judge should accept it as being true unless the car dealer disputes it.

Investigate the possibility of a "secret warranty." After a model has been in production for awhile, a pattern of problems or failures may develop. Manufacturers are extremely sensitive to complaints in "high problem" areas—if for no other reason than to head off a possible federal safety recall. As a result, the manufacturer may have issued a "service bulletin" and created an adjustment program that extends the warranty or offers to pay for repair of conditions that substantially affect the vehicle's durability, reliability, or performance. Here's how you can find out about service bulletins and adjustment programs:

- Dealers must post a notice in the showroom or other areas with information on how to obtain service bulletins.
- You can search the National Highway Traffic Safety Administration's database of technical service bulletins at www.safercar.gov (click on "Vehicle Owners").
- If you go to the dealer for repair of a condition covered by an adjustment program, the dealer must inform you of the program's terms.
- The manufacturer must notify eligible owners about an adjustment program within 90 days after adopting it.

If your vehicle has a serious problem but the manufacturer hasn't issued a service bulletin or adopted an adjustment program (or you can't find out about either), talk to people at independent garages that specialize in repairing your model. Especially if they tell you the problem is widespread and that the manufacturer has fixed it without charge for some persistent customers, your next step is to write a demand letter to the car dealer and manufacturer. (See Chapter 6.) Mention that if your problem is not taken

care of, you will sue in small claims court and you will subpoena all records having to do with this defect. This may well cause the manufacturer to settle with you. If not, follow through on both threats.

> EXAMPLE: Bruno bought an expensive European car that repeatedly had engine problems while under the manufacturer's written warranty. Each time, Bruno brought it into the dealer's repair shop and adjustments were made that seemed to fix the problem. A few months after the written warranty ran out, the engine died. Even though the car was only a little over a year old and had gone less than 50,000 miles, both the dealer and the parent car company refused to repair or replace it. Their refusals continued even though the owner repeatedly wrote to them, demanding action. How does Bruno deal with his problem?
>
> First, because he needed his car, he had the repairs made. Second, although the repairs cost slightly more than the small claims limit, he decided he would scale down his claim and sue for the small claims maximum to save the extra expense and hassle of finding a lawyer and suing in regular court.
>
> At the hearing, both Bruno and his wife testified about their trials and tribulations with the car. They gave the judge copies of the several letters they had written to the dealer, one of which was a list of the dates they had taken the car to the dealer's shop while it was still under warranty. They also produced a letter from the owner of the independent garage that finally fixed the engine, stating that when he took the engine apart, he discovered a defect in its original assembly. The new car dealer testified only that his mechanics had done their best to fix the car when it was under the written warranty. He then contended that, once the written warranty had run out, he was no longer responsible. The dealer made no effort to challenge the car owner's story, nor did he bring his own mechanics to court to testify to how they had repaired the car while it was still under warranty. Bruno won and the dealer was ordered to reimburse him for the repair costs.

Used Vehicles From Dealers

Successfully suing used vehicle dealers can be tricky. Unlike new vehicle dealers, who are usually somewhat dependent upon their reputation in the community for honesty, a fair percentage of used vehicle dealers don't have

a good reputation to start with and survive by becoming experts at self-protection.

The principal self-protection device employed by used vehicle dealers is the "as is" designation in the written sales contract. The salesperson may praise a car to the sky, but when you read the contract, you will see it clearly stated that the seller takes absolutely no responsibility for the condition of the vehicle and that it is sold "as is."

To successfully sue a used car dealer, you must be able to prove that:

- you suffered a financial loss (this is not hard if you had to pay for repairs), and
- the dealer is legally responsible for your damages.

This second point is often harder to prove. Almost surely, the used car dealer will testify that he or she had no way of knowing how long a ten-year-old Dodge would last and that, for this very reason, the car was sold "as is." The dealer will then show the judge the written contract that not only contains the "as is" designation, but also "this written contract is the entire agreement between the parties and no oral statements or representations made by the dealer or any salesperson are part of the contract."

How can you fight this sort of cynical semi-fraud? It's difficult to do after the fact. The time for self-protection is before you buy a vehicle, when you have the opportunity to have it checked by an expert and to get a vehicle history report. There are a lot of online resources for checking a vehicle's history, particularly if you have the Vehicle Identification Number (VIN). In addition, you have the opportunity to refuse to close the deal unless the salesperson's claims about the great condition of the car are put in the contract. Of course, after the damage has been done, good advice such as this isn't worth much. If you have just been cheated on a used car deal, you want to know what, if anything, you can do now. Here are some suggestions.

Your state's lemon law may apply to used vehicles. In some states, the lemon law applies to used as well as new cars. Check to see if your situation is covered.

Argue fraud. If the car broke almost immediately after you took it out of the used car lot, you can file in small claims court and argue that you were

defrauded. Your theory is that, no matter what the written contract said, there was a clear implication that you purchased a car, not a junk heap. When the dealer produces the "as is" contract you signed, argue that it is no defense to fraud. (For more discussion of fraud, see Chapter 2.)

Did the dealer make promises? If the dealer made any promises, either in writing or orally, about the good condition of the vehicle, he or she may be required to live up to them. Why? Because, as noted in Chapter 2, statements about a product that you rely on as part of deciding whether to purchase the product constitute an express warranty that the dealer breaches if the promise turns out to be a lie. This is true even if the seller had you sign a contract with an "as is" statement that disclaims all warranties, because an "as is" statement does not disclaim an express warranty if one is made. The key to winning this sort of case is to produce a witness to the dealer's laudatory statements about the vehicle, copies of ads that state the car is in good shape, and anything else that will back up your story.

There also may be an implied warranty. There are two types of implied warranties. One type—the implied warranty of fitness—means that the vehicle is warranted to work for a particular purpose (say, consistency). The more common implied warranty is for merchantability. Here, you would argue that the car you bought was so defective that it didn't meet the reasonable standards expected of even a used car. (See Chapter 2 for more on warranties.)

A radical remedy: Give the car back and stop payment. You may consider having the car towed back to the lot and then refusing to make future payments. This option should be considered only in an extreme situation, but it does shift the burden of taking legal action to the other side, at which point you can defend on the basis of fraud (see above). If you take this approach, be sure you have excellent documentation that the car was below any reasonable expectations. And be sure to write a letter detailing the circumstances surrounding your extreme difficulties with the dealer, along with a convincing statement that, taken as a whole, the dealer's conduct amounts to consumer fraud. Send copies to the dealer and the bank or finance company to whom you pay your loan. Of course, you will probably have already made a down payment, so even in this situation you may wish to initiate action in small claims court to try to recover it.

CAUTION

Your credit rating will suffer. If you stop making payments, it will appear as a default on your credit report and will affect your credit score significantly, so think very carefully before choosing this course of action.

TIP

How to find signs of fraud. If you really suspect that you have been defrauded, have your car checked by an experienced mechanic who will be willing to write a letter explaining the findings. If the mechanic can find affirmative evidence that you were cheated, you will greatly improve your small claims case. The mechanic might, for example, find that the speedometer had been tampered with in violation of state law, or that a heavy grade of truck oil had been put in the crankcase so that the car wouldn't belch smoke. Also, this is the sort of case where subpoenaing documents might help. Specifically, you might wish to subpoena the car dealer's records, including any that indicate the dealer's purchase price and the condition of the car when it was purchased. It might also be helpful to learn the name of the car's former owner, with the idea of contacting that person. You can also check the car's history through an online service (search the Internet for "vehicle history"), which can tell you whether the car was stolen or salvaged, or was used as a rental or a taxi. (See Chapter 2 for more on fraud.)

Consider other remedies besides small claims court. These can include checking with your state department of consumer affairs or the local department of motor vehicles to see if used car lots are regulated. In many states, the department of motor vehicles licenses used car dealers and can be very helpful in getting disputes resolved, particularly where your complaint is one of many against the same dealer for similar practices. Also, contact your district attorney's office. Most now have a consumer fraud division, which can be of great help. If you can convince someone at the fraud division that what happened to you smells rotten, or if your complaint happens to be against someone they have already identified as a borderline criminal, they will likely call the used car dealer in for a chat. In theory, the D.A.'s only job is to bring a criminal action, which will be of no direct aid in getting your money back, but in practice, negotiations can often result in restitution. In plain words, this means that the car dealer may be told, "Look, you're right on the edge of the law here (or maybe over the edge). If

you clean up your act, which means taking care of all complaints against you and seeing that there are no more, we will close your file. If you don't, I suggest you hire a good lawyer, because you are going to need one."

Used Vehicles From Private Parties

Normally, it is easier to win a case against a private party than against a used vehicle dealer. This often runs counter to both common sense and fairness, as a private party may be more honest than a dealer. But fair or not, the fact is that a nondealer is usually less sophisticated in legal self-protection than a pro. Indeed, in most private party sales, the seller does no more than sign over the title slip in exchange for the agreed-upon price without any formal contract.

Too often, trouble develops soon after you purchase the vehicle and you must pay money for unexpected repairs. As is true with a used vehicle purchased from a dealer, your problem usually is not with proving that you suffered a loss. Instead, the key to winning is to show the judge that the seller of the vehicle is responsible for making your loss good. To do this, you normally must prove that the seller claimed that the vehicle was in better shape than it really was, and that you relied on these promises when you purchased it. The seller will almost certainly claim that he or she told you the car was being sold "as is." Remember, however, that an "as is" statement does not invalidate an express promise made about the car's condition.

> **EXAMPLE:** Barbara, a 20-year-old college student, bought a used BMW motorcycle from John. She sued John for $2,150 in repair costs, claiming that the motorcycle was in far worse shape than he had advertised. In court, she ably and convincingly outlined her conversations with John about the purchase of the motorcycle, testifying that he repeatedly told her that the cycle was "hardly used." She hadn't gotten any of John's promises in writing, but she did a creative job of developing and presenting what evidence she had. This included:
> - a copy of her letter to John that clearly outlined her position (see letter below)
> - copies of repair bills (and estimates) dated within two weeks of her purchase of the cycle, the lowest of which came to $2,150

- a copy of John's newspaper ad, which read: "BMW 500 c.c., almost new—hardly used—excellent condition—$7,500."
- a letter from the mechanic who worked on the motorcycle for Barbara (see letter below).

In court, Barbara outlined for the judge what happened and emphasized that she had saved for six months to get the money to buy the motorcycle. True, testimony about financial hardship isn't relevant, but a quick tug on the judge's heartstrings never hurts. Next, John had his turn. His testimony consisted mostly of some vague philosophy about machinery. He kept asking, "How could I know just when it would break?" When the judge asked him specific questions about the age, condition, and previous history of the cycle, he clammed up. When the judge asked him if he had, in fact, made specific guarantees about the condition of the bike, John began a long explanation about how when you sell things, you "puff them up a little." The judge decided in Barbara's favor based on her clear presentation and the two documents she presented supporting her case.

In used car transactions, it's often one person's word against another's, particularly if there's no written warranty or advertisement. Any shred of tangible evidence that the seller really did make an express oral warranty as to the condition of the car and that the seller relied on those statements to make the purchase can be enough to shift the balance to your side. Of course, if you have a friend who witnessed or heard any part of the transaction, her testimony will be extremely valuable. Getting a mechanic to check over a vehicle and then testify for you is also a good strategy. Sometimes you can get some help from publications that list wholesale and retail prices for used cars. Some people bring these publications into court to back up their assertion that they paid above the "Blue Book" price for a used car "because the car was represented to be in extra good shape." This type of evidence doesn't constitute much in the way of real proof that you were ripped off, but it is helpful to at least show the judge that you paid a premium price for unsound goods.

Demand Letter

14 Stockton Street
Moline, IL 12233

January 27, 20xx

John Malinosky
321 South Zaporah
Moline, IL 12233

Dear Mr. Malinosky:

This letter is a follow-up to our recent phone conversation in which you refused to discuss the fact that the 2010 BMW motorcycle I purchased from you on January 15 is not in the "excellent condition" that you claimed.

To review: On January 12, I saw your ad for a motorcycle that was "almost new—hardly used—excellent condition" in the local flea market newspaper. I called you, and you told me that the cycle was a terrific bargain and that you would never sell it except that you needed money for school. I told you that I didn't know much about machinery.

The next day, you took me for a ride on the cycle. You told me specifically that:

1. The cycle had just been tuned up.

2. The cycle had been driven less than 30,000 miles.

3. The cycle had never been raced or used roughly.

4. If anything went wrong with the cycle in the next month or two, you would see that it was fixed.

Relying on these statements, I bought the cycle from you for $7,500.

I had the cycle less than a week when the brakes went out. When I had them checked, the mechanic told me that the transmission also needed work (I confirmed this with another mechanic—see attached estimate). The mechanic also told me that the cycle had been driven at least 75,000 miles (perhaps a lot more) and that it needed a tune-up. In addition, he showed me caked mud and scratches under the cycle frame that indicated to him that it had been driven extensively off the road in rough terrain and had probably been raced on dirt tracks.

Demand Letter (continued)

The lowest estimate to do the repairs was $2,150. Before having the work done, I called you to explain the situation and to give you a chance to arrange for the repairs to be made, or to make them yourself. You laughed at me and said, "Sister, do what you need to do—you're not getting one dime from me."

Again I respectfully request that you make good on the promises you made to me on January 15. I relied on the truth of your statements when I decided to buy the bike. I enclose a copy of the mechanic's bill for $2,150, along with copies of several higher estimates that I received from other repair shops.

Sincerely,

Barbara Parker

Barbara Parker

Witness Letter

February 3, 20xx

To Whom It May Concern:

It's hard for me to get off work, but if you need me, please ask the judge to delay the case a few days. I have been in the motorcycle-repair business for 20 years, and have repaired hundreds of BMWs. The BMW that Barbara Parker brought to me was in fair shape at best. It's impossible to be exact, but given that the brakes and transmission were completely shot, I would conservatively guess it had been driven at least 75,000 miles. And given the damage to the underside of the bike, it was definitely driven a lot of those miles on dirt.

Respectfully submitted,

Honker Green

Al "Honker" Green

Bad Debts: Initiating and Defending Cases

Many small claims cases involve bad debts—a claim that the defendant owes the plaintiff money. Usually this means a bill for goods or services hasn't been paid, but it also can involve failure to pay a promissory note (for example, a loan from a friend or relative) or even a civil fine for something as simple as the failure to return a library book. The plaintiff wins the vast majority of these cases, often because the defendant defaults. This illustrates how effective small claims court can be as part of any business's collection strategy. Individuals also use small claims court to sue over goods or services that are shoddy, not as promised or ordered, or not delivered at all.

TIP

Even bad checks for small amounts may be worth pursuing. A bad check may be worth three times its face value. Every merchant is stuck with a bad check now and then. In many states, special laws allow a person receiving a bad check to obtain a judgment for a significant amount of money in damages in addition to the amount of the check, sometimes up to three times the amount of the check.

But paradoxically, small claims court can also work well for a defendant who puts on a spirited defense because the person believes he or she owes no money or the plaintiff is asking for too much. In large part this is because, unlike formal court, in small claims, defendants don't need to file complicated paperwork or jump through other legal hoops to present their side of the story. Indeed, all a defendant has to do is show up on the appointed day and make a convincing, well-documented presentation.

Some professionals, like doctors, dentists, and lawyers, don't use small claims court to collect unpaid bills because they think it takes too much time. Businesspeople who don't use small claims court as part of a self-help debt collection strategy must normally either write off the loss or turn the bill over to a collection agency. But small claims court actions can often be handled with very little time and expense once you get the hang of them. And in many states, businesses can delegate the job of actually appearing in court.

TIP
Unincorporated businesses can often send a representative to small claims court. Oftentimes, a bookkeeper, financial manager, or other employee of a sole proprietorship or partnership can appear and present a case in small claims court if the case can be proved by presenting a business record (showing that a bill hasn't been paid, for example), and if there is no other issue of fact involved in the case. And, in many states, a corporation or limited liability company has the right to send any authorized employee, officer, or director, and a partnership may send a partner, to court.

Who Should Appear in Court?

Small claims courts vary from state to state in terms of who can sue to collect unpaid bills. As listed in the state-by-state appendix, some states:

- allow bill collectors (called "assignees") to use small claims court
- ban bill collectors, but let lawyers carry out much the same task by representing multiple creditors, or
- ban both bill collectors and lawyers, only allowing businesses to sue on their own behalf.

Even among the states where businesses can't hire third parties but must represent themselves to sue on bad debt claims, there are important differences. For example, a few states entirely prohibit corporations from suing in small claims court, while others make it difficult for unincorporated businesses to send anyone but an owner or partner to court. However, most states allow corporations to sue and make it reasonably easy for both incorporated and unincorporated businesses to designate a bookkeeper or other employee to handle court appearances. (See Chapter 7 for more on who can sue in small claims court.)

After first checking the summary of rules in the appendix and on your state's website, contact your small claims court clerk and find out exactly what rules govern bill collection activities in your state. If you are a business, talk to other businesspeople (or business associations, such as the chamber of commerce) to learn practical strategies to cope with these rules. Also, if you are in a state where bill collectors or lawyers do small claims collection work,

you will want to find out how much they charge and how efficient they are and then compare this information to the time and energy it would take for you to do it yourself. Because bill collectors and lawyers typically charge from 20%–50% of any money they collect, you may conclude that you want to do this work yourself.

In many states, a business owner does not have to personally appear in court but can send an employee. Where money is owed, a bookkeeper or financial manager is normally a good choice, because the person can testify that a valid contract existed and the defendant has not paid the promised amount. However, if the defendant shows up and defends on the basis that the goods or services were defective, delivered late, or otherwise not acceptable, the bookkeeper is likely to be at a serious disadvantage; he or she probably has no firsthand knowledge of anything except that the check was not in the mail. For example, if you own a graphics business and are suing on an unpaid bill in a situation where you expect the defendant to show up in court and falsely claim you did lousy work, you will need to have someone in court who knows the details of the particular job. Typically, this should be the employee who dealt with the customer and did the work.

From the Plaintiff's Point of View

The job of the plaintiff who sues for nonpayment of a debt is often easy. That's because in the majority of cases, the debtor doesn't show up. In the absence of a defendant, the plaintiff needs only to introduce evidence that a valid debt exists and has not been paid. To accomplish this, present written proof of the debt in the form of a contract, work order, promissory note, or purchase order signed by the defendant. Even if a debt is based on an oral contract, it's usually easy to get a judgment because the defendant isn't present to contradict the plaintiff's version of events.

Here are a few suggestions for plaintiffs who plan to sue to collect a debt.

When It Doesn't Pay to Sue

Although using small claims court to collect a bad debt often makes sense, there are exceptions. Here are the principal ones:

When there isn't enough money at stake. For disputes involving a few hundred dollars or less, for businesses, the costs of filing, preparing, and presenting a small claims case are likely to be high relative to what they are likely to recover. Of course, this is doubly true if you doubt that a court judgment will be collectible.

When you won't be able to collect the judgement. As discussed in more detail in Chapters 3 and 24, when the defendant has a job, bank account, investments, or real estate, a court judgment is fairly easy to collect. However, some people are broke and unemployed and are likely to stay that way. A significant percentage of the adult U.S. population lives below the poverty level. Even those living above the poverty level, however, may not have money or property that can be easily collected. One thing is sure—you don't want to spend your time and energy suing someone who is not likely to have enough money to pay the resulting judgment. Better to write off the debt and tighten up your credit-granting procedures.

When you want or need to get along with the person in the future. Any court action, even a small claims lawsuit, tends to aggravate a dispute, resulting in more anger between the parties. This isn't a big problem when dealing with people or businesses you don't plan to have future contact with. But in other circumstances, such as where a relative or local business owes you money, it's possible that your ongoing relationship with a debtor may be more important than collecting all that you are owed. It may make sense to try to minimize conflict by trying to work out your dispute through mediation. (See Chapter 6.)

Ask for Your Money Before You Sue

Writing an effective letter demanding payment may prompt the debtor to send a check. You should always send a demand letter before filing in small claims court (and your letter may be helpful in explaining your case to the judge). Unfortunately, instead of doing this, many businesses rely on fill-in-the-blanks past-due notices and letters purchased from commercial sources. While sending one of these is better than nothing, it's far more effective to write your own, more personal letter (see the sample demand letter in Chapter 6)—or at least to customize a form letter enough so that it's clear it is aimed at the debtor. But be aware that if you regularly demand payment

of business debts, you'll have to comply with laws to protect the debtor from overzealous collection techniques, guard the debtor's privacy, govern communications with the debtor, and more. For the legal dos and don'ts of collecting bills, see *Legal Guide for Starting & Running a Small Business,* by Fred S. Steingold (Nolo).

> **TIP**
> **Plan in advance to counter any claim that your bill wasn't paid for a good reason.** If you provide goods or services, it's wise to include a statement on all your bills and collection letters requesting that the debtor notify you if goods are defective or services are substandard. Bring copies of these notices to court. Then if the debtor shows up and, for the first time, claims he or she didn't pay because the goods or services were somehow defective, you will be prepared to counter this claim. Do this by first showing the judge your many notices asking that any problem be brought to your attention and then testifying that the defendant never made a complaint. This should go far toward convincing the judge that the defendant is fabricating, or at least exaggerating, the current complaint in an effort to avoid paying you.

Bring Your Case Promptly

For maximum success in collecting on bad debts, file suit as soon as you conclude that informal collection methods are unlikely to work. You'll be pleasantly surprised that a small but significant number of debtors will quickly pay up—or call you to work out a payment plan—to avoid having a court judgment appear in their credit records. Fast action is also advisable for other reasons, the most important being that people who owe you money are likely to have other debts as well and may be considering bankruptcy. The quicker you act, the faster you'll get a judgment and be eligible to start collection activities, like wage garnishment or property attachment.

In addition, if you file promptly, you will avoid having to worry about whether you are within the legal filing deadline, called the statute of limitations. Depending on the state and the type of debt, this usually is anywhere from one to four years. (There is a discussion of the statutes of limitations applicable to different sorts of debts in Chapter 5.)

Installment Debts

If you lend money or sell an item with payments to be made in installments, and a payment or two is missed, you normally are entitled to sue only for the amount of the missed payments, not the whole debt. Before you can sue for the entire amount, you must wait until all payments are missed. However, there is a major exception to this rule: You can immediately sue for 100% of the debt—plus any interest—if your contract contains an acceleration clause. This is a statement that if one payment is missed, the whole debt becomes due. To see whether this type of provision is present, carefully read your installment sales contract and consider rewriting it to include such a clause.

Written Contracts

Most debts are based on written contracts. The contract may be a purchase order, credit agreement, lease, or formal contract. It normally makes no difference what your document is called, as long as you have something in writing with the defendant's signature.

Always bring your written documentation to court on the day your case is heard and be ready to show it to the judge. Also, bring any ledger sheets, computer printouts, or other business records documenting the payments that have been made or missed. Bring an extra copy for the judge and defendant.

It's important to be organized; you don't want to show up with botched records or become flustered when closely questioned by the judge. The courtroom is not the place to straighten out a poor accounting system.

Oral Contracts

Generally, a debt based on an oral contract is legal as long as the contract was (or could have been) carried out in one year and is not for the sale or mortgage of real estate or the sale of goods (personal property) worth more than $500. (See Chapter 22 for more on written documentation requirements for the sale of goods.) Of course, it may be hard to prove the debt exists if the defendant flat out denies that he or she borrowed the money or bought the goods or services. Your best bet is to attempt to come

up with some written documentation that your version of what occurred is true. For example, even if there is no written agreement, the defendant may have provided you with a down payment check or a letter asking for more time to pay. Either would be a huge help in convincing the judge that a debt exists. Or, when you write a letter demanding payment before you sue (see Chapter 6), include a description of the oral agreement and existing debt along with a phrase like "If my understanding is incorrect in any way, please contact me in writing or by phone by [date]." If the debtor doesn't dispute your version of events, then bring a copy of your letter to court and tell the judge you never got a reply, if that's truly the case.

If you can't come up with anything in writing, try to think of a person who has firsthand knowledge of the debt and who is willing to testify. For example, if you asked for your money and the defendant said in the presence of a friend, "I know I owe you $1,000. I'll pay you next month," or even, "Too bad you will never get your money back," or anything similar that indicates that the loan existed, bring your witness to court or if that's not possible have the witness write a letter explaining what that person heard, and show the letter to the judge.

If you don't have a witness, consider whether you can establish the debt's existence by looking at the debtor's actions. It is often particularly easy to do this when you haven't been paid for services you provided in a commercial context. After all, if the other party accepted your labor, there is almost always an implication that payment is expected.

EXAMPLE: Jane, a commercial illustrator, works as a freelancer for a number of ad agencies, publishers, and other clients. One day she gets a call from Harold, a dress designer, asking her to do a series of drawings of his new line of evening wear. Jane does the drawings and submits her bill for $2,000. Harold refuses to pay, claiming both that payment was conditional on the drawings being published in a fashion magazine (they weren't) and that even if a contract did exist, Jane is charging too much. Jane files in small claims court. The judge has no trouble finding the existence of an oral contract based on Harold's admission that he asked Jane to do the work. However, the judge only awards Jane $1,400, because she can't document her claim that she was to be paid $100 an hour, and Harold made a convincing presentation that illustrators with similar qualifications customarily charge no more than $70 per hour.

 RELATED TOPIC
More on contract cases. See "Breach of Contract Cases" in Chapter 2 for more on oral and implied contracts.

From the Debtor's Point of View

If you are the one being sued for nonpayment of a debt, don't assume you'll automatically lose your case. If you show up with well-thought-out, convincing defenses, the judge may reduce the amount the plaintiff asked for, or may even rule that no debt exists.

A prominent study of small claims court cases found that when a defendant shows up to contest a case, the plaintiff's chance of winning 100% of the amount asked for declines substantially. ("Small Claims and Traffic Courts," by John Goerdt (National Center for State Courts).) In fact, defendants win outright in about one-quarter of debt cases and often pay half or less of what the plaintiff asked for.

Here are some examples of cases in which the defendant succeeded in whole or part:

EXAMPLE 1: A local hospital sued an unemployed man for failure to pay an emergency room bill for $678. It seemed like an open and shut case—the person from the hospital had all the proper records, and the defendant hadn't paid. Then the defendant told his side of it. He was taken to the emergency room suffering from a superficial but painful gunshot wound. Because it was a busy night and he was not about to die, he was kept waiting four hours for treatment. When treatment was given, it was minimal, and he suffered later complications that might have been avoided if he had been treated more promptly and thoroughly. He said he didn't mind paying a fair amount, but that he didn't feel he got $678 worth of care in the 20 minutes the doctor spent with him. The judge agreed and gave judgment to the hospital for $250, plus court and service of process costs. After the defendant explained that his only income was his unemployment benefits, the judge ordered that he be allowed to pay the judgment at the rate of $25 per month.

EXAMPLE 2: A large local tire retailer sued a woman for not paying the balance on a tire bill. She had purchased eight light truck tires manufactured by a major tire company and still owed $612. The tire company representative

presented the judge with the original copy of a written contract along with the woman's payment record, and then waited for judgment. The woman, who ran a small neighborhood gardening and landscaping business, produced several advertising flyers from the tire company that strongly implied that the tires would last at least 40,000 miles. She then testified and presented a witness to the fact that the tires had lasted less than 25,000 miles before wearing out. The defendant also had copies of four letters she had written over the past year to the headquarters of the tire company in the Midwest complaining about the tires. Both in the letters, and in court, she repeatedly stated that the salesperson at the tire company told her several times that the tires were guaranteed for 40,000 miles. Putting this all together, the judge declared the total price of the tires should be prorated on the basis of 25,000 miles and, after figuring what the defendant had already paid, gave the tire company a judgment for only $350, instead of the $612 requested. The woman wrote a check on the spot and departed feeling vindicated.

EXAMPLE 3: A rug company sued a customer for $1,486 and produced all the necessary documentation to show that the carpet had been installed and that no payment had been received. The defendant testified that the rug had been poorly installed, with a seam running down the center of the room. He brought pictures that left little doubt that the rug installer was either incompetent or completely thoughtless. The defendant also presented drawings that illustrated that there were several better ways to cut the carpet to fit the room. The rug company received nothing.

Of course, the real point of these examples is not to be found in their individual fact situations—yours will surely differ. Rather, they illustrate that if you can convince the judge that goods or services were substandard, chances are you'll win at least a partial victory.

Common Defenses

As discussed in more detail in Chapter 2, below are some defenses in cases where you are sued for nonpayment:

Breach of contract. The other party failed to live up to (perform) the terms of the contract within the correct period of time, with the result that you are no longer obligated to keep your payment obligation. For example, you

contracted to have your kitchen counter replaced using white ceramic tile, and ended up with beige plastic tile. Or, you ordered a cake from a website and it arrived looking nothing like the picture.

> ⓘ **CAUTION**
> **Trivial defects won't void a contract.** To succeed with a breach of contract defense, you must show that the other party's breach was significant enough that it prevented you from receiving all or at least a substantial amount of the benefits that you wanted from the contract. For example, if you order light yellow flowers for a wedding and refuse to pay the bill because cream-colored flowers are delivered, you can be pretty sure the judge will decide in favor of the flower vendor, especially if you used the flowers. By contrast, if you order yellow flowers and receive dark red ones that obviously clash with your color scheme, your chances of winning would be much better.

Fraud. The other party intentionally lied to you about a key fact in a transaction. For example, you purchased a used car with 75,000 miles on the odometer. Later, you meet the vehicle's first owner who says it really had gone 125,000 miles and that the odometer said so when he sold it to the used car dealer who sold it to you.

Breach of warranty. An express or implied warranty (assurance) made by the seller of goods is breached. For example, a roofer claims in writing that your new roof will last 20 years. In fact, it leaks in the first big storm.

Violation of statute. Many federal and state laws require the seller of a particular type of goods or services to comply with specific rules. For example, federal regulations provide that a door-to-door seller of goods and services that cost more than $25 must give you notice of your right to cancel the purchase within three business days, along with a cancellation form. (There are a few exceptions.) If he fails to do so, your right to cancel continues indefinitely. For example, if you buy an expensive vacuum cleaner from a door-to-door salesperson and ask (in writing) to cancel the deal the next day, you have a good defense if the vacuum cleaner company sues you for nonpayment.

EXAMPLE: TopHat Models, a New York modeling agency, sued Mary P., claiming she had not paid the agency's $1,000 fee for creating a portfolio of

"professional quality photographs." The photos were designed to help Mary obtain employment as a model. In her defense, Mary claimed that TopHat had violated New York State's employment agency licensing law (N.Y. Gen. Bus. Law § 170 and following) by falsely claiming it would help her find modeling jobs and in fact making no effort to do so. After concluding that TopHat was primarily a scheme designed to get consumers to overpay for photographs and that it had not attempted to find Mary modeling work, the court agreed and ruled that Mary owed nothing.

Evidence to Defend Your Case

To successfully defend a suit claiming you owe money, you'll normally need to document a very good reason why the goods or services you received were inadequate or some other reason why you are not legally required to pay. This means you'll need to do more than tell the judge a sad story. If shoddy goods are involved, show them to the judge or bring a picture or written report from an expert. (See Chapter 14.) If you received truly bad service, bring a witness or other supporting evidence to court. For example, suppose the new paint on your recently refinished boat immediately began to chip and peel and, as a result, you notified the boat yard that you would not pay for the job. In case you are later sued, you will want to take pictures clearly showing the problem and get a written opinion from another boat refinisher stating the work was substandard as well as an estimate to fix or redo the job. If a company misrepresented a product or service to you, it is very helpful if you can find others who were also victims who will either go to court with you to tell the judge a similar story to yours, or give you a letter you can take to court, describing the false statements they were given.

Appearing in Court

You may have a tactical advantage at the hearing if the person who appears in court on behalf of the creditor is not the same person with whom you dealt. For example, if you state that a salesperson told you X, Y, and Z, the salesperson probably won't be present to state otherwise. This may tilt a closely balanced case to you. It is perfectly appropriate for you to point out to the judge that your opponent has only books and ledgers, not firsthand

knowledge of the situation. The judge may sometimes postpone the case until another day to allow the creditor to present the testimony of the employee you dealt with, but often this is impossible because the person in question has moved on.

TIP

You can ask for a little more time to pay. In some states, the judge has considerable discretion to order that a judgment be paid in installments. If you are financially pressed, installment payments can obviously be extremely helpful, because as long as you meet the payment schedule, the creditor can't initiate a wage levy (garnishment) or other collection activity. So don't be shy about asking the judge to establish time payments—the judge won't know that you want them if you don't ask. Even if you don't make your request in court, it may not be too late. Some courts allow you to file a request to pay a judgment in installments after the hearing.

Vehicle Accident Cases

t is a rare small claims session that does not include at least one fender bender. Unfortunately, these cases are often badly prepared and presented, with the result that the judge commonly makes a decision at least partially by guesswork.

> **TIP**
>
> **File personal injury cases in formal court.** Unless it's very minor, personal injuries don't belong in small claims court, as they will involve claims for far more money than the small claims maximum. And in states that have no-fault insurance, personal injury cases may not be allowed in court at all unless you've first complied with the requirements of your state's no-fault insurance law.

The average vehicle accident case that ends up in small claims court doesn't involve personal injury but is about damage to one or both parties' vehicles. And, unless the drivers' respective car insurance companies are battling it out (which is very rare in small claims court), the claimants are typically the drivers themselves. Whether they are uninsured, carry insufficient coverage, or their policies don't apply to the accident case for some other reason, most drivers will find themselves personally on the financial hook if they lose their small claims case. That's one reason why these cases are extremely hard fought. Another reason is that so often both drivers in an accident are convinced the other driver was at fault.

Chapter 2 explains the legal concept of negligence. Please reread this material. To recover in a vehicle accident case, you have to prove either that the other person was negligent (careless) and you were driving safely or, if both of you were negligent, that you were less so. Normally, dealing with concepts of negligence in a vehicle accident is a matter of common sense; you probably have a fairly good idea of the rules of the road and whether you or the other driver was at fault. One key is whether you or the other party was cited for breaking a law having to do with highway safety. (See "Determining Fault," below.) When a safety-related law is broken, negligence is usually presumed.

> CAUTION
> **Check rules in no-fault states.** States with no-fault insurance laws generally require that auto accident disputes—especially those involving less serious injuries—be submitted to the no-fault administrative system, not to the court. Check your state's rules.

You can still win, or at least partially win, a case involving negligence even if you were not completely in the right. Under the doctrine known as comparative negligence, if the other person was significantly more at fault than you were, you may still have a good case. (See Chapter 2 for more on comparative negligence.)

Who Can Sue Whom?

The owner of a vehicle is the person who should file a claim for damage done to the vehicle, even if that person wasn't driving when the accident occurred. The lawsuit should be brought against the negligent driver and—if the driver is not also the vehicle's owner—against the registered owner as well. To find out who owns a car, contact the state Department of Motor Vehicles. As long as you can tell them the license number, they can tell you the registered owner. (See "Motor Vehicle Accident Cases" in Chapter 8.)

Was There a Witness?

Because the judge has no way of knowing what happened unless one or more people tell the story, a good witness can make or break your case. It is better to have a disinterested witness than a close friend or family member, but any witness is far better than none. If the other person is likely to have a witness who supports his or her point of view (even though it's wrong) and you have none, you will have to work extra hard to develop other evidence. Reread Chapter 14 for more information on witnesses. If you can't get your eyewitness to show up in court voluntarily, try to get that person to give you a written statement of what he or she saw, and present that as evidence.

Police Accident Reports

When you have an accident and believe the other person was more at fault than you were, it is almost always wise to immediately call the police so that a police report can be prepared. (In some areas, however, accident reports are only prepared if someone claims to be injured.) A police report might be admissible as evidence in small claims court; however, the court might not allow it in under the evidentiary theory of hearsay. If possible, you'll stand a better chance bringing in the officer who prepared the report, as well as any witnesses who made statements that support your position.

So, if an accident report was made, buy a copy for a few dollars from the police station. If it supports you, try to bring in the actual parties. If you can't do so, bring the police report to court. If it doesn't support you, be prepared to refute what it says (such as with eyewitness testimony) and argue that it's hearsay and shouldn't be admitted. If both an eyewitness and a police report are against you, you might want to rethink the idea of a lawsuit.

Determining Fault

Chapter 2 explains the general concept of negligence. That discussion is fully applicable to motor vehicle cases. Negligence can also be determined by showing that the other driver caused the accident (in whole or in part) as a result of safety-related violations of driving laws. For instance, if Tommy runs a red light (prohibited by driving laws) and hits a car crossing the intersection, Tommy is presumed to be negligent unless he can offer a sufficient excuse for his action. On the other hand, if Tommy is driving without his seatbelt (also prohibited) and has an accident, the seatbelt violation cannot be said to have caused the accident and therefore can't be used to presume negligence.

If there is a police report, the reporting officer will have noted any driving law violations that occurred during the accident. The report may even conclude that a driving violation caused the accident. Obviously, if the police cited the other driver, this is terrific evidence that you'll want to show to the judge. If there is no police report, you may wish to do a little research on your own. Your state's vehicle code is available online on Nolo's website (at www.nolo.com; click on "Legal Research" and look for "State Law

Resources"), in most large public libraries, and in all law libraries. You can use its index to review dozens of driving rules that may have been violated by the other driver. If you discover any violations that can fairly be said to have contributed to the accident, call them to the attention of the judge. (For more tips on legal research, see Chapter 25.)

> ⓘ **CAUTION**
> **Beware! Professional drivers have an incentive to bend the truth.**
> Be particularly on your guard when you are opposing a bus or truck driver. Many of these people risk job-related consequences if they are found to be at fault in an accident. As a result, they often deny fault automatically. Judges usually know this and are often unsympathetic when a bus driver says that there has never been a time when he didn't "look both ways twice and count to ten" before pulling out from a bus stop. Still, it never hurts to ask the driver in court whether there is any demerit system or other penalty at his or her work for being at fault in an accident.

Diagrams

With the exception of witnesses and police accident reports, the most effective tool in presenting an accident case is a good diagram. Many good cases have been lost because the judge never properly visualized what happened, and several iffy cases won because plaintiffs made persuasive drawings. It is an excellent idea to draw a diagram of what happened as part of your presentation, so try to find out if the courtroom has some kind of white board or blackboard you can use for this purpose. If you are nervous about your ability to do this, prepare your diagram in advance and bring it to court. Use crayons or magic markers and draw on a large piece of paper about three feet square. Do a good job with attention to detail. When it's your turn to speak, ask the judge for permission to display your drawing (this will be easy if you have attached it to a piece of cardboard or similar stiff surface).

For example, suppose you're involved in an intersection accident—you collide with another car coming from the right. You'd want to draw the intersecting streets, showing the lane separators and any stop signs or signals, and use arrows to indicate the lines of travel. Draw any obstructions, such as trees and other vehicles.

Photos

Photographs are very helpful in auto accident cases. This is especially true if they back up your story about how an accident occurred. For example, if you claim that you were sideswiped while you were parked, a photo showing a long series of scratches down the side of your car is likely to be convincing. Assuming they help you tell a convincing story, it can also be effective to show the judge pictures of the defendant's car and the scene of the accident.

Estimates

Whenever you attempt to recover money for damage done to your vehicle, it is important to show the judge several estimates for the cost of repairs. Three is usually a good number. If you have already had the work done, bring your canceled check or receipt from the repair shop along with the other estimates. Be sure to get your estimates from reputable shops. If, for some reason, you get an estimate from someone you later think isn't competent, simply ignore it and get another. You have no legal responsibility to get your car fixed by anyone suggested to you by the person who caused the damage. Indeed, common sense often dictates that you don't. Unfortunately, you can't recover money from the other party to cover the time you put in to get estimates, take your car to the repair shop, or appear in court.

In addition to damage to your car, you can also recover money for the fair market value of anything in your car that was destroyed. You must be prepared to establish both the fact of the damage and the dollar amount of the loss. (See Chapter 4 for a discussion of how to do this.) You can also recover money for the cost of alternate transportation while your car is disabled. However, a judge will usually only allow car rental fees for the minimum period of time it reasonably should have taken to get your car fixed. Thus, if it normally would take two days to get a fender fixed, you would only be entitled to reimbursement for renting a car for that time, not the days it took for an overworked body shop to get around to it.

⚠ CAUTION
Defendants should be on their guard against plaintiffs who try to pad their repair bill. Sometimes, plaintiffs will try to fix existing damage to their car as part of getting legitimate accident work done. If you think the plaintiff is asking for too much money, try to develop evidence to support your belief. For example, if you can present evidence that the plaintiff's car was already damaged at the time of your accident, but that the plaintiff is suing you for 100% of all repair costs, the judge should award less—maybe a lot less—than the amount he or she is demanding. Also, remember that the plaintiff is only entitled to get repairs worth up to the total value of the car before the accident. If the car was worth only $1,500 and the repairs would cost $2,500, the plaintiff is only entitled to $1,500. (See Chapter 4.)

Your Demand Letter

As in almost every other type of small claims court case, you should write a letter to your opponent, with an eye to the judge reading it, that proposes settlement. See the sample letters in Chapter 6. A Sample Demand Letter After Auto Accident is shown below.

Appearing in Court

Here's how a motor vehicle accident case can be presented in court:

Clerk: *"Next case,* McClatchy v. Rugg. *Please come forward."*

Judge: *"Please tell me what happened, Ms. McClatchy."*

Sandy McClatchy: *"Good morning. This dispute involves an auto accident that occurred at Rose and Sacramento Streets on the afternoon of August 15, 20xx. I was coming uphill on Rose (that's east) and stopped at the corner. There is a four-way stop sign at the corner. I turned right, or south, on Sacramento Street, and as I was doing so, Mr. Rugg ran the stop sign on Sacramento and crashed into my front fender. Your Honor, may I use the blackboard to make a quick diagram?"*

Judge: *"Please do, I was about to ask you if you would."*

Sandy McClatchy: (makes a drawing as suggested in "Diagrams," above, points out the movement of the cars in detail, and answers several questions from the judge): *"Your Honor, before I sit down, I would like to give you several*

Sample Demand Letter After Auto Accident

18 Channing Way
Eugene, OR 12345

August 27, 20xx

R. Rigsby Rugg
27 Miramar Crescent
Eugene, OR 12345

Dear Mr. Rugg:

On August 15, 20xx, I was traveling eastbound on Rose Street in Eugene, Oregon, at about 3:30 on a sunny afternoon. I stopped at the stop sign at the corner of Rose and Sacramento and then proceeded to turn right (south) on Sacramento. As I was making my turn, I saw your car going southbound on Sacramento. You were about 20 feet north of the corner of Rose. Instead of stopping at the stop sign, you proceeded across the intersection and struck my car on the front left fender. By the time I realized that you were coming through the stop sign, there was nothing I could do to get out of your way.

As you remember, after the accident the Eugene police were called and cited you for failure to stop at a stop sign. I have a copy of the police report, and it confirms the facts as I have stated them here.

I have obtained three estimates for the work needed to repair the damage you caused to my car. The lowest is $612. I am proceeding to get this work done because I need my car fixed as soon as possible.

I will appreciate receiving a check from you as soon as possible. If you wish to talk about any aspect of this situation, please don't hesitate to call me, evenings at 486-1482.

Sincerely,

Sandy McClatchy
Sandy McClatchy

items of evidence. First, I have a copy of the police accident report from the Eugene police, which states that Mr. Rugg got a citation for failing to stop at the stop sign in question. Second, I have some photos that show the damage to the front fender of my car. Third, I have my letter to Mr. Rugg trying without success to settle this case. Finally, I have several estimates as to the cost of repairing the damage to my car. As you can see from my canceled check, I took the lowest one (hands copies of each piece of evidence to bailiff to give to judge)."

Judge: *"Thank you, Ms. McClatchy. Now, Mr. Rugg, it's your turn."*

R. Rigsby Rugg*: "Your Honor, my case rests on one basic fact. Ms. McClatchy was negligent because she made a wide turn into Sacramento Street. Instead of going from the right-hand lane of Rose to the right-hand or outside lane on Sacramento Street, she turned into the center lane on Sacramento Street.* (Mr. Rugg moves to the blackboard and points out what he says happened.) *Now it might be true that I made a rolling stop at the corner. You know, I really stopped, but maybe not quite all the way—but I never would have hit anybody if she had kept to her own side of the road. Also, your Honor, I would like to say this—she darted out; she has one of those little foreign cars and instead of easing out slow like I do with my Lincoln, she jumped out like a rabbit being chased by a red fox."*

Judge: *"Do you have anything else to say, Ms. McClatchy?"*

Sandy McClatchy: *"I am not going to even try to argue about whether Mr. Rugg can be rolling and stopped at the same time. I think the policeman who cited him answered that question. I want to answer his point about my turning into the center lane on Sacramento Street, instead of the inside lane. It is true that, after stopping, I had to make a slightly wider turn than usual. If you will look again at the diagram I drew, you will see that a car was parked almost to the corner of Sacramento and Rose on Sacramento. To get around this car, I had to drive a little farther into Sacramento before starting my turn than would have been necessary otherwise. I didn't turn into the center lane, but as I made the turn, my outside fender crossed into the center lane slightly. This is when Mr. Rugg hit me. I feel that since I had the right of way and I had to do what I did to make the turn, I wasn't negligent."*

Judge: *"Thank you both—you will get my decision in the mail."*

(The judge decided in favor of Sandy McClatchy and awarded her $612 plus service of process and filing costs.)

Landlord-Tenant Cases

By using small claims court, tenants in most states can sue for money damages over a whole host of landlord violations—failure to return a cleaning or damage deposit, invasion of the tenant's privacy, violation of the duty to provide safe and habitable premises, and rent control violations, to name but a few. In addition, a group of tenants or neighbors can individually (but simultaneously) sue a landlord who tolerates an illegal or even legal but highly annoying situation on the rental property. For example, if ten tenants sue a landlord who tolerates drug dealing for $7,500 each, the landlord would face $75,000 worth of lawsuits.

Although the majority of cases are initiated by tenants, landlords also can and do use small claims court—for example, to sue a former tenant for damages done to the rental property. In some states, it is also possible for a landlord to use small claims court to evict a tenant. (See Appendix A for state-by-state information.) This is an exception to the general rule that only money damage cases can be handed down by small claims court—but it's an exception landlords may find hard to take advantage of, as discussed in "Evictions for Nonpayment of Rent," below.

Further Reading on Landlord-Tenant Law

To minimize your chances of ending up in small claims court and to more effectively fight your case if a dispute does end up in court, we highly recommend the following Nolo books. These provide detailed state-specific information on landlord-tenant law and checklists and forms to avoid disputes involving security deposits, housing code violations, late rent and rent withholding, inspections (tenants' privacy rights), discrimination, illicit tenant activity, and more.

- For tenants: *Every Tenant's Legal Guide*, by Janet Portman and Marcia Stewart.
- For property owners and managers: *Every Landlord's Legal Guide*, by Marcia Stewart, Ralph Warner, and Janet Portman.
- The Landlords and Tenants centers on Nolo.com also include many charts with state laws, including security deposit limits and rent rules, and useful articles on topics such as evictions.

Security Deposit Cases

Disagreements about whether a landlord properly withheld all or part of a tenant's security deposit account for a large percentage of the landlord-tenant disputes that end up in small claims court.

Problems involving security deposits often arise like this:

- the tenant moves out, making what the tenant considers to be a reasonable effort to clean the place
- the landlord keeps all or part of the deposit, stating that the place was left damaged or dirty, and
- the tenant is furious, claiming the landlord is illegally withholding the deposit.

If the tenant and landlord can't reach a compromise, the tenant's best remedy is to sue the landlord for the money withheld, leaving it up to the small claims court judge to decide who is telling the truth.

Whether you're a tenant filing a case or a landlord defending one, it's important to understand state law on security deposits.

State Deposit Laws

State law often dictates how large a deposit a landlord can require, how it may be used, when and how it must be returned, and more. In some states, landlords must offer to perform a "pre-move-out inspection," which gives tenants notice of—and time to fix—damage or uncleanliness, thus avoiding a deduction. In most states, it is up to the landlord to prove that dirty or damaged conditions justified keeping all or part of a deposit. Often, state law also provides that if a deposit is not returned within a specified time after the tenant moves out (usually somewhere between 14 and 30 days, depending on the state), the tenant is entitled to receive the entire deposit back.

If the landlord acted in bad faith in retaining the deposit (by deliberately and unjustifiably withholding the deposit despite repeated requests to follow the law), the tenant may be entitled to extra ("punitive") damages over and above the actual amount of the withheld deposit. Whether the tenant actually gets these extra damages is up to the judge. After checking your

state's rule, which may specifically describe the conduct that will support a request for punitive damages, you may decide to ask for those extra damages. See the Nolo website at "Legal Research," "State Law Resources" for your state's laws.

Deposit Cases From the Tenant's Point of View

How should a tenant prepare a case involving a landlord's failure to return a deposit? Ideally, preparation should start when you move in. Any damaged or dirty conditions should be noted in the lease or rental agreement, or an attached inventory or checklist, both of which should be signed by both you and the landlord (in some states, these inventories are required by law). You should also take photographs or videos of substandard conditions and have neighbors or friends look the place over. When you move out and clean up, you should do much the same thing—take photos or videos, have friends (or another tenant in the building) check the place over, keep receipts for cleaning materials, and, once the place is cleaned up, try and get the landlord to agree in writing that it is in satisfactory condition or that the earlier noted areas of damage are all there is.

Now let's assume that you are a tenant, and your former landlord has not returned your $900 security deposit even though you moved out more than three weeks ago, having paid all your rent, given proper notice, and "passed" the move-out inspection. Start by writing the landlord a letter like the one shown below.

> CAUTION
>
> **Be specific when requesting the return of a deposit.** If your landlord has returned only part of your security deposit, deducting more for cleaning or damages than you thought was reasonable, your demand letter should detail exactly why you believe the deductions were improper. For example, if the landlord says a door was damaged and cost $200 to fix, you might claim that the work could have been done competently for $75. If you get no satisfactory response from your landlord, file your case.

Sample Letter Demanding Security Deposit

October 25, 20xx

Adam Anderson
Anderson Realty Co.
10 Rose Street
Anytown, [state] 12345

Dear Mr. Anderson:

As you know, until September 30, 20xx, I resided in Apartment #4 at 1700 Walnut Street and regularly paid my rent to your office. When I moved out, I left the unit cleaner than it was when I moved in. During the move-out inspection, you told me the place looked fine.

As of today, I have received neither my $900 security deposit nor any accounting from you for that money. Please be aware that I know my rights under [*state law*] § [xxx]. If I do not receive my money within the next week, I will regard the retention of this deposit as showing "bad faith" on your part and shall sue you, not only for the $900 deposit plus interest, but also for the $1,800 punitive damages allowed by law. May I hear from you soon?

Sincerely,

Farrah Shields
Farrah Shields
456 Main Street
Anytown, [state] 12345

Whom Should Tenants Sue in Security Deposit Cases?

A tenant who knows who owns the building should sue this person or business. However, sometimes it is hard to know whom to sue, because rent is often paid to a manager or other agent instead of the owner. In most states, multiple occupancy buildings must have ownership information posted on the premises, or list the name of the owner (or the owner's agent for purposes of suit) on the lease or rental agreement. If you are in doubt as to who owns your unit, you are probably safe if you sue the person to whom you pay your rent.

On court day, a well-prepared tenant should show up in court with as many of the following pieces of evidence as possible:

- Date-stamped photos or a video of the apartment showing how it looked when you moved in, including any dirt or damage that already existed. (If you don't have these, it's not fatal; if you do, it helps.)
- A copy of the pre-move-out inspection report, if one was done.
- Photos or a video (again, date-stamped) of the apartment showing clean conditions when you moved out.
- A copy of an inventory of conditions upon moving in and moving out, signed by the landlord and tenant, if one or both was prepared.
- Receipts or canceled checks for any cleaning supplies used in the final cleanup.
- A copy of your written lease or rental agreement.
- A copy of a demand letter to the landlord, such as the sample set out above, showing that you made the required demand before suing.
- One or, preferably, two witnesses who were familiar with the property, saw it after you cleaned up, and will testify that it was in good shape. Incidentally, the testimony or written statements of people who actually scrubbed an oven or toilet are particularly effective. If you also have a witness who saw the place when you moved in and who will say that it wasn't perfectly buffed (or that damage already existed), so much the better.

The Landlord's Perspective: Defending Deposit Cases

Your best protection against spending hours haggling over security deposits is to follow the law scrupulously when a tenant moves out. It is your responsibility to return the deposit within the number of days legally required or explain why you are withholding some or all of it. But no matter how meticulous you are about properly accounting for your tenants' deposits, sooner or later you may be sued by a tenant who disagrees with your assessment of the cost of cleaning or repairs. This section shows landlords how to defend themselves in tenant-initiated small claims court cases.

Within the time limit set by your state's law, after inspecting the premises and documenting any dirty or damaged conditions, send the tenant a written itemization of deductions for repairs, cleaning, and unpaid rent. Include details on the costs of any cleaning or damage repair, including a reasonable hourly charge if you or your employees do any necessary cleaning or repainting, and an itemization if work is done by an outside firm. Keep receipts for costs of repairs such as new carpets or repainting. If you use an outside cleaning service, ask the service whether they will testify in small claims court, if necessary, or at least write a letter describing what they did in detail in case the tenant contests your deposit deductions.

Before your court hearing, you should gather all the evidence you have that the premises needed cleaning or were damaged. It's important to understand that you, the landlord, have the legal burden of proving these facts. If you fail to do that, the tenant will win. In other words, all a former tenant needs to prove to win is that a residential tenancy existed, that he or she paid you a deposit, and that you didn't return all of it.

To make a winning case, a landlord should show up in court with as many of the following items of evidence as possible:

- Date-stamped photos or a video of the premises before the tenant moved in, showing how clean and undamaged the place was.
- Photos or a video taken at the pre-move-out inspection, if any, and then after the tenant left, that show a mess or damage.
- Copies of inventory sheets (if any were prepared) detailing the condition of the rental unit when the tenant moved in and out, signed by the landlord and tenant. (These are particularly valuable if they

show that an item that is now broken was in good shape when the tenant moved in.)

- A copy of your written lease or rental agreement.
- An itemization of hours spent by you, or your repair or cleaning people, working on the unit, complete with the hourly costs for the work.
- A copy of the written security deposit itemization(s) (pre-move-out and post-move-out) you sent the tenant, with details about the deductions.
- Any damaged items that can be brought into the courtroom (for example, a curtain with a cigarette hole would be effective evidence).
- Receipts for professional cleaning or repair services.
- One, or preferably two, witnesses who were familiar with the property, saw it just after the tenant left, and who will testify that the place was dirty or that certain items were damaged. People who helped in the subsequent cleaning or repair, or the new tenant who saw the place before you cleaned it, are likely to be particularly effective witnesses. Written statements or declarations under penalty of perjury can be used, but they aren't as effective as live testimony. A sample written statement is shown below.

The Landlord's Perspective: Suing When the Deposit Is Depleted

Most of the security deposit cases in small claims court involve tenants arguing for their return, and landlords defending their use of the money. Occasionally, landlords go to small claims court as plaintiffs, when the departed tenant has left damage or dirty conditions that the security deposit can't cover entirely. For example, if your tenant leaves you with $2,000 worth of damage and cleaning, but the deposit comes to only $1,500, you'll be out of pocket $500 unless you sue.

Few landlords pursue tenants in small claims court over relatively small amounts for three very good reasons: Either they can't find the tenant, the amount at issue isn't worth their time and trouble to go after, or they know the tenant is "judgment-proof" and won't be able to pay anyway. But if you're in the rare position of knowing where to find your departed tenant, the tenant has some wherewithal, and the amount at issue is significant, you may wish to file.

Sample Declaration

Declaration of Paul Stallone

I, Paul Stallone, declare:

1. I am employed at A & B Maintenance Company, a contract cleaning and maintenance service located at 123 Abrego Street, Tucson, Arizona. Gina Cabarga, the owner of an apartment complex at 456 Seventh Street, Tucson, Arizona, is one of our accounts.

2. On May 1, 20xx, Gina asked me to go to the premises at 456 Seventh Street, Apartment 8, to shampoo the carpets. When I entered the premises, I noticed a strong odor, part of which seemed like stale cigarette smoke. An odor also seemed to come from the carpet.

3. When I began using a steam carpet cleaner on the living room carpet, I noticed a strong smell of urine. I stopped the steam cleaner, moved to a dry corner of the carpet, and pulled it from the floor. I then saw a yellow color on the normally white foam-rubber pad beneath the carpet. I also smelled a strong urine odor, apparently caused by a pet (probably a cat) having urinated on the carpet. On further examination of the carpet, I noticed similar stains and odors throughout the carpet and pad.

4. In my opinion, the living room carpet and foam-rubber pad underneath need to be removed and replaced and the floor should be sanded and sealed.

5. I declare under penalty of perjury under the laws of the State of Arizona that the foregoing is true and correct.

Dated: June 15, 20xx

Signature: _____
 Paul Stallone

Prepare your case, this time as a plaintiff, in much the same way as you would prepare a defense to deposit withholding, described in the section above. You'll need the same kind of evidence—proof of damage caused by this tenant (it must not be preexisting) along with invoices from a repairperson or cleaning establishment documenting the money you had to spend to deal with the mess. You'll also need to prove that you collected a specific sum as a security deposit. If the security deposit available to you, minus proper deductions, does not cover the legitimate expenses you incurred in cleaning or repairing, and you wrote the tenant a demand letter requesting those additional expenses, you'll have met your burden. It will be up to the judge, of course, to determine whether your expenses were needed, or whether they fall within the regular refurbishing that all rentals need to remedy the normal wear and tear that all tenants cause.

Unpaid Rent and Former Tenants

Landlords sometimes go to small claims court to sue former tenants—those who have already moved out—for unpaid rent, when the security deposit isn't sufficient to cover the amount. These cases arise when:

- the tenancy is month-to-month, and the tenant has left without giving the required 30 days' notice, or
- the tenant has a lease, but has broken it by leaving before its term is up.

> **CAUTION**
> **Take care of your reputation.** If you are a landlord with many rental units and regularly use a local small claims court, make particularly sure that every case you bring is a good one. You do not want to lose your credibility with the court by ever appearing to be unfair or poorly prepared.

Unpaid Rent and Month-to-Month Tenants

Month-to-month tenants must give at least the legally required number of days' notice of their intent to move out, and must pay rent during those days. For example, if the notice period is 30 days, and the landlord receives notice on the 20th, that tenancy will end 30 days later. If the tenant pays

rent on the first of the month, he or she will owe prorated rent for 20 days of the next month. If the tenant doesn't pay and simply moves out, the landlord could sue for those 20 days' worth of rent, assuming the security deposit is too small or already depleted due to needed repairs or cleaning.

Landlords in these situations rarely find it sensible to go to court over a month's (or less) rent, unless their total losses are augmented by having to deal with major damage as well. If you are a landlord and find yourself in this position, follow the advice above for preparing a case when you sue over damage or uncleanliness. You'll need to also prove that the rent was not paid, by showing that your rent ledger, for example, does not include an entry for that month.

When the Tenant Has No Defense

Often the tenant has moved away and doesn't bother to show up in court. If this happens, the landlord briefly states his or her case and, assuming it's credible, will win by default. (See Chapter 15.) Sometimes the tenant does show up but presents no real defense (often hoping only to be allowed to pay the judgment in installments). (See Chapter 24.) Again, the landlord should easily prevail.

The landlord should bring the lease or rental agreement to court and simply state the time periods for which rent is due but unpaid. Nothing else is required unless the tenant presents a defense, as discussed below.

Unpaid Rent and Tenants With Leases

Tenants who leave without legal justification before the expiration of a fixed-term lease (whether or not they notify the landlord that they're leaving) and refuse to pay the remainder of the rent due under the lease are said to have "broken the lease." This means the tenant is liable for the rent for the entire lease term (except where the landlord breaches an important lease provision first). However, the tenant's responsibility for paying all rent still due under the lease when he or she leaves early is limited in most states by the landlord's duty to "mitigate damages." Stated in plain English, the landlord has a legal duty to try to find a new tenant as soon as reasonably possible to limit the financial loss.

What all this adds up to is that a landlord whose tenant breaks a lease with no legally recognized reason is entitled to:

- the remaining rent due under the lease, minus
- any portion of that amount that the landlord can reasonably obtain by rerenting the unit, plus
- any reasonable advertising expenses incurred in finding a new tenant, plus
- charges for necessary repair and cleaning after the tenant moves out.

A landlord can deduct the total cost of these items from the tenant's security deposit (see "Security Deposit Cases," above) and sue for the remainder in small claims court. (See Chapter 4 for a discussion of the "mitigation of damages" concept.)

Former Tenants' Defenses to Unpaid Rent

Lease-breaking tenants may have a defense to a landlord's suit for unpaid rent—rent the landlord would have collected had the tenant stayed in the rental. Landlords file these lawsuits when there's considerable time left on the lease, and their reasonable efforts, if legally required (see the section above), have failed to produce a new tenant (perhaps because the market is soft, or the rental just isn't that attractive). As explained above, landlords usually don't bother filing suit unless they can find the tenant, have some reason to think that they can actually collect if they win, and are confident that the tenant has no legal defense for failing to stay through the end of the lease.

Tenants may have legal justification for breaking a lease and leave early— for example, if the tenant is the victim of domestic violence or is entering active military service. The most common defense to breaking a lease is the tenant's claim that the rental was uninhabitable under state law. Landlords must offer and maintain "fit and habitable" premises, and if they fail to do so, their failure justifies the tenant's lease-breaking. To successfully raise this defense, the tenants must prove that they did not cause the problem themselves, the defects were serious enough to threaten health or safety or constituted a lack of basic services, and the landlord had been given a reasonable amount of time to fix the problem.

Tenants Suing Cotenants for Unpaid Rent

When two or more people rent property together and all sign the same rental agreement or lease, they are cotenants. Each cotenant shares the same rights and responsibilities under the lease or rental agreement. For example, each cotenant, regardless of agreements the tenants make among themselves, is liable to the landlord for the entire amount of the rent. But being cotenants together does not establish one cotenant's legal right to sue the other cotenant for his share of the rent. In order to do that, the cotenants need to have an agreement between them that specifies how much each will contribute to the total rent. A cotenant who doesn't pay his share, as specified in the agreement, may be sued by the other cotenant(s) in small claims court.

> **EXAMPLE:** James and Helen sign a month-to-month rental agreement for an $800 apartment. They agree between themselves to each pay half of the rent. After three months, James moves out without notifying Helen or the owner, Laura. As one of the two cotenants, Helen is still legally obligated to pay all the rent and may be able to recover James's share by suing him in small claims court. Laura, the owner, may serve Helen, the tenant, with a notice to pay the whole rent or leave (or face eviction).

Rent Control Cases

In the cities in New York and California that have rent control laws, a landlord who charges illegally high rent can be sued by the tenant not only for the excess rent charged, but for a punitive amount as well (often several times the overcharge).

Drug Dealing and Other Crimes

Landlords have some degree of legal responsibility to provide secure housing. This means they must take reasonable steps to:

- protect tenants from would-be assailants, thieves, and other criminals
- protect tenants from the criminal acts of fellow tenants
- warn tenants about dangerous situations they are aware of but cannot eliminate, and

- protect the neighborhood from their tenants' illegal activities, such as drug dealing.

When landlords don't live up to this responsibility, they may be liable for any injuries or losses that befall tenants as a result.

A tenant or neighbor also may sue the landlord for maintaining or allowing a "nuisance"—a serious and persistent condition that adversely affects the tenant's (or neighbor's) enjoyment of the property—even if no physical injury occurs. For example, a tenant plagued by the stench of a pile of garbage because the landlord hasn't provided enough garbage cans for the apartment building can sue the landlord for the annoyance and inconvenience of putting up with the smell.

Tenants Band Together

Increasingly, tenants have gotten together to hold landlords accountable for failing to fulfill their legal responsibility to maintain rental property in a habitable condition. For example, tenants and homeowners have extended this group action approach to sue landlords for failing to protect tenants and neighbors from drug dealers, neighborhood gangs, or other tenants who are creating excessive noise, running an illegal business, or throwing trash in common areas. Similarly, homeowners have filed multiple suits to collect damages from neighbors who allow their teenage children to create disturbances that keep the neighborhood awake all night.

As noted in "Class Actions (Group Lawsuits)" in Chapter 7, this technique of using small claims court for groups of individual actions became popular after a neighborhood group successfully banded together to bring hundreds of small claims suits against the City of San Francisco to recover damages for the nuisance created in their neighborhood by the noise from the city airport (*City & Co. of S.F. vs. Small Claims Division, San Mateo Co.*, 190 Cal.Rptr. 340 (1983)).

Despite the fact that this approach is legal and effective, some judges have greeted the filing of many simultaneous lawsuits with verbal disapproval. Nonetheless, a number of claimants in such cases have been successful in obtaining a quick and inexpensive resolution of their neighborhood disputes

when other channels for solving their problems had failed. It appears that unless society or the legal system creates another efficient, economic alternative for dealing with neighborhood problems such as these, small claims court judges will be facing a growing number of this type of claims whether they like it or not.

One problem that often arises in this type of case is how much to sue for. Assuming the annoyance is serious and persistent and the landlord or other source of the problem does not take reasonable steps to reduce or eliminate it after receiving a written demand to do so, it often makes sense for each claimant to sue for the small claims maximum and let the judge scale this back if the court feels that a lower amount is appropriate.

The Obnoxious Landlord

Occasionally, a particular landlord can get pretty obnoxious. This is also true of plumbers, physics teachers, and hair stylists, but because this chapter is about landlord-tenant disputes, we will concentrate on these folks.

Typically, tenants have problems with landlords who cannot stop fidgeting and fussing over their property. Smaller landlords tend to develop this problem to a greater extent than do the larger, more commercial ones. Nosy landlords are always hanging around or coming by, trying to invite themselves in to look around and generally being pests. In addition, a tenant may also run into a manager or owner who sexually harasses tenants or is on a power trip.

A landlord or manager who is difficult or unpleasant to deal with can make a tenant's life miserable. There are no laws that protect a tenant from a landlord's disagreeable personality, and when tenants have no lease, they are especially unprotected from all but the most outrageous invasions of privacy, sexual harassment, or trespass (discussed just below). However, if the landlord or manager's conduct is truly obnoxious, courts in some states recognize that tenants have a right to sue for the intentional infliction of emotional distress. (See Chapter 4 for advice on determining the dollar amount of a suit for emotional or mental distress.)

The Landlord's Right of Entry and the Tenant's Right of Privacy

Tenants are easily and understandably upset when they feel their privacy is invaded. Landlords, on the other hand, have a legal right to enter their rental units in certain situations. Sometimes a tenant's need to be left alone and a landlord's need to enter conflict. If they do, it is extremely important that both parties understand their rights.

About half the states have access laws specifying when and under what circumstances landlords may enter tenants' premises. Typically, there are only four broad situations in which a landlord may legally enter while a tenant is still in residence. They are:

- to deal with an emergency
- to make needed repairs (or assess the need for them)
- to show the property to prospective new tenants or purchasers, or
- when the tenant gives permission (for example, invites the landlord to enter).

In most instances (emergencies and invitations by tenant excepted), a landlord can enter only during "normal business hours" (usually considered to be 9 a.m. to 5 p.m. Monday through Friday, though some people claim that Saturday should be a business day) and then only after "reasonable notice," which is presumed to be 24 hours.

If a landlord does not follow these rules, a tenant's first step is to politely ask the landlord to do so. If violations persist, a follow-up letter is in order. If this doesn't help, it is possible to sue in small claims court if the landlord's conduct is persistently outrageous. The specific claims that a tenant might make against a landlord in such a situation include: invasion of privacy, trespass, harassment, violation of the tenant's right to enjoy his or her home free from the landlord's unreasonable interference, or intentional or negligent infliction of emotional distress.

A tenant who sues a landlord for entering the tenant's unit without permission may have a hard time proving much in the way of money damages. (A judge will want to know why the landlord's improper entry justifies a good-sized monetary award.) However, if a tenant can show a repeated pattern of trespass (and the fact that the tenant asked the landlord

to stop it) or even one clear example of outrageous conduct, he or she may be able to get a substantial monetary recovery.

As a tenant who feels you've been trespassed upon, how much do you sue for? There is no easy answer, but one approach is to keep or reconstruct a list (or diary) of each incident, complete with a fair amount of detail about the distress it caused you. Then read it over and assign a reasonable dollar value to each hour of distress. For example, if a landlord's repeated illegal entries into your house caused you 75 hours of serious upset, and you value your time at $25 per hour, you would sue for $1,875.

If you are a landlord being sued, but believe that your entry or conduct was legal, you should be able to document this. For example, if a tenant claims that you entered his or her apartment without 24-hour notice, then you should be able to show a copy of a formal 24-hour notice to enter to make needed repairs that you sent to your tenant (notes you took documenting related phone conversations would also be useful). You could also ask a repairperson or cleaning service to testify (either in person or in writing; see Chapter 14) as to the date and time that person entered the rental unit, which should be at least the legally required amount of time after you delivered the notice. Or, you may be able to explain that the urgent nature of the repair required you to enter sooner.

But what if you are a landlord whose tenant repeatedly refuses to let you or your employees enter during normal business hours for one of the legitimate reasons cited above? In such a situation, you can legally enter anyway, provided you do so in a peaceful manner. Bring someone along who can later act as a witness in case the tenant claims some personal property is missing.

Discrimination

Federal laws make it illegal for a landlord to refuse to rent to a tenant or to engage in any other kind of discrimination (such as requiring higher rent or larger deposits) on the basis of any group characteristic such as race, color, religion, national origin, familial status (includes families with children younger than 18 and pregnant women), disability, and gender (includes sexual harassment). In some states and localities, additional characteristics, such as gender identity and sexual orientation, are protected. A landlord who

attempts to or actually terminates someone's tenancy for a discriminatory reason, or who discriminates in providing services such as the use of a pool or other common area, is also acting illegally.

The discriminated-against tenant can use the landlord's behavior as a defense to an eviction lawsuit as well as a basis for suing the landlord for monetary compensation and an order directing the landlord to stop the discriminatory behavior. Even an innocent owner whose agent or manager discriminates without the owner's knowledge can be sued and found liable. A landlord who unlawfully discriminates against a tenant or prospective tenant may end up in federal or state court, including small claims court, or before a state or federal housing agency, facing a tenant's allegations of discrimination.

Most of these cases involve amounts in excess of the small claims maximum. If you've experienced discrimination, your most effective remedy is to file an administrative claim through the Department of Housing and Urban Development (HUD), or to sue the offending landlord in formal court. For more information on how to spot and prove discrimination, see *Every Tenant's Legal Guide,* by Janet Portman and Marcia Stewart (Nolo). To find a lawyer who handles this type of lawsuit, contact a tenants' rights or civil rights organization in your area.

Evictions for Nonpayment of Rent

In some states, it is legal to do some types of evictions (known technically as "unlawful detainer," "summary dispossess," or "forcible entry and detainer," depending on the state) in small claims court. A few larger cities even have separate landlord-tenant courts that amount to small claims courts for this specific purpose.

Landlords should have a simple and cheap way to free themselves of tenants who don't pay their rent. But in states that don't have special landlord-tenant courts, the only practical method is to file an unlawful detainer action in formal court. Traditionally, this has required the expense of a lawyer, though more and more landlords are learning to handle their own eviction actions.

Formal court, though less friendly to nonlawyers than small claims court, may actually be preferable when you have a choice. The small claims court rules, even in those states where evictions are allowed, tend to limit a landlord's rights when it comes to getting the tenant out in the minimum time and getting a judgment for the maximum amount of rent and other damages. In a few states' small claims courts, a losing tenant even has an automatic right to appeal the eviction judgment and to stay in the rental unit while the appeal is pending, despite the fact that the tenant isn't paying rent and hasn't posted bond.

So before you bring an eviction action in small claims court, find the answers to the following questions by reviewing your state's small claims court rules (see Chapter 25 for tips on painless legal research):

- If you win an eviction order, can you get the sheriff or marshal to enforce it immediately?
- If the defendant appeals, can he or she stay in the dwelling while the appeal is pending?
- Can you sue for enough damages to fully or at least mostly cover your legitimate claim for back rent and damages to the premises?
- If the defendant can stay in the dwelling during an appeal, is there a requirement that he or she must post some money in the form of a bond that will go to you to cover lost rent if the appeal fails?

If you decide to go ahead with an eviction in small claims court, you must prove that the rent was not paid and that a pay-or-quit notice was properly served. Bring a copy of this notice to court along with an appropriately completed Proof of Service form. The fact that a tenant is suffering from some hardship, such as illness, poverty, birth of a child, and so on, is not a defense to failure to pay rent. Possible tenant defenses are discussed above. In most states, the tenant may claim, as a defense, that the rental property was uninhabitable. But remember, a tenant cannot legally raise the existence of a defect for the first time on the day of the court hearing. The landlord must be given reasonable notice that a defect exists before the tenant withholds rent or makes repairs.

Miscellaneous Cases

By now you should have a pretty clear idea of how a small claims case should be researched and presented. The facts of each situation will vary, but the general approach will not. This chapter will very briefly discuss a few of the common types of cases not covered in the previous few chapters. Unfortunately, given the huge number of fact situations that commonly result in small claims disputes, it still may not cover your situation in detail. It will be up to you to adapt the approaches outlined in Chapters 13–20.

Clothing (Alteration and Cleaning)

It's surprising how often you'll encounter people in small claims court clutching an injured garment. All too often, people react with a level of indignation out of proportion to the monetary loss when a favorite item is damaged. Unfortunately—no matter how much we love a favorite coat, dress, or sweater—winning a significant amount of money in a case involving clothing is difficult. That's because—as also discussed in Chapter 4—while it's often fairly easy to prove that the defendant mutilated your garment, most used clothing simply isn't worth much. Remember: in theory, at least, you are only legally entitled to the fair market value of the item of clothing just before it was damaged or destroyed, not to its replacement value. To get more, you'll normally need to engage the sympathies of the judge.

Here are some ways to handle a clothing case:

- Bring the damaged clothing to court. It's hard for a tailor to say much in his or her own defense when confronted with a coat two sizes too big or featuring three sleeves.
- Be ready to prove the original purchase price with a canceled check, newspaper ad, or credit card statement. If the item was purchased at a pricey store, let the judge know where.
- If you only wore the damaged or destroyed item a few times, make sure the judge knows it. For example, if you paid $500 for a good-quality suit jacket you planned to wear to work 50 to 100 times over the next three years and a dry cleaner screwed it up after just five wearings, try to get the judge to value it at close to $500.

- Be sure that the person you are suing (tailor, cleaner, seamstress) really caused the problem. As noted in the example of the suede coat in Chapter 2, some problems that develop during cleaning or alterations may be the responsibility of the manufacturer.

> **TIP**
> **Don't let the cleaners take you to the laundry!** Cleaners are particularly apt to offer "proof" from "independent testing laboratories" that the damage caused to your garment during cleaning was really the fault of the manufacturer. Because these labs work almost exclusively for the dry-cleaning industry, the idea that they are independent is a joke. If you are faced with one of these reports, ask the defendant:
> - "How much did you pay the testing lab for the report?"
> - "How many times have you used the same testing lab before?"
> - "How did you know about the testing lab (for example, does it place ads in dry cleaners' trade journals that say, 'Let us help you win in court')?"

Dog-Related Cases

No question, dogs can be frustrating, especially to people who don't own dogs. As a result, lots of dog-related cases end up in small claims court. Because many of these involve neighbors who will benefit by maintaining or establishing a pleasant relationship, trying to work out the dispute through mediation is almost always a good first step. (See Chapter 6.) Also, before heading to court, check whether the dog-related incident is covered by the dog owner's homeowners' or other insurance policy.

Dog Bites

Many states have dog-bite statutes that make dog owners completely liable for injuries their dogs cause—no ifs, ands, or buts. Some statutes cover only injuries occurring off the owner's property. Also, some statutes cover only bites, whereas others apply to any injury (for example, the dog jumps on you, scratches you, or knocks you over) or property damage (for example, the dog digs up your rose garden). Do a little research online to find out whether your state has a dog-bite statute. If it does, your task in court could be a lot easier.

If your state doesn't have a dog-bite statute, the old common law rule probably applies. This means you'll have to prove that the owner was aware of, or should have been aware of, the fact that the dog was likely to injure someone. So, if you're bitten by a dog and can show that the dog had snarled, snapped, and lunged at people before, and the owner knew about it but let the dog run free anyway, the owner is probably liable (unless you provoked the dog).

Also be ready to prove the extent of the injury, where it occurred, and the amount of your losses. As discussed in Chapter 4, this consists of the value of any uncompensated time you took off from work, out-of-pocket medical expenses, property damage (for example, a ripped coat), and the value of your pain and suffering.

Barking Dogs

The problem of barking dogs is often regulated by city or county ordinance. Sometimes there is a separate ordinance involving animals; in many places, dogs are covered by a general noise ordinance. Look up the law to find out the specifics and whether your city or county government will help enforce it. In addition, the owner of a barking dog that interferes with your ability to enjoy your home has committed a civil wrong (tort) called a nuisance. As with any other tort, the dog's owner is responsible for compensating people harmed by the nuisance. (For more information about suing someone for causing a nuisance, see Chapter 2.)

If you can't work something out through negotiation or mediation and you file in small claims court, you will face two main challenges:

Establishing that the barking dog really has damaged your ability to enjoy your property. One good way to do this is to get a number of neighbors to write letters or, better yet, testify in court to the fact that the dog is truly a noisy menace. (Don't forget to bring a copy of the local dog-barking ordinance to establish that the owner is also a law breaker.) Also, if your city has cited the dog's owner for violating the noise ordinance, make sure the judge knows about it.

Proving money damages. Establishing financial losses caused by a noisy dog is obviously a subjective task. One approach is to try to put a money value on each hour of your lost sleep. For example, if you can convince the judge

that each hour you lie awake is worth a certain amount (perhaps $10 or even $20), your damages will quickly add up. As a backup to your oral testimony about how miserable it is to be denied sleep by a howling canine, keep a log of the dates and times you are awakened and present it to the judge. In one case, six neighbors kept a log for 30 days detailing how often a particular dog barked after 10 p.m. The number, which was over 300, was influential in convincing the judge to give the plaintiffs a good-sized judgment.

RESOURCE
More on dog problems. *Every Dog's Legal Guide: A Must-Have Book for Your Owner*, by Mary Randolph (Nolo), answers common legal questions about biting, barking, leash laws, problems with veterinarians, and other common dog-related problems. You will also find a number of interesting dog-related articles on Nolo's website.

Damage to Real Estate (Land and Buildings)

If you own real property (land and structures) that has been damaged by another person or by a force of nature, chances are that you won't turn first to small claims court to cover your loss. That's because virtually all landowners have property insurance, primarily because most owners have a mortgage or a loan secured by the land. Mortgagors and lenders will not finance a purchase of real property or make a loan secured by land unless the borrower obtains and maintains sufficient property insurance. Even those owners whose land is unencumbered by mortgages or loans have property insurance—it's the obvious, smart way to protect their investment.

Property insurance comes in three basic types: basic coverage, covering just a few perils, or causes; broad coverage, which covers more perils, and all-risk coverage, which covers all perils except specified ones. All three types exclude damage from nuclear hazards, earthquakes, and floods, though you can sometimes buy separate policies to cover some excluded perils. All property insurance comes with a deductible—the higher your deductible, the lower your premium. And all policies include a policy limit—the most that the insurance company will pay for a loss.

Even though you have property insurance that will cover the damage your property has suffered, you may still have small claims court in your future.

Here's how that can happen: Suppose your commercial building is damaged when your neighbor's sewer line ruptures, sending water down the hill and into your first floor. Most property policies will cover in this situation—they won't consider this a flood, which is, in insurance lingo, the result of a "sudden inundation" of water from the sky. Let's say your property insurance covers the $10,000 worth of damage to the walls, floors, and basement, but you've had to pay for $1,500 worth of the damage, because that's your deductible.

Your insurance company has the right to go after the neighbor to recoup the money it's paid you. With a large claim, they'll do just that—and happily for you, they will also demand the deductible that you had to cover. If they collect, they will write a check to you, reimbursing you for the deductible you were stuck with.

But not all claims are worth pursuing. Naturally, the smaller the claim, the less inclined the insurance company will be to spend the time and money to go after the responsible party. Suppose the damage in this example amounted to only $2,500. Your company would be out-of-pocket (they'd pay you) only $1,000 ($2,500 minus your $1,500 deductible). It may not be worth their time to pursue your neighbor over such a small sum. You, however, would like that $1,500, so you can apply it to repairs. And this is where small claims court comes in.

To recover from your neighbor, you'd have to convince the judge that the neighbor acted carelessly, or negligently, when it came to maintaining his sewer pipes. Did he know that they were already leaking (great news for you)? Did he know that they were ancient and at risk of breaking at any time (again, information in your favor). Or were they new, or almost-new, and failed because they were installed improperly—in other words, there was no reason for the neighbor to suspect they'd break? The more you can show that your neighbor knew, or should have known, that this was an accident waiting to happen, the more likely it would be that you'd prevail.

Police Brutality

Until relatively recently, a citizen's complaint of police brutality fell on deaf—or nonexistent—ears. Many police and sheriff's departments had internal complaint mechanisms, but they were staffed by officers, not neutral third parties. Starting in the 1970s, however, the concept of citizen police

review boards became increasingly popular. Typically, these boards are made up of nonpolicemen who hear appeals from the internal complaint process. The most effective have the power to subpoena witnesses, compel testimony, and make recommendations as to punishment. Review boards do not generally have the power to order officers to pay damages, but starting with a complaint and an appeal to the board, if necessary, may significantly affect your ability to eventually go to court and obtain money damages, as explained below. Most major cities (covering about 80% of the population) have citizen review boards (for a partial list, visit the website of the National Association for the Civilian Oversight of Law Enforcement, www.nacole.org, or call your city government and inquire).

If you feel that you've been seriously mistreated by a police officer, start by consulting an attorney. Unlike many of the cases explained in this book, which are relatively simple variations on contract disputes or personal or property damage, police brutality cases are very complex, involving municipal immunity from lawsuits and confidentiality of police records, for example. For this reason, they are expensive to bring, and unless you have a very good case, an attorney will not invest time in it (attorneys are typically paid "on contingency," which means that they won't be paid for their time if they lose).

If an attorney will not take your case (or, in some instances, even if you find one who will), the next step may be to file an internal complaint with the police department. If you lose, consider appealing to the review board. Depending on the powers given the board by the legislation establishing it, you may learn a lot about your case and the defendant-policeman. And that information could be key if you later decide, whether or not the policemen is disciplined internally, to pursue a civil action and ask for monetary damages.

Many civil rights attorneys will recommend going through the internal complaint-review board process simply in order to get information, known in legalese as "discovery." If your experience with the board is fruitful—if you appear to have a good case, by unearthing lots of good evidence about the policeman's background and the details of your encounter—you may be able to find an attorney who will represent you, even if you were turned away before. There's good reason to hire a pro, because these cases can be hard to prove and involve tricky legal issues, as noted above.

On the other hand, if you've lost before the board and have nothing much to show an attorney except your own version of what happened, the lawyer

will probably decline to represent you. If you go it alone in small claims court, you'll probably be outgunned by city attorneys and policemen who are adept at testifying. The few cases that show up in small claims court usually lose.

Defamation

Many states have placed an outright ban on bringing libel and slander cases in small claims court. However, even in states where you can bring a defamation case in small claims court, oftentimes judges don't take them seriously, because most untrue statements don't result in serious damage.

To prevail, you need to show that the statement made about you was false, that others saw or heard it and understood that it was about you, and most importantly, that the statement significantly harmed your reputation. In addition, if you are a public figure (politician, actor, media celebrity), you not only need to show that the statement was false, but also that the defendant either knew it was false or made it in reckless disregard of whether or not it was true. In short, the fact that the defendant's statement was just plain wrong isn't enough to make you a winner if you are a public figure.

> **EXAMPLE:** Your nutty neighbor tells everyone on the block you are an idiot. You wonder if you have grounds to sue. Probably not, because chances are you haven't been harmed—after all, everyone in the neighborhood knows your neighbor is a kook, so it's probable that no one has taken his comments seriously. However, if he writes and distributes a leaflet all over town that falsely accuses you of having sex with minors, your chances of winning are much better. There are several reasons why: Being accused of a sex crime is much more likely to damage your reputation than being called an "idiot"; the fact that the defamatory statement is printed on a flyer makes it easier to prove; and the wider distribution of the printed fliers makes it more likely that at least some people who receive the flyer won't know that the writer isn't very reliable and therefore may take it seriously.

> **RESOURCE**
> **There are many intricacies to defamation law.** To learn more, start with online resources such as the Legal Information Institute-Cornell Law School website (www.law.cornell.edu); or buy a law student course outline on torts (a negligent or intentional "wrong" that results in damage). These are carried by all law bookstores (usually located near law schools) and most public law libraries.

Internet Transactions

We love the Internet, don't we? We shop at home and have packages delivered to the front door. We create websites for our small businesses and communicate with friends and family through social media. And some of us do much of our work over the Internet, as well. Technology has definitely changed how we live, work, and communicate.

But what about when something goes wrong? The package doesn't arrive or is different than advertised. Or perhaps you agree via email to write a restaurant review for a local magazine, and you email the article on time to the editor, but never receive payment. Are these types of problems any different from the face-to-face disputes we've discussed in the rest of this book? Can you use small claims court to get compensation from a person or business you've dealt with only over the Internet?

The answer is, maybe. As with face-to-face disputes, your ability to sue in small claims court for a wrong you suffered via an Internet transaction depends on where the person or business you want to sue is located. As you recall from Chapter 9, you cannot automatically sue someone in small claims court when you have suffered an economic loss. The court has to have power over that particular party, which basically depends on where the person or business lives, works, or has an office. If your Internet-related dispute is with a person or business located in your state, then you shouldn't have a problem. However, only under specific circumstances can you sue a nonresident in your state's small claims court.

If the person or business does not regularly do business with state residents over the Internet (in other words, if the transaction at issue is a one-time event), then you will not be able to sue in your local small claims court, because that person does not live, work, or regularly do business in-state; it is therefore fundamentally unfair to ask that party to travel to your state to defend itself from a lawsuit.

If, however, the person or business regularly transacts with Internet customers in your state, then you should be able to bring your lawsuit in your local small claims court. In the context of Internet transactions, what does it mean to "regularly do business" in a state? The courts are actively discussing this issue, and different judges have different opinions, but here are some basic guidelines:

- Does the website conduct direct sales over the Internet (versus referring customers to offline distributors, retail stores, or other resellers)?
- At the time of the transaction, did the person or business know what state you were a resident of—for example, did you fill out a form with your address or have a package shipped to you?
- Does the person or business do a lot of business with state residents?
- Does the person or business have any offices or employees in-state, even though its main "location" is on the Internet?
- Does the person or business send employees or agents into your state to conduct business?
- Does the person or business advertise or solicit business in your state?
- Does the person or business have a registered agent for service of process in your state? (See Chapter 11 for instructions on finding out if a business has a registered agent.)

If your answer to all or most of these questions is yes, then you will probably be successful in bringing your case against the party in your local small claims court. The only other issue is whether, as a condition of your transaction, you entered into a "Terms and Conditions" agreement with the website owner that establishes where you can bring a dispute.

EXAMPLE 1: Mary Mallone lives in Vermont and sells handmade jewelry to customers around the world via her website. She designed the website herself, and the computer files are stored on a Web hosting company, Web-R-Us, located in Colorado. She signed a contract with Web-R-Us to provide her with this service and regularly uploads new files for her website to Web-R-Us's computers in Colorado from her computer in Vermont. The contract also requires that all disputes be resolved by arbitration in Colorado. When customers visit her website, they can make purchases online, and that information is temporarily stored on Web-R-Us's computers until it is transmitted to Mary. One day, due to the carelessness of a Web-R-Us employee, the office floods and the computers are ruined. As a result, Mary loses 15 jewelry orders that were stored on Web-R-Us's computers. Can Mary sue Web-R-Us in Vermont for losing $2,000 worth of jewelry orders even though its offices are in Colorado?

No. The contract establishes where all disputes must be brought. Mary will have to take her case to an arbitrator in Colorado.

An Internet business can also be subject to jurisdiction for purposefully causing an injury in the state. If someone uses the Internet to cause an injury in one state, the person causing the damage may be hauled into court in the state where the injury occurred. In cases where the connection between the activity and the injury is not completely clear, courts also look for evidence that the activity was "purposefully directed" at the resident of the forum state or that the person causing the injury had contacts with the state.

EXAMPLE 2: James lives in California. He buys new gears for his brand new $3,000 bicycle from a bicycle parts distributor on eBay, Will Wheely. Will, who is based in Nevada, sells almost all his inventory via eBay. The gears are defective, and James crashes, ruining the bicycle. James finds out that Will Wheely bought the gears from Big Gear, Inc., a bicycle parts manufacturer in Florida that does occasional business in California. James later learns that both Will and Big Gear were aware that the gears had a defect. Can James sue either Will Wheely or Big Gear in California small claims court to get compensation for his busted bike?

Yes. James can sue both Will and Big Gear in California. Even though neither potential defendant is a California resident, they each purposefully caused an injury in the state by placing the gears in commerce in California.

CAUTION
Nonresidents will fight your attempt to sue them in your state's small claims court. It's a tremendous hassle for a nonresident to travel to defend a lawsuit, which is why the courts have strict rules stating that a person must already do regular business in a state in order to be sued there. (See Chapter 9 for information on how a nonresident defendant might challenge such a lawsuit.)

Consumer Complaints About Internet Transactions

If an Internet transaction goes wrong, you might consider filing an official complaint against the person or business, either in addition to or instead of filing a lawsuit. The Federal Trade Commission accepts complaints about consumer Internet transactions. Visit www.ftc.gov and go to "File a Consumer Complaint."

Disputes Between Small Businesses

More and more small business owners are turning to small claims court to settle business disputes when they have been unable to reach an acceptable compromise through negotiation or mediation. Small claims court offers them speed and cost efficiency. In several states, business-friendly changes in the law are making it easier for businesses to use the court efficiently. For example, New York state has established a separate commercial small claims court in Manhattan and other areas. Unfortunately, other states still block businesses' efforts to use small claims courts to resolve their disputes. For example, in California, a business entity may not bring more than two lawsuits for more than $2,500 each (for a total of $5,000) in a 12-month period. (A sole proprietor can ask for up to $10,000 in a single case, but other limitations apply.) And in some other states—including Pennsylvania—incorporated businesses are required to be represented by an attorney under certain circumstances, which prevents incorporated businesses from saving money by handling their own legal affairs.

This chapter focuses on how to handle substantive disputes between businesses in small claims court. Typically, these center on a claim that one party's work for the other was done poorly, late, or not at all. (Cases involving the simple failure to pay a bill are covered in Chapter 18.) Although many disputes between small businesses involve a failure to pay money, a significant number are more complicated. Commonly these more complex disputes involve people who have had a continuing business relationship and find themselves in the midst of a major misunderstanding that goes beyond the refusal to pay a bill. Often, both parties are in court because they feel badly used—perhaps even ripped off or cheated—by the other.

A surprising variety of businesspeople use small claims court for small business disputes. They include:

- A dentist who was furious at a dental equipment wholesaler who passed off slightly used equipment as new.
- An architect who wasn't paid for drawing preliminary plans for a small retail complex when the development failed to get financing.
- A phototypesetter who refused to pay her former accountant because she disputed the value of the latter's services.
- A landscape designer who tried to enforce an oral agreement, which he claimed allowed him to increase his fee when he accommodated a client by making changes to final plans.

- An author who claimed that her publisher had taken too long to publish her book.
- A client who claimed that his lawyer's incompetence was a prime reason he had to pay too much to settle a case.

Remember: You Didn't Always Hate the Other Guy

Although the disputes listed above seem very different, they all have one thing in common: In each situation, the disputing parties previously enjoyed a friendly business or personal relationship. And in each case, at least part of the reason the plaintiff brought the dispute to court was that he or she was just plain mad at the defendant.

Disappointment is a significant factor driving many small business disputes. But feeling let down by the other party doesn't help you evaluate whether you have a good case. Nor does it help you prepare for court or collect your money should you win. In fact, aside from its value in goading you to take action, disappointment often gets in the way of the clear thinking necessary to make good decisions. It follows that your first job is to try to cool your emotions. If you are having trouble doing this, enlist another businessperson as your mentor. Carefully explain both sides of the dispute. Then ask your mentor for a frank evaluation of both the merits of the argument and whether there really is enough at stake to warrant taking the case to court.

TIP

Mediation may offer the best way to settle your dispute. Assuming you really do have a good case and the defendant is solvent, going to small claims court is a quick and cost-effective way to put dollars in your pocket. But like all courts, small claims court tends to polarize disputes and deepen enmities. In some circumstances—especially where businesspeople will benefit from working together, or from at least being civil to each other in the future—attempting to arrive at a compromise settlement through mediation is a better initial choice. (See Chapter 6 for more on mediation.)

Organizing Your Case

When it comes to preparing for court, small business owners normally have two advantages over run-of-the-mill mortals. First, as a matter of course, they maintain a record-keeping system. Depending on the type of business, this typically includes a good filing system to maintain bids, contracts, and customer correspondence, as well as a bookkeeping system that tracks payables and receivables. Taken together, these resources normally contain considerable raw material helpful to proving a small claims case. The second advantage is more subtle but no less real. It involves the average businessperson's organizational skill—that is, the ability to take a confused mess of facts and organize them into a coherent and convincing narrative. Of course, when one businessperson sues another, those advantages often cancel out, meaning that both sides are likely to be well organized and prepared.

Other sections of this book explain how to decide whether you have a good case (Chapter 2) and, assuming you do, how to prepare and present it in court (Chapters 13–21). There is no point in repeating this information, so instead the rest of this chapter will supplement it with material of particular interest to small businesses.

Contracts—The Most Common Case

In the majority of business cases one business claims that the other has broken a contract. (See Chapter 2 for more on contract law.) If you're facing this issue, take a close look at any contract involved in your case. Specifically, ask yourself what were your obligations and expected benefits from the deal? What was the other person supposed to do and how was that person going to benefit?

What is a written contract? It need not be a formal negotiated document with both parties' signatures at the end. Under the Uniform Commercial Code (UCC)—which has been adopted in all states and applies to the sale of goods but not services—a contract can be a letter or other written document that doesn't even state the price or time of delivery, only that the parties agree on the sale of goods and the quantity of goods sold. If it meets

this modest requirement, any letter, fax, or other writing can constitute a contract. (See "The Sale of Goods," below.)

> EXAMPLE: Hubert, a pest control operator, sends a fax to Josephine, the business manager of a company that manufactures rodent traps, saying, "I would like to order 1,000 gopher traps at $14 per trap." Josephine faxes back, "Thank you for your order. The traps will be sent next week." There is a contract. Indeed, even if Josephine didn't reply but instead promptly sent the traps, a contract would be formed based on the circumstances of the transaction.

Usual business practices and customs in a particular field are also commonly viewed as being part of a contract and can be introduced as evidence in small claims court to support or thwart your case. Thus, if Hubert ordered rodent traps in February and Josephine didn't send them until September, Hubert could present evidence to the judge that everyone in the rodent control business knows that traps are only saleable in the summer when rodents attack crops, and that Josephine's failure to deliver the traps in the correct season constituted a breach of contract.

Finally, keep in mind that contracts can be, and often are, changed many times as negotiations go back and forth and circumstances change. The important agreement is the most recent one.

Oral Contracts Are Usually Legal

Most oral contracts—except those for the sale of real estate or goods (tangible property) worth $500 or more, or those that can't be carried out in one year—are legal and enforceable if they can be proven. But when nothing has been written down, proving that a contract existed can sometimes be difficult. An exception to this rule applies when you did work for someone and weren't paid (for example, you are a commercial photographer and spend a day taking pictures of a hat designer's new creations), because the judge is likely to agree with your contention that, by implication, the designer must have noticed what you were doing, and you wouldn't have done the work unless the person had promised to pay you.

The Sale of Goods

The Uniform Commercial Code (UCC), adopted by all states, contains special rules affecting contracts for the sale of goods. It requires you to produce something in writing if you want to enforce a contract for a sale of goods and the price is $500 or more, but it also provides that this writing can be very brief—briefer than a normal written contract. Under the UCC, the writing need only:

- indicate that the parties have agreed on the sale of the goods, and
- state the quantity of goods being sold.

If terms such as price, time and place of delivery, or quality of goods are missing, the UCC fills them in based on customs and practices in the particular industry. And where specially manufactured goods are ordered, the UCC doesn't require any writing at all once a party makes a significant effort toward carrying out the terms of the contract.

> EXAMPLE: A restaurant calls and orders 200 sets of dishes from a restaurant supply company. The dishes are to feature the restaurant's logo. If the supply company makes a substantial beginning on manufacturing the dishes and applying the logo, the restaurant can't avoid liability on the contract simply because it was oral.

Presenting Your Evidence in Court

In business disputes, the problem is often having *too much* evidence, rather than too little. Your job is to separate the material that is essential to proving your case from that which is less important. Organize both your oral presentation and the backup written evidence around the heart of the dispute, rather than trying to first fill in all the background information.

> EXAMPLE: Alice, the owner of Ames Country Inn, hires Ted, an interior decorator, to freshen up the decor of her bed and breakfast. Ted submits an estimate, which Alice verbally accepts by telephone. Later, Alice stops by Ted's office to drop off a set of detailed architectural drawings. Ted works for three days on the new decor plan before Alice suddenly calls and cancels the deal because, "on second thought, I don't like the colors you are proposing." After

Ted's bills are not paid and his demand letter is ignored, Ted files in small claims court, asking for three days' pay plus the money he spent on supplies. In court, Ted very sensibly begins his presentation like this: "Your Honor, the defendant hired me to prepare a detailed plan to redecorate the Ames Country Inn. I worked on the job for three days and bought $200 worth of supplies before she canceled our contract. Today, I'm asking for a judgment for my normal rate of pay of $80 per hour for the 24 hours I worked, plus the $200 for supplies. The total is $2,120."

Of course, there is more to Ted's story, which means, after stating the crux of his claims, he will need to fill in the key points. Ted should next make these points:

- He and Alice had worked together before, and his work had always been acceptable and paid for.
- He really did the 24 hours of work he claimed, as documented by drawings and worksheets he brings to court.
- He has canceled checks covering an itemized list of supplies he purchased for the job ready to show the judge.

This should be enough to make Ted a winner. But as is true of all small claims litigants, Ted should also try to anticipate and deflect what he thinks will be the other side's key points. For example, in this instance, if Ted is pretty sure Alice is going to claim she canceled because Ted was using a design theme and colors she had specifically ruled out, he would be wise to make it clear that no such restrictions were contained in their contract.

Many businesspeople have employees, partners, or business associates who have intimate knowledge of the dispute. By all means, bring them to court as witnesses. A witness who is knowledgeable about the transaction is almost always worth more than a stack of documentary evidence.

EXAMPLE: Assume Ted's assistant, Doris, attended a preliminary meeting with Alice at which Ted asked Alice for a list of her suggestions. Also assume Doris can truthfully testify that when the subject of color came up, Alice just waved her hand and said, "You know I don't like purple too much, but it's really up to you—you're the designer." Aided by Doris's testimony, Ted should be a winner, even if Alice claims he violated their agreement not to use purple.

In some situations, having a witness testify as to the normal business practices in an industry field can also be helpful. Thus, if in your industry goods are normally shipped within five to 15 days after an order is received (unless written notice of a delay is sent), but the person you are having a dispute with claims you still must pay for goods that were shipped 90 days after your order was received, it would be a good idea to present an expert witness—or a letter from someone knowledgeable about relevant business practices—who could testify that unfilled orders are never good for more than 30 days.

A Case Study—Proving a Contract Exists

Now let's review a typical small business case with an eye toward identifying good strategies. Don Dimaggio is a successful architect and industrial designer who heads his own small company, which specializes in designing small manufacturing buildings. He prides himself on doing highly innovative and creative work. Recently Don did some preliminary design work for an outfit that wanted to build a small candle factory. When they didn't pay, he was out $8,500. In Don's view, the dispute developed like this:

> *"Ben McDonald, who makes custom candles, had a good year and wanted to expand. He called me and asked me to rough out a preliminary design. McDonald claims now that we never had a contract, but that's simply not true. What really happened is that McDonald authorized me to do some preliminary work before his company got their financing locked down. When interest rates went through the roof, the whole deal collapsed. I had already completed my work, but they refused to pay. My next step was to get Stephanie Carlin, a lawyer who has done some work for me, to write McDonald a letter demanding payment. When that didn't do any good, I took Stephanie's advice and filed a small claims court suit against McDonald. True, I had to scale my claim back to $7,500, the small claims maximum. But I obviously couldn't afford to pay Stephanie $200 an hour to file in formal court, so it seemed like the best approach."*

Don's most immediate problem was that he had never used small claims court before. He wasn't sure how he needed to prepare, but knew, at the very least, he had to develop a coherent plan—if for no other reason than to overcome his anxiety. Here is how the attorney he hired coached him to do this:

RW: *"Your first job is to establish why McDonald owes you money. Presumably it's because he violated an agreement that he would pay you for your work."*

DD: *"True, but unfortunately, nothing was written down."*

RW: *"Oral contracts to provide services are perfectly legal if they can be proven, and judges typically bend over backward to see that freelancers get paid. But don't be so sure you have nothing in writing. Tell me, how did McDonald contact you?"*

DD: *"Mutual friends recommended me to him. He phoned me and we talked a couple of times. There was some back and forth about how much I would charge for the whole job and how much for parts of it. After a little garden-variety confusion, we decided that I would start with the preliminary drawings and be paid $8,500. If the whole job came through and we felt good about one another, I would do the entire thing. On big jobs, I always insist on a written contract, but this one was tiny and I couldn't see wasting the time. McDonald just stopped by with someone else from his business, and we hashed out the whole thing in person."*

RW: *"Did you make notes?"*

DD: *"Sure. In fact, I made a few sketches, and they gave me specifications and sketches they had already made."*

RW: *"Do you still have those?"*

DD: *"Of course, in a file along with a couple of letters they sent later thanking me for my good ideas and making a few suggestions for changes. And of course, I have copies of the detailed drawings I made and sent them."*

RW: *"Well, that's it."*

DD: *"What do you mean, that's it?"*

RW: *"You've just told me that you can prove a contract exists. The combination of the sketches McDonald provided and the letters someone at his company wrote to you pretty convincingly prove they asked you to do the work. Of course, it helps your case that the law presumes that when a person is asked to do work in a situation where compensation is normally expected, he must be paid when the work is completed."* (In legalese, this presumption is called quantum meruit. See Chapter 2.)

DD: *"That's all there is to it? I just tell the judge what happened and I win?"*

RW: *"Not so fast. First, let me ask if you are sure you can present your case coherently. After you make your opening statement, you need to back it up with*

the key facts that show that McDonald hired you, that you did the work, and that he broke the contract by failing to pay you. (As discussed throughout this book, because so many people do a poor job making their oral presentation, make sure that you practice ahead of time.) *Ask a savvy friend to serve as your pretend judge. Then present your case as if you were in court. Encourage your friend to interrupt and ask questions, since that's what a judge will likely do. Finally, be sure you have organized all your evidence, especially the plans and letters, so you are ready to present them to the judge at the appropriate time."*

DD: *"What about McDonald? Is he likely to show up?"*

RW: *"Many cases involving money being owed result in defaults, meaning the person being sued ignores the whole proceeding.* (See Chapter 15.) *But you know that McDonald claims he doesn't owe you the money, so it's my guess he will probably show up and claim no contract existed. Therefore, you should be prepared to counter the points he is likely to make."*

DD: *"You're right. Although it's a total crock, he will probably claim I agreed to do the work on speculation that he would get financing and that since the job fell through, he doesn't owe me anything."*

RW: *"And if your case is typical, McDonald will also probably try to claim your work was substandard. That way, even if you prove that a contract existed, the judge may award you less than you asked for."*

DD: *"But they wrote me that my design was of excellent quality."*

RW: *"Great, but don't wait until they raise the issue. Because you are pretty sure this point will come up, emphasize in your opening statement how pleased McDonald was with your work and present the letter to the judge. Now, what about McDonald's argument that there was no deal in the first place? Do you ever do preliminary work without expecting to be paid unless the deal goes through? And is that a common way to operate in your business?"*

DD: *"Me? Never! I don't have to. I suppose some designers do, or at least prepare fairly detailed bid proposals without pay, but I have so much work coming my way these days, I'm turning jobs down right and left, so when I do submit a bid, I make it clear to all potential clients that I charge for preliminary drawings. In this situation, as I said, we agreed on the price in advance."*

RW: *"What about witnesses to that conversation?"*

DD: *"Well, Jim, my partner, sat in on one of the early discussions. We hadn't agreed on the final price yet, but we weren't too far apart."*

RW: *"Was it clear to Jim that you intended to charge for your work and that McDonald knew you did?"*

DD: *"Yes, absolutely."*

RW: *"Great, bring Jim to court with you as a witness. Here is how I would proceed. Organize your statement as to what happened so it takes you no longer than five minutes to present it to the judge. Bring your sketches, and most importantly, the sketch that McDonald made, along with the letters they sent you, and show them to the judge. (See Chapter 15.) Then introduce your partner and have him state that he was present when money was discussed."*

This little scenario is a simplified version of a real case. What happened? The small claims court judge awarded Don the entire amount he requested, and McDonald paid it.

A Case Study—Personal Services Contract

Finally, let's review another typical small claims dispute. Toni, a true artist when it comes to graphics, doesn't understand dollars and cents. Recognizing this, she never prepares her own tax returns. For the past several years, she has turned all of her tax affairs over to Phillip, a local C.P.A. They discussed price the first year, but after that Toni just paid Phillip's bill when the job was done.

One spring, things went wrong. As usual, Toni's records weren't in great shape, and she was late in getting them to Phillip. By this time Phillip, who was overly busy, put Toni's tax return together quickly, without discussing it with her in detail. When Toni saw the return, she was shocked by the bottom line. She felt that she was being asked to pay way too much.

She called Phillip and reminded him of a number of deductions that she felt he had overlooked. There was some discussion of whether Phillip should have known about these items or not. Things began to get a little edgy when Phillip complained about Toni's sloppy records and her delay in making them available, and Toni countered by accusing Phillip of doing a hurried and substandard job. But after some more grumpy talk back and forth, Phillip agreed to make the necessary corrections. In a week this was done and the return was again sent to Toni.

While her tax liability was now less, Toni was still annoyed, feeling that not all of the oversights had been corrected. Toni called Phillip again and this time they quickly got into a shouting match. When Phillip finally and reluctantly agreed to look at the return a third time, Toni replied, "Hell no, I'm taking my business to an accountant who can add."

True to her word, Toni did hire another accountant, who made several modifications to her return, resulting in a slightly lower tax liability. The second accountant claimed that because he needed to check all of Phillip's work to satisfy himself that it was correct, he ended up doing almost as much work as if he had started from scratch. As a result, he billed Toni for $2,300, saying that this was only $500 less than if he had not had the benefit of Phillip's work.

Phillip billed Toni $3,000. Toni, still furious, refused to pay. Phillip then sent Toni a demand letter asking to be paid and stating that most of the problems were created by Toni's bad records. He added that he had already made a number of requested changes and had offered to make relatively minor final changes at no additional charge. Phillip also suggested in his letter that he was willing to try to mediate the claim using a local community mediation center that charged very low fees.

When Toni didn't answer the letter, Phillip filed suit. Here is how Phillip should prepare the case:

Phillip's Case

Step 1. Phillip has already written a clear demand letter (see Chapter 6 for a discussion of how to do this) and suggested mediation—a good idea, as both he and Toni work in the same small city and Phillip has an obvious interest in not turning Toni into a vocal enemy. Unfortunately, Toni didn't bite on Phillip's suggestion of mediation.

Step 2. Phillip knows that Toni's business makes money, so he is pretty sure he can collect if he wins, which of course should be a big consideration in deciding whether to file any small claims case. (See Chapter 3.)

Step 3. In court, Phillip's main job will be to prove that he did a job that was worth $3,000 and to refute Toni's likely contention that his work was so bad it amounted to a breach of their contract. Bringing copies of the tax returns he prepared for Toni as well as his own worksheets is probably

the simplest way for Phillip to accomplish this. He should not present the returns to the judge page by page, but as a package. The purpose is to indicate that a lot of work has been done, without going into details.

Step 4. Phillip should then testify as to his hourly rate and how many hours he worked. He should emphasize that extra hours were required because Toni did not have her records well organized. To illustrate his point, Phillip should present to the judge any raw data Toni gave him that he still has (for example, a shoebox full of messy receipts). If he no longer has Toni's material, he might create something that looks like it, carefully pointing out to the judge that this is a simulation of Toni's data, not the real thing.

Step 5. By testifying that he was hired to do a job, that he did it, and that he wasn't paid, Phillip has presented facts necessary to establish a breach of contract case. However, he would be wise to go beyond this and anticipate at least some of Toni's defenses, which will almost surely involve the claim that Phillip broke the contract by doing poor quality work and doing it late. In addition, Phillip should anticipate Toni's backup claim that he charged too much and that the judge should award him less than $3,000. Phillip could attempt to take the sting out of Toni's likely presentation by saying something along these lines:

> "Your Honor, when I finished my work, my client pointed out that several deductions had been overlooked. I believed then and believe now that this was because the data she provided me with was disorganized and inadequate, but I did rework the return and correct several items that were left out. When my client told me that she felt the revised draft needed additional changes, I again told her that I would work with her to make any necessary modifications. It was at this point that she refused to let me see the returns and hired another accountant. In my professional opinion at this stage, very little work remained to be done—certainly nothing that couldn't be accomplished in an hour or two.
>
> "Now, as to the amount charged—it took me ten hours to reconstruct what went on in the defendant's business from the mess of incomplete and incoherent records I was given. At $90 per hour, this means that $900 of my bill involved work that had to be done prior to actually preparing the return. Taking into consideration the difficult circumstances, I believe I charged fairly for the work I did and that I did my work well."

Toni's Case

Okay, so much for looking at what happened from the point of view of the indignant accountant. Now let's see how Toni, the upset graphic artist, might deal with the situation.

Step 1. For starters, Toni made a mistake by refusing to negotiate or mediate with Phillip. Especially since this is the sort of dispute over the quality of work where a judge is likely to enter a compromise judgment, it would have saved time and anxiety for both her and Phillip to at least try to arrive at a compromise outside of court. (See Chapter 6.)

Step 2. Once Toni has decided not to try to settle the case, she should write a letter of her own, rebutting Phillip's demand letter point by point. (See Chapter 6.) She should bring a copy of this letter to court and give it to the judge as part of her presentation. The judge doesn't have to accept Toni's letter (it's not really evidence of anything but the fact that she rejected Phillip's request for payment), but more often than not, the judge will look at both parties' letters.

Step 3. Next, Toni should testify that she refused to pay the bill because she felt that Phillip's work was so poor that she didn't trust Phillip to finish the job. To make this point effectively, Toni should testify as to the details of several of the tax issues Phillip overlooked. For example, if Toni provided Phillip with information concerning the purchase of several items of expensive equipment for which Phillip didn't claim depreciation, this would be important evidence of poor work. But Toni should be careful to make her points about tax law in a relatively brief and understandable way. She won't gain anything by a long and boring rehash of her entire return. One good approach might be for Toni to submit pertinent sections of IRS publications or a privately published tax guide outlining the rules that require equipment to be depreciated.

Step 4. Toni should next present more detailed evidence that supports her claim that Phillip did poor work. The tax return as correctly prepared by the new accountant would be of some help, but it would be even better to have the second accountant come to court to testify about the details of Phillip's substandard work. Unfortunately for Toni, professionals are commonly reluctant to testify against one another, so this may be difficult to arrange. But Toni should at the very least be able to get a letter from the new

accountant outlining the things that he found it necessary to do to change the return as prepared by Phillip.

Step 5. Toni should also present to the court her canceled checks, establishing the amounts she paid Phillip for the last several years' returns—assuming, of course, that Phillip's previous bills were substantially less. For example, if Toni had been billed $1,700 and $1,900 in the two previous years, it would raise some questions as to whether Phillip's bill of $3,000 for the current year was reasonable.

> 💡 **TIP**
>
> **Both Toni and Phillip should be prepared to answer the judge's questions.** Especially in a case like this one involving a technical subject, the judge is almost sure to interrupt both Toni's and Phillip's presentations and ask for details. So in addition to preparing and practicing presenting their cases before a critical friend, both Phillip and Toni should be prepared to answer likely questions and then smoothly return to presenting their cases.

This story is based on a real case. Here's what happened. The judge gave Phillip a judgment for $1,800. The judge didn't explain his reasoning but apparently felt that there was some right on each side. He split the difference with a little edge to Phillip; probably because Toni hired Phillip in the first place and had worked with him for several years, she was on somewhat shaky ground claiming he was incompetent. This sort of compromise decision, where each side is given something, is common in small claims court and again illustrates the wisdom of the parties' negotiating or mediating their own compromise. Even if Toni and Phillip had arrived at a solution where one or the other gave up a little more than the judge ordered, there would have been a savings in time and aggravation that probably would have more than made up the difference.

Judgment and Appeal

The Judgment

In most states, the decision in your case will be mailed to the address on record with the clerk any time from a few days to a few weeks after your case is heard. The exception to this rule is when one side doesn't show up and the other wins by default. Default judgments are normally announced right in the courtroom.

RELATED TOPIC

See Chapter 15 for information on how to set aside a default. For information on how to get a court judgment after a mediated settlement isn't carried out, see Chapter 6.

The truth is that in the vast majority of contested cases, the judge has already made a decision at the time the case is heard and jots down the decision before the parties leave the courtroom. Decisions are sent by mail because the court doesn't want to deal with angry, unhappy losers in court, especially those few who might get violent. However, despite the fact that an occasional person may be upset, some judges are willing to announce and explain their decisions in court, on the theory that both parties are entitled to know why a particular decision was reached. One judge explained his policy in this regard as follows: "The only time I don't announce my decision in court is when I have phoning or research to do before finalizing it, or if I feel that the losing party will be unnecessarily embarrassed in front of the audience."

JUDGE'S TIP

Don't be flummoxed by the judge who takes everything under submission and sends the results by mail. If, when you receive the decision, you have questions about it, consider writing to the judge (send a copy to your opponent) with a respectful request for a further explanation of the judge's reasoning. Most judges will respond.

> **TIP**
> **Legal jargon note.** Now that a judgment has been entered, we need to expand our vocabulary slightly. The person who wins the case (gets the judgment) now becomes the judgment creditor, and the loser is known as the judgment debtor.

Often, when a judgment is entered, the losing party feels that the judge would surely have made a different decision if he or she hadn't gotten mixed up, overlooked a crucial fact, or failed to understand an argument. In the vast majority of cases this is not true. Even if you had an opportunity to argue the whole case over, there is little likelihood that you would change the judge's mind. Or put another way, chances are good the judge did understand your side of the case but simply didn't agree that you were in the right. (See "The Appeal," below, for information about your appeal rights.)

If you sued more than one person, the judgment should indicate whom the judgment is against and for how much. Some defendants may not owe anything, or their financial liability may be limited to a stated amount. If so, this is the maximum you can collect from them. However, in most instances where a judgment is against two or more defendants, they will be jointly and severally liable. This means that each defendant is 100% on the hook for the entire amount. For example, if you receive a $1,000 judgment against two defendants, you may collect it in any proportion from either defendant (for example, you could collect $800 from one defendant and $200 from another). If you collect a disproportionate amount from one defendant, that person is left with the task of evening things out. (In this example, the defendant who paid the $800 could sue the other for $300.)

> **TIP**
> **The words joint and several liability may not appear on the judgment.** A judgment against two or more defendants will often simply list the names of the judgment debtors. This means they are jointly and severally liable for the entire amount. In cases where one defendant's judgment debt liability is limited (say to $200), the judgment will make that clear.

Paying the Judgment

In most states, the judge may order that the loser be allowed to pay the winner in installments over a period of time, rather than all at once. The judge normally won't make this sort of order unless you request it. Be sure the judge knows that if you lose, you wish to pay in installments. You might put your request this way:

- "In closing my presentation, I would like to say that I believe I have a convincing case and should be awarded the judgment, but in the event that you rule for my opponent, I would like you to allow me time payments of no more than [*an amount convenient to you*] per month."

Or, if you have no real defense:

- "Your Honor, I request that you enter the judgment against me for no more than [*an amount convenient to you*] per month."

If you neglect to ask for time payments in court and wish to make this request after you receive the judgment, first contact the other party to see whether the person will voluntarily agree to accept the money on a schedule under which you can afford to pay. If the other party agrees, it is wise to write your agreement down and each sign it. Some courts also have a form for you to fill out.

If your opponent is an all-or-nothing sort of person and refuses payments, promptly contact the court clerk and ask that the case again be brought before the judge—not as to the facts, but only to set up a payment schedule you can live with. The clerk should arrange things for you, but if there is a problem, write a letter like the one below to the judge. (See "Sample Letter to Judge Requesting Installment Payments," below.)

In some states, the judgment debtor may pay the amount of the judgment directly to the small claims court, which will then notify the judgment creditor. This procedure is helpful for a judgment debtor who doesn't want to deal directly with the prevailing party or doesn't know the person's current address. Contact your small claims clerk to find out whether your court has a direct pay procedure.

Sample Letter to Judge Requesting Installment Payments

October 17, 20xx

Honorable Felix Hamburg

Judge of the Small Claims Court

111 Center Street

New York, NY 12345

Re: *Elliot v. Toller*

 Index No. _____

Dear Judge Hamburg:

I recently appeared before you in the case of *Elliot v. Toller* (Index No. _____).
Mr. Elliot was awarded a judgment in the amount of $526. Paying this amount
all at once would be nearly impossible because of [*state reason, such as lack of
employment or illness*]. I can pay $25 per month.

Please change the order in this case to allow for a $25 per month payment. If it
is necessary for me to make this request in court, please inform me of the time I
should be present.

Sincerely,

John Toller

John Toller

TIP
Notify the court when you move. It's important to keep your current address on file if you've won a lawsuit but haven't yet been paid. That way, you won't miss out on your money in a situation where the losing party pays the court and the court can't find you.

Satisfaction of Judgment

Once a judgment is paid, whether in installments or a lump sum, a judgment creditor (the person who won the case) must acknowledge that the judgment has been paid by filing a Satisfaction of Judgment form with the court clerk. Doing this makes it clear to the world (and especially credit rating agencies) that the person who lost the case (the judgment debtor) has met the obligation. (See sample form, below.)

Judgment creditors who have also recorded a lien on real property (see Chapter 24), must make sure the lien is removed. Ask the small claims clerk for more information about how to do this.

If a judgment creditor receives payment in full on a judgment but fails to file a Satisfaction of Judgment form, the judgment debtor will want to send a written demand that this be done. A first-class letter is adequate. If, after written demand, the judgment creditor still doesn't file within the required number of days of the request (usually between 15 and 30—check your local rules) and without just cause, many states allow the judgment debtor to recover all actual damages he or she suffers as a result of the failure (for example, denial of a credit application). In addition, some states will penalize the judgment creditor by requiring a payment of a set amount of money to the judgment debtor.

Below is a sample Satisfaction of Judgment form used in California. Again, it should be signed by the judgment creditor when the judgment is paid, and then filed with the court clerk. Don't forget to do this; otherwise, you may have to track down the other party later.

Sample Acknowledgment of Satisfaction of Judgment

EJ-100

ATTORNEY OR PARTY WITHOUT ATTORNEY *(Name, State Bar number, and address):*
After recording return to:

Andrew Printer, Judgment Creditor
1800 Marilee Street
Fremont, CA 94536

TELEPHONE NO.:
FAX NO. *(Optional):*
E-MAIL ADDRESS *(Optional):*
ATTORNEY FOR *(Name):*

SUPERIOR COURT OF CALIFORNIA, COUNTY OF Alameda
STREET ADDRESS: 600 Washington Street, 3rd Floor
MAILING ADDRESS:
CITY AND ZIP CODE: Oakland, CA 94607
BRANCH NAME:

FOR RECORDER'S OR SECRETARY OF STATE'S USE ONLY

PLAINTIFF: Andrew Printer	CASE NUMBER:
DEFENDANT: Acme Illusions, Inc.	002006

ACKNOWLEDGMENT OF SATISFACTION OF JUDGMENT
[X] FULL　　[] PARTIAL　　[] MATURED INSTALLMENT

FOR COURT USE ONLY

1. Satisfaction of the judgment is acknowledged as follows:
 a. [] Full satisfaction
 (1) [X] Judgment is satisfied in full.
 (2) [] The judgment creditor has accepted payment or performance other than that specified in the judgment in full satisfaction of the judgment.
 b. [] Partial satisfaction
 The amount received in partial satisfaction of the judgment is $
 c. [] Matured installment
 All matured installments under the installment judgment have been satisfied as of *(date):*

2. Full name and address of judgment creditor:*
 Andrew Printer
 1800 Marilee Street, Fremont, CA 94536

3. Full name and address of assignee of record, if any:
 N/A

4. Full name and address of judgment debtor being fully or partially released:*
 Acme Illusions, Inc., 100 Primrose Path, Oakland, CA 94602

5. a. Judgment entered on *(date):* 7/21/20xx
 b. [] Renewal entered on *(date):*

6. [X] An [X] abstract of judgment [] certified copy of the judgment has been recorded as follows *(complete all information for each county where recorded):*

COUNTY	DATE OF RECORDING	INSTRUMENT NUMBER
Alameda County	8/14/20xx	21

7. [] A notice of judgment lien has been filed in the office of the Secretary of State as file number *(specify):*

NOTICE TO JUDGMENT DEBTOR: If this is an acknowledgment of full satisfaction of judgment, it will have to be recorded in each county shown in item 6 above, if any, in order to release the judgment lien, and will have to be filed in the office of the Secretary of State to terminate any judgment lien on personal property.

▶ *Andrew Printer*

Date: 8/14/20xx

*(SIGNATURE OF JUDGMENT CREDITOR OR ASSIGNEE OF CREDITOR OR ATTORNEY**)*

Page 1 of 1

*The names of the judgment creditor and judgment debtor must be stated as shown in any Abstract of Judgment which was recorded and is being released by this satisfaction. ** A separate notary acknowledgment must be attached for each signature.

Form Approved for Optional Use
Judicial Council of California
EJ-100 [Rev. January 1, 2005]

ACKNOWLEDGMENT OF SATISFACTION OF JUDGMENT

Code of Civil Procedure, §§ 724.060, 724.120, 724.250

> ⟨💡⟩ **TIP**
>
> **It's easy to get a copy of a Satisfaction of Judgment form.** If either party ever needs it (for example, to correct an out-of-date credit report), the court clerk will provide a certified copy of a filed Acknowledgment of Satisfaction of Judgment form. This form proves that the judgment was paid.

Sometimes judgment debtors forget to get the judgment creditor to sign the Satisfaction of Judgment form when they pay a judgment, only to find that they can't locate the judgment creditor later. If this happens and you need the form to clean up your credit record or for some other reason, you can get it if you present the court clerk with proof the judgment was paid. The following documents will help:

- A canceled check or money order written subsequent to the date of the judgment by you, the judgment debtor, for the full amount of the judgment, or a cash receipt for the full amount of the judgment signed by the judgment creditor after the date the court awarded judgment.
- A statement (see the sample below) signed by you under penalty of perjury stating all of the following:
 - The judgment creditor has been paid the full amount of the judgment and costs.
 - The judgment creditor has been asked to file an Acknowledgment of Satisfaction of Judgment form and refuses to do so or can't be located.
 - The document attached (for example, the check or money order) constitutes evidence of the judgment creditor's receipt of the payment.

The Appeal

Unlike small claims court itself, where rules and procedures are remarkably the same throughout the United States, the rules that cover appeals from small claims court judgments vary greatly from one state to the next. A few allow no appeal. New York allows an appeal of a judge's decision but not an arbitrator's. California, Massachusetts, and a few other states allow a losing defendant to appeal but do not permit the person who brought the suit (the plaintiff) to do so, except to appeal from counterclaims initiated by the defendant. In the appendix you will find a very brief summary of the appeal procedures of every state.

Sample Statement of Debtor Regarding Full Payment of Judgment

My name is John Elliot. On January 11, 20xx, a judgment was awarded against me in small claims court in Ithaca, New York (Case # 1234). On March 20, 20xx, I paid Beatrice Small, the prevailing party, $1,200, the full amount of this judgment [*or, if payments were made in installments—"I paid Beatrice Small, the prevailing party in this action, installments of the following amounts on the following dates:* _____ , *concluding with a final payment of $*_____ *on March 20, 20xx."*]

I attach to this statement a canceled check [*or other proof that the judgment was paid*] for the full amount of the judgment endorsed by Beatrice Small. [*If payment was made by money order or cash (with a receipt), modify this statement as needed. If payment was made in installments, modify this statement as needed and enclose copies of all canceled checks.*]

Beatrice Small did not voluntarily file a Satisfaction of Judgment. When I tried to contact her, I learned that she had moved and had left no forwarding address. [*If the judgment creditor refuses to sign a Satisfaction of Judgment form, or is otherwise not available to do so, modify this statement as necessary.*]

I declare under penalty of perjury under the laws of the State of _____ _____ that the foregoing is true and correct.

DATED: June 4, 20xx.

John Elliot

CAUTION
You can't appeal if you didn't show up in small claims court. Appeal rights are almost always restricted to those who showed up in small claims court, argued their case, and lost. If you defaulted (didn't show up), you normally can't appeal unless and until you get the default set aside. Normally, you must file paperwork to do this almost immediately, or the small claims judgment will become final and unappealable. (See Chapter 15.) Filing a request to set aside a default judgment normally *does not* extend the time allowed to appeal.

You may have heard that some higher court judges consider small claims appeals to be a nuisance and try to discourage them by routinely upholding the original judgment. There's very little truth to this. Most judges will give you a fair hearing on appeal if you are well prepared and able to present a convincing case. Therefore, if you believe you were victimized by a bad decision in small claims court and your case involves enough money to make a further investment of time and energy worthwhile, go ahead and appeal if your state's rules allow it.

Determining whether you are eligible to appeal is important, but it is only part of the information you need. It is just as important to determine what kind of appeal is permitted in your state. Some states allow an appeal only on questions of law, while others allow the whole case to be replayed from scratch. Let's pause for a moment and look at some of the differences.

New Trial

In several states, either party can appeal and have the case heard over from scratch. In other states, only the defendant can appeal (in most cases), but if the defendant does file an appeal, the whole case is presented again by both sides as if the first hearing hadn't occurred.

When a whole new hearing is allowed on appeal (it's called a trial de novo), you simply argue the case over, presenting all necessary witnesses, documents, and testimony. Starting from scratch is required because records often aren't kept at small claims court hearings. However, in some courts, judges record hearings, and these recordings are available to the judge who considers the appeal as part of the reargument of the case.

Questions of Law

In many states, appeals can be based only on questions of law, not on the facts of the case. (See the appendix.) What's the difference between law and facts? It's best illustrated with a couple of examples.

> EXAMPLE 1: You sue your mechanic in small claims court, claiming that he botched a repair job on your car. After listening to both sides, the judge rules for the mechanic, concluding that the repairs were made properly and something else was wrong with your car. You disagree, contending that the repairperson really did mess up the job. You are not eligible to appeal, because this is a factual dispute.

> EXAMPLE 2: You are a tenant suing for the return of a cleaning deposit withheld by the landlord. The court agrees with you and awards you the amount of the deposit plus $500 in punitive damages. The landlord appeals, claiming that under the law of your state, the judge only has the power to award punitive damages in the amount of $250. Because this appeal claims a mistake was made in applying the law, it is proper and will be considered.

In most states, appeals made on the basis of a mistake of law must be supported by a written outline of what the claimed mistakes are. This can put nonlawyers at a disadvantage, because they are unfamiliar with legal research and legal writing techniques. Start by contacting the court clerk and requesting all forms and rules governing appeals. Although it's important to take these seriously and do your best to comply, the good news is that most appellate judges will consider any well-reasoned written statement you submit claiming the small claims judge made a legal error.

RELATED TOPIC
Some legal research tips. Check out Chapter 25 for pointers on how to learn about the laws that apply to your appeal.

Here is a brief example of appropriate paperwork:

Sample Appeals Statement

Appeal from Small Claims Judgment #_____ ,
Based on Legal Error

Under the laws of the state of _____ , a small claims judgment may be set aside if it is based on a legal error or mistake. In my personal injury case, the court incorrectly applied the statute of limitations, because it did not take into consideration the fact that I was a minor when the accident occurred.

My case is based on a personal injury I suffered on January 23, 2015, when I was 17 years and two months old. The small claims judge dismissed my case because it was not filed within one year after my injury, as is required by the statute of limitations. This was an incorrect application of the law.

It's true that under the terms of Code of Civil Procedure, Section 340, a personal injury case must normally be filed within one year of the date of the injury, which in my case occurred on January 23, 2015. However, Sec. 352 of the Code of Civil Procedure also states: "If a person entitled to bring an action, mentioned in Chapter 3 of this title, be, at the time the cause of action occurred, ... under the age of majority ... the time of such disability is not a part of the time limited for the commencement of the action."

Because I was still a minor until November 23, 2016 (when I turned 18), under the terms of Code of Civil Procedure, Section 352, it was from this date (not from January 23, 2015) that the court should have begun counting the one-year statute of limitations for personal injury actions. Therefore, I was entitled to file my case until November 22, 2017. In fact, because I filed on June 27, 2017, I was well within the allowed time.

In conclusion, I request that the judgment in this case be vacated and that I be granted a new small claims court hearing.

Filing and Presenting Your Appeal

If you haven't already done so, it is absolutely essential that you obtain and study a copy of your state's small claims appeal rules. They vary considerably, especially between those states where you can only appeal questions of law and those where you are entitled to a completely new trial.

File Promptly

In all states, appeals must be filed promptly (usually within ten to 30 days), so wherever you are, don't delay. In many states, you must file a notice of appeal within 30 days after the court clerk mails the judgment to the parties (or hands it over, if a decision is made in the courtroom). This means that if the decision was mailed, there will be less than 30 days to file an appeal from the day that the defendant receives the judgment. In some states, appeals must be filed within ten days.

CAUTION
Don't oversleep in Washington, DC, or Rhode Island! You'll have only two days to appeal your small claims court decision in Rhode Island, and three days in Washington, DC. Luckily, weekends and holidays don't count.

You'll need to consult your state statute to find out when to start counting your time to appeal. Because many states start counting from the date the judgment was mailed, this date, which should appear on the judgment, is critical. If, for some reason, your judgment doesn't show up within the number of days in which you are allowed to appeal, call the small claims clerk immediately and request help getting an extension of time to file your appeal.

Appeals must usually be filed using a form supplied by the small claims court.

Appeal Fees

The appeal fee is often higher than the original filing fee. If you ultimately win your appeal (that is, get the original decision turned around in your favor), you can add these court costs to the judgment. In many states, the party filing an appeal must post a cash bond (or written guarantee by financially solvent adults) to cover the amount of the judgment if he or she loses.

Doing It Without a Lawyer

You are entitled to have an attorney in the appeals court. By definition, your small claims case is not worth big bucks, so you will probably decide it is not cost-efficient to hire one. Indeed, there should be little practical reason for an attorney, as you probably have an excellent grasp of the issues by this time.

JUDGE'S TIP
It doesn't take a lawyer to make a good impression in an appeal. A prepared, respectful, and self-represented litigant can often make just as impressive a showing at a small claims appeal as a lawyer would.

But what if your opponent hires a lawyer? Aren't you at a disadvantage if you represent yourself? Not necessarily. As noted in "Presenting Your Appeal," below, in many states the appeals court must follow informal rules similar to those used in small claims court. This puts you on a relatively equal footing, even if your opponent has a lawyer. If you have prepared carefully, you may even have an advantage: You carry with you the honest conviction that you are right. If, despite this commonsense view of the situation, you still feel a little intimidated, the best cure is to go watch a few small claims appeals. Ask the court clerk when they are scheduled. Watching the process should persuade you that you are perfectly capable of handling your own appeal.

Presenting Your Appeal

On appeal, both sides should give careful thought to how their presentation can be improved. This is particularly true if you are the person who lost. Ask yourself: Did the judge decide against me because I presented my case poorly or because I didn't support my statements with evidence? Or did the judge simply misapply the law? To answer these questions, you may have to do some additional legal research. (See Chapter 25 for some tips on how to do this.)

JUDGE'S TIP
Read the case file before your appeals hearing. The file is a public record, and you have a right to see it (ask the small claims clerk how to get a copy). You'll be better prepared if you know what material the appeals judge has read.

Sometimes the trial judge will leave notes in the file that the appeal judge will be reading. If so, you'll want to know that and adjust your case accordingly.

Once you have decided how to improve your case, practice presenting it to an objective friend. When you are done, ask your friend which parts of your presentation were convincing and which need more work.

Some Cures for Prehearing Jitters

What should you do if you see that your appeal will be conducted in a style you find intimidating?

- Read *Represent Yourself in Court: How to Prepare & Try a Winning Case*, by Paul Bergman and Sara Berman (Nolo). This book explains how to conduct a contested civil trial in a formal courtroom setting, including how to present testimony and cross-examine witnesses. It should quickly increase your comfort level.
- Ask the judge, in advance, to conduct your appeal as informally as possible. You can do this on the day of your hearing or, better yet, by writing a brief, polite letter to the court ahead of time. Explain that, as a nonlawyer, you are thoroughly prepared to present the facts of your case, but because you are unfamiliar with formal rules of evidence and procedure, you would appreciate it if your small claims appeal could be conducted so that a citizen who has not spent three years at law school is given a fair opportunity to be heard.
- During your small claims appeal, if there is some procedure you don't understand, politely ask the judge for an explanation. If necessary, remind the judge that, as a taxpayer and a citizen, you are entitled to understand the rules and procedures that control the presentation of your case.

In some states, small claims appeals can be presented to the judge just as informally as any small claims court case. At the other extreme, some states' small claims court appeal rules require that an appeal be conducted with all the pomp and circumstance of a regular trial court case. Because procedures can differ even within the same state, this book can't tell you exactly what

type of hearing you will face. So, again, it is important to take the time to check out exactly what type of appeal hearing rules you will encounter. For example, you may learn you'll need to be prepared to present your testimony while sitting in the witness box. You may also have to question your witnesses using the formal lawyer style you have seen so often on TV, and introduce evidence according to a strict, step-by-step script.

> **CAUTION**
> **Jury trials.** A few states permit jury trials on appeal. Most states don't. Check with your court clerk and the appendix.

Further Appeals

If a defendant loses the appeal, there is usually no right to file a second appeal. However, it is sometimes possible to file an extraordinary writ (a special request for review based on extraordinary circumstances) to a court of appeal claiming that either the small claims court or first appeals court made a serious legal mistake in handling the case (for example, the court had no power to consider the issues involved in your case). In some states, the lower court judge may have the power to recommend that the court of appeal hear your case. But because of the relatively small amounts of money involved, extraordinary writs based on small claims judgments are almost never filed. And when they are, they are seldom granted. For these reasons, this procedure isn't covered here.

Collecting Your Money

ou won. Congratulations! You undoubtedly want to collect every penny from the opposing party, pronto. If the other party is cooperative, that won't be much trouble. But some defendants have figured out that typically the court will not make them pay unless you take action. That's where this chapter comes in, explaining when you can start your collection efforts and how to enforce your judgment. With a little patience and some careful planning, you should be able to collect—by garnishing wages, attaching the defendant's bank account, or taking other legal steps.

> CAUTION
> **Don't harass the debtor.** Businesses that regularly attempt to collect debts for another business's consumer customers are subject to the federal Fair Debt Collection Practices Act (15 U.S.C. §§ 1692–1692p), and in most states, subject to similar state laws. These laws protect consumer debtors from abusive or unfair conduct. Basically, the rules prohibit conduct such as calling the debtor so often that it is harassing, causing the debtor's phone to ring continuously, using profane language, or badmouthing the debtor in the community. Some state laws apply even if you are doing your own collections. If you plan to do your own collections, you should consult with a lawyer and/or review your state law carefully. (Of course, it's fine to talk about the judgment to officials who are helping with the collection process.) Even if you are trying to collect debts not covered by these consumer protection laws, other more general laws may apply if you use abusive or unfair tactics, so it's best to avoid inappropriate conduct.

The Timing of Collecting Your Money

Wait until the dust settles before beginning your collection efforts. This means different things in contested cases and default cases.

Contested Cases

If the defendant appeared in court, fought the case, and lost, you may have to wait to see whether there is an appeal before you start trying to collect the judgment amount. Some states prohibit collection efforts while a defendant can still appeal. Other states do not require you to wait, but it is a good

idea to wait anyway. Trying to collect may spur the defendant to appeal the judgment. Depending on your state's rules, an appeal must normally be filed within ten to 30 days. (See the appendix.)

TIP
Exception. In a few states, no appeals are allowed, and in several more, only a losing defendant can appeal. (See the appendix.) If the other party can't appeal, you can begin collection activities immediately.

After the allowed time to appeal has passed, check with the small claims court clerk to make sure that the defendant hasn't appealed. If the defendant has appealed, then you will get notice in the mail of the appeals hearing date. (Learn more about appeals in Chapter 23.)

Some states don't stop you from collecting while you are waiting for the appeal to be decided. Others do. Again, even if you can collect, you may be better off waiting. A defendant is likely to take the appeal more seriously, if for example, you are trying to take money out of his or her paycheck before the appeal hearing. On the other hand, if the law doesn't stop you from collecting before the appeal is decided, and you believe the defendant may be using the time to hide assets, you may want to act quickly to collect what you can. After the appeals court makes its decision, it will notify the small claims court. If the appeal was decided in your favor, you can proceed to enforce the judgment immediately.

Default Judgments

If you got your judgment because the defendant defaulted (that is, didn't show up), the defendant usually can't appeal without first asking the court to set aside or vacate the default. Most defendants who didn't show up in the first place don't bother to do this. Nevertheless, in some states, you may have to wait out the time period during which the losing party is allowed to ask the court to set aside the default judgment. (See Chapter 15 for more on setting aside default judgments.) And even if waiting isn't required, it's always a good idea if you are in a state that allows defendants a certain number of days in which to ask the court to set aside the default judgment.

The reason is simple: If you move to collect your judgment immediately, you may alert the defendant to try to set it aside.

If the defendant loses on the request to set aside the judgment, then appeals that decision, in some states you may have to wait until the court decides that appeal before you can begin to enforce your judgment.

How to Collect

Once the relevant waiting period is up, what should you do? There are a few possibilities.

Ask for Payment

Start by asking politely for your money. This works in many cases, especially if you have sued a responsible person or business. If you don't have personal contact with the party who owes you money, try a note like the sample below.

Sample Request for Payment

> P.O. Box 66
> Bangor, Maine 12345
> February 15, 20xx
>
> Mildred Edwards
> 11 Milvia Street
> Bangor, Maine 12345
>
> Re: *Toller vs. Edwards* (Small Claims Case No. 200600)
>
> Dear Mrs. Edwards:
>
> As you know, a judgment was entered against you in small claims court on January 15 in the amount of $1,457.86. As the judgment creditor, I would appreciate your paying this amount within ten days.
>
> Thank you for your attention to this matter.
>
> Very truly yours,
>
> *John Toller*
> John Toller

Payment Through the Court

Your judgment debtor may be willing to pay up—but may not want to deal directly with you. In some states, the judgment debtor can pay the judgment to the court instead. Contact your small claims court clerk to find out whether this is an option in your state. If so, it might make sense to write a short note explaining that payment can be made to the court. (See the sample letter, below.) The court may charge the debtor for this service. Once the court receives payment, it will notify you. If you fail to claim the payment within a certain amount of time, the state will probably get to keep the money—which is an important reason to keep your current address on file with the court.

Collecting the Money

If you receive no payment after sending a polite note, you will have to get serious about collecting your money—or forget it. The emphasis in the previous sentence should be on the word "you." To many people's surprise, the court will not enforce your judgment and collect the money for you—you have to do it yourself.

Fortunately, a few of the ways to legally collect money from a debtor are relatively easy—if the debtor has any money in the first place. Hopefully you gave some thought to collection before you brought your case. If you only now realize that your opponent doesn't have the money to buy a toothbrush, let alone pay off your judgment, you are better off not wasting more time and money trying to get your money, at least for the present. In some situations, you may want to sit on your judgment with the hope that your judgment debtor will show signs of economic life sometime in the future. But if the debtor owns real estate, you'll want to immediately put a lien on the property so that money from a sale will go to pay your judgment, even if the only property the person currently owns is a residence that is exempt from being sold. (See "Property Liens," below.)

Sample Payment Request With Information
on Making Payments to the Court

P.O. Box 18-C

Bangor, Maine 12345

July 2, 20xx

Donald Lee

Donald Lee Industries

14 Western Avenue, S.W.

Bangor, Maine 12345

Re: *Andrews vs. Lee* (Small Claims Case No. 200600)

Dear Mr. Lee,

As you know, a judgment was entered against you in small claims court on June 25 in the amount of $4,112.87. If you would prefer to pay the small claims court rather than pay me directly, you can do so. However, please be aware that the court may charge a small fee for processing your payment. To arrange payments directly to the court, contact the small claims clerk at _[name and address of court where small claims case was decided]_.

As an alternative, you can send the payment directly to me. I would appreciate your handling this matter within ten days from the date of this letter.

Thank you for your consideration.

Very truly yours,

Alice Andrews

Alice Andrews

TIP

Collection rules are getting tighter. A few states are putting teeth into their collection rules. In New York, if a judgment debtor who is solvent doesn't pay three or more small claims court judgments that were based on a repeated course of conduct or the debtor's business transactions, a judgment creditor can get triple the judgment as damages, plus attorneys' fees. Contact the small claims court clerk to see about any collection rules in your jurisdiction.

When the Debtor Pays by Check

Always make copies of any checks the debtor sends you as partial payment on your judgment. If the debtor fails to pay the entire judgment, you'll need to find a collection source for the unpaid portion—and the debtor's bank account is a great place to start. (See "Levying on Wages, Bank Accounts, and Other Property" below.) Your copy of the check will show the debtor's bank, branch, and account number.

If the debtor's check bounces, you may, depending on your state's law, be entitled to:

- Sue in small claims court for the original amount of the bounced check plus damages. First, you must follow your state's detailed procedures, usually including sending a demand letter to the debtor (often by certified mail).
- See whether your county's district attorney's office has a check diversion program. To avoid prosecution, the person who wrote a bad check must make the check good and comply with other rules. You cannot seek damages if you enlist the district attorney's help—but you'll be spared the hassle of another lawsuit.

Installment Payments

When a court orders a judgment to be paid in installments and the judgment debtor misses one or more payments, the person holding the judgment (the judgment creditor) has the right to collect the missed payments immediately. But here is the problem: The judgment creditor can't collect the rest of the

judgment (the part that hasn't come due yet) unless the court first sets aside the installment payment provisions and makes the entire judgment due and payable.

> **EXAMPLE:** Phoebe gets a judgment against Ted for $3,000. The judge grants Ted's request to pay the judgment in installments of $300 per month. Ted misses the first payment, and Phoebe hears he plans to move out of state. She can immediately move to collect the $300. But to collect the rest, Phoebe must either wait until each subsequent payment is missed (and then try to collect each one) or go back to court and ask the judge to set aside the installment payments portion of the judgment so that she can collect it all.

To set aside an installment judgment, call the small claims clerk's office and find out whether the court has a form for this purpose. Below is a sample form you can copy if your court doesn't have its own form. File the original form with the small claims clerk, have a copy served on the debtor, and follow up with a Proof of Service form. (See Chapter 11.)

Judgments Against Government Agencies

If you have a small claims judgment against a government agency, typically you can't use any of the enforcement procedures outlined in the rest of this chapter. Instead, you'll need to follow special procedures to collect. Public entities include your state government, counties, cities, school districts, public authorities, and any other political subdivisions in the state.

Procedures differ slightly from state to state. As soon as you are awarded a judgment against a government agency, you can contact the agency to get information about its payment procedures. In many states, you must take the following steps to collect a judgment from a government agency:

1. Prepare a written declaration under penalty of perjury stating the following:
 • the fact that you have a judgment in your favor
 • the name of the government agency that owes the judgment
 • that you desire payment, and
 • the amount of the judgment.

Sample Request to Set Aside Payment Terms

CITY OF _____ , SMALL CLAIMS COURT

[*Plaintiff's name*] , PLAINTIFF VS. [*Defendant's name*] , DEFENDANT

CASE NO. _____

MOTION OF JUDGMENT CREDITOR

TO SET ASIDE TERMS FOR PAYMENT OF JUDGMENT

The undersigned hereby declares the following:

1. The judgment was entered in the above-entitled action on [*date*] against the judgment debtor(s) _____ [*name(s)*] _____ in the amount of: $ _____ principal, $_____ interest, and $_____ costs.

2. The judgment bore terms for payment of the above amount as follows: $_____ to be paid on _[*date*]_ and $_____ to be paid on _[*date*]_ . (Complete the applicable item below.)

 - No "grace period" for late payments was stated on the judgment.
 - If payment is (specify): _____ days late, the entire balance is due and owing.

3. The judgment debtor(s) has defaulted in payment of the judgment, and the balance owing is $_____ , including interest and costs awarded at the time of judgment. The last payment by the judgment debtor(s) was made on _[*date*]_ in the amount of $_____ .

4. The judgment creditor therefore petitions the court for an order setting aside the terms for payment of the judgment so that execution on the entire balance of the judgment may issue forthwith.

5. I, the undersigned, am [*specify: "the judgment creditor," or "the agent for the judgment creditor"*] .

I declare under penalty of perjury under the laws of the State of _____ that this declaration is true and correct.

Date: _____

Signature of declarant: _____

Print name of declarant: _____

NOTICE TO THE JUDGMENT DEBTOR(S):

If you dispute any allegation made in this motion, you must file a declaration in opposition to the motion with the small claims court within 10 days of the mailing of this motion.

The sample declaration below contains all this information.

2. Get a certified copy of the judgment from the small claims court clerk.

3. Contact the agency that owes you money and find out the fee to collect the judgment.

4. Take or send the declaration, copy of the judgment, and the fee to the office or individual the agency you have the judgment against identifies as the correct place to send the documents.

5. You may be required to deliver a notice to the judgment debtor (the same government agency) where you filed a request for payment, even though doing so is redundant. To play it safe, have a friend mail photocopies of the declaration, the judgment, and a completed proof of service form to the government agency.

As with any judgment, it may be better to wait until the time to appeal has passed before asking for payment.

6. Keep the original proof of service and your copies of the declaration and judgment in a safe place.

The government agency will notify its treasurer or controller, who will pay you or deposit the money with the court. Make sure that you have your current address on file with the court—otherwise, you may never get paid.

Sample Declaration

I, Steven Nakamura, declare as follows:

1. I have a judgment against the City of Los Angeles (Los Angeles Small Claims Court case #11212).

2. I desire payment according to the terms of the judgment.

3. The exact amount required to satisfy the judgment is $2,312, plus interest at the rate allowable by law from February 16, 20xx, until the judgment is paid in full.

I declare under penalty of perjury under the laws of the State of California that this declaration is true and correct.

Dated: February 16, 20xx _____

 Steven Nakamura

Finding the Debtor's Assets

Collecting your small claims judgment isn't too difficult if the judgment debtor has some money or property and you know where it is. But what do you do if you suspect that money or other assets exist but you have no idea how to find them? For example, you may know a person works, but not where, or that he or she has money in the bank, but not which one.

Judgment Debtor's Statement

Wouldn't it be nice to simply ask the judgment debtor a few questions about his or her assets? Well, in many states the loser (judgment debtor) must fill out a form listing the judgment debtor's assets. (See "Sample Judgment Debtor's Statement of Assets," below.) Typically, the judgment debtor must send a completed copy of this form to the person who won the case (the judgment creditor) within a certain number of days after the judgment is mailed out by the clerk—unless the judgment debtor pays off the judgment, appeals, or asks the judge to reverse a default judgment. If the judgment debtor fails to complete the statement (which, unfortunately, is all too common), the judgment creditor may be able to ask the court to hold the debtor in contempt of court, and even issue a bench warrant for his arrest. Ask a small claims adviser how to ask the court to hold the debtor in contempt.

Order for Examination

If the judgment debtor doesn't fill out the Statement of Assets form when required to do so (or if no such form exists), another tool is available in most states. The judgment creditor can ask the court clerk to issue an order requiring the judgment debtor to appear in court in person to be questioned. In some states, this is called an order for examination or judgment debtor's examination. This order, which must be properly served on the judgment debtor, requires the debtor to show up in court and provide the information personally. Typically, if the debtor fails to show up, the judge can issue a bench warrant for the person's arrest.

Sample Judgment Debtor's Statement of Assets

<table>
<tr><td>**MAIL TO THE JUDGMENT CREDITOR**
DO NOT FILE WITH THE COURT</td><td>**SC-133**</td></tr>
</table>

JUDGMENT CREDITOR (the person or business who won the case) *(name):*

JUDGMENT DEBTOR (the person or business who lost the case and owes money) *(name):*

SMALL CLAIMS CASE NO.:

NOTICE TO JUDGMENT DEBTOR: You *must* (1) pay the judgment or (2) appeal or (3) file a motion to vacate. If you fail to pay or take one of the other two actions, you must complete and mail this form to the judgment creditor. If you do not, you may have to go to court to answer questions and may have penalties imposed on you by the court.	**AVISO AL DEUDOR POR FALLO JUDICIAL: Usted debe (1) pagar el monto del fallo judicial, o (2) presentar un recurso de apelación o (3) presentar un recurso de nulidad.** Si usted no paga el fallo o presenta uno de estos dos recursos, deberá llenar y enviar por correo este formulario a su acreedor por fallo judicial. Si no lo hace, es posible que deba presentarse ante la corte para contestar preguntas y pagar las multas que la corte le pueda imponer.

INSTRUCTIONS

The small claims court has ruled that you owe money to the judgment creditor.

1. You may appeal a judgment against you only on the other party's claim. You may *not* appeal a judgment against you on *your* claim.
 a. If you appeared at the trial and you want to appeal, you must file a *Notice of Appeal* (form SC-140) within 30 days after the date the *Notice of Entry of Judgment* (form SC-130 or SC-200) was mailed or handed to you by the clerk.
 b. If you did not appear at the trial, before you can appeal, you must first file a *Notice of Motion to Vacate Judgment and Declaration* (form SC-135) and pay the required fee within 30 days after the date the *Notice of Entry of Judgment* was mailed or handed to you. The judgment cannot be collected until the motion is decided. If your motion is denied, you then have 10 days after the date the notice of denial was mailed to file your appeal.
2. Unless you **pay the judgment or appeal the judgment or file a motion to vacate, you must fill out this form and mail it to the person who won the case** within **30 days** after the *Notice of Entry of Judgment* was mailed or handed to you by the clerk. Mailing this completed form does not stay enforcement of the judgment.
3. If you lose your appeal or motion to vacate, you must pay the judgment, including postjudgment costs and interest. As soon as the small claims court denies your motion to vacate and the denial is not appealed, or receives the dismissal of your appeal or judgment from the superior court after appeal, the judgment is no longer suspended and may be immediately enforced against you by the judgment creditor.
4. Unless you have paid the judgment, complete and mail this form to the judgment creditor within **30 days** after the date the clerk mails or delivers to you (a) the denial of your motion to vacate, or (b) the dismissal of your appeal, or (c) the judgment against you on your appeal.

If you were sued as an individual, skip this box and begin with item 1 below. Otherwise, check the applicable box, attach the documents indicated, and complete item 15 on the reverse.

a. ☐ *(Corporation or partnership)* Attached to this form is a statement describing the nature, value, and exact location of all assets of the corporation or the partners, and a statement showing that the person signing this form is authorized to submit this form on behalf of the corporation or partnership.

b. ☐ *(Governmental agency)* Attached to this form is the statement of an authorized representative of the agency stating when the agency will pay the judgment and any reasons for its failure to do so.

JUDGMENT DEBTOR'S STATEMENT OF ASSETS

EMPLOYMENT

1. What are your sources of income and occupation? *(Provide job title and name of division or office in which you work.)*

2. a. Name and address of your business or employer *(include address of your payroll or human resources department, if different):*

 b. If not employed, names and addresses of all sources of income *(specify):*

3. How often are you paid?
 ☐ daily ☐ every two weeks ☐ monthly
 ☐ weekly ☐ twice a month ☐ other *(explain):*
4. What is your gross pay each pay period? $
5. What is your take-home pay each pay period? $
6. If your spouse earns any income, give the name of your spouse, the name and address of the business or employer, job title, and division or office *(specify):*

Page 1 of 2

Form Adopted for Mandatory Use
Judicial Council of California
SC-133 [Rev. January 1, 2011]

JUDGMENT DEBTOR'S STATEMENT OF ASSETS
(Small Claims)

Code of Civil Procedure,
§§ 116.620(a), 116.830
www.courts.ca.gov

Sample Judgment Debtor's Statement of Assets (continued)

CASH, BANK DEPOSITS

7. How much money do you have in cash?. $
8. How much other money do you have in banks, savings and loans, credit unions, and other financial institutions either in your own name or jointly *(list):*

Name and address of financial institution	Account number	Individual or joint?	Balance
a.			$
b.			$
c.			$

PROPERTY

9. List all automobiles, other vehicles, and boats owned in your name or jointly:

Make and year	License and vehicle identification (VIN) numbers	Value	Legal owner if different from registered owner	Amount owed
a.		$		$
b.		$		$
c.		$		$
d.		$		$

10. List all real estate owned in your name or jointly:

Address of real estate	Fair market value	Amount owed
a.	$	$
b.	$	$

OTHER PERSONAL PROPERTY *(Do not list household furniture and furnishings, appliances, or clothing.)*

11. List anything of value not listed above owned in your name or jointly *(continue on attached sheet if necessary):*

Description	Value	Address where property is located
a.	$	
b.	$	
c.	$	

12. Is anyone holding assets for you? ☐ Yes. ☐ No. If yes, describe the assets and give the name and address of the person or entity holding each asset *(specify):*

13. Have you disposed of or transferred any asset within the last 60 days? ☐ Yes. ☐ No. If yes, give the name and address of each person or entity who received any asset and describe each asset *(specify):*

14. If you are not able to pay the judgment in one lump sum, you may be able to make payment arrangements with the person or business who won the case (the judgment creditor). State the amount that you can pay each month: $, beginning on *(date):* . If you are unable to agree, you may also ask the court for permission to make installment payments by filing a *Request to Make Payments* (form SC-220).

15. I declare under penalty of perjury under the laws of the State of California that the foregoing is true and correct.

Date:

▶

_____ _____
(TYPE OR PRINT NAME) (SIGNATURE)

Mail or deliver this completed form to the judgment creditor at the address shown on the* Notice of Entry of Judgment *form.

There are usually some limits to your use of this procedure. You can't require the judgment debtor to travel too far to participate, for example.

Collecting Judgments Across State Lines

What if your judgment debtor moves to another state, or you discover that he or she owns property or assets elsewhere? Collecting on the judgment will become less convenient, but it is still possible. The majority of states have enacted what's called the Uniform Enforcement of Foreign Judgments Act, creating standard procedures for going after a debtor's assets or property across state lines.

Here's how it ordinarily works: Say you file your small claims case in Illinois and get a judgment for $2,500. When you try to collect, you discover that the debtor has moved to Florida. In order to start your collection efforts, you will need to file your judgment in Florida, the new state. The procedure there, as in most states, is that you mail a certified copy of the original judgment to the Florida court clerk (usually in the area of the state where the judgment debtor lives), along with an affidavit showing your and the judgment debtor's names and addresses. (Some states vary this routine, so check with the court clerk first.)

Once the court receives the certified copy and affidavit, your filing becomes a valid part of the court record. The court may notify the judgment debtor of your filing, or you may need to serve notice on the judgment debtor. When this is done, you can proceed with your collection efforts, following the collection laws of the new state.

TIP

Ask for relevant documents. You may want the judgment debtor to bring certain documents to the examination. Bank statements, vehicle records, and documents regarding property ownership may be helpful in trying to collect. To do this, you must ask the clerk to issue a subpoena for documents. (See Chapter 14 for more information.)

> **TIP**
> **At the debtor's examination, in many states the judgment creditor can ask whether the debtor has any cash in his or her possession.** If so, the judge may issue a "turnover order," authorizing you to take the cash right then and there to satisfy at least a portion of the debt. You will probably need to request the court to issue a turnover order.

Levying on Wages, Bank Accounts, and Other Property

This section discusses a number of ways to collect a court judgment. One or more may work easily and quickly. However, some judgment debtors hide assets or are otherwise difficult to collect from. If you face this situation and believe the judgment debtor may own or buy real property, your best bet may be to establish a lien against that property and wait until the judgment debtor tries to sell the property. (See "Property Liens," below, for details on how to do this.)

> **TIP**
> **Think twice before using a collection agency.** If you don't want to bother pursuing the debtor, you can turn your debt over to a real collection agency. However, this probably doesn't make much sense, as the agency will often take up to 50% of what it can collect as its fee. And unless you are a regular customer, the agency probably won't treat your debt with much priority unless it believes your judgment will be easy to collect. Of course, if the debt is easy to collect, you should be able to do the job yourself and pocket the collection fee.

If you know where the judgment debtor works, you are in good shape. In most states, you are generally entitled to get approximately 25% of a person's net wages to satisfy a debt. (But if a person has a very low income, the amount you may recover can be considerably less than 25% and possibly nothing at all.)

324 | EVERYBODY'S GUIDE TO SMALL CLAIMS COURT

Wage garnishments are not allowed in some states. In others, they are limited to, for example, 10% of a debtor's gross wages, 25% of net wages, or a multiple of the minimum wage, whichever is less. Some other states make it difficult to garnish the wages of a head of family if the family has a low income and needs all of it to survive. The sheriff's or marshal's office in your area can supply you with the rules in your state, or you can check online.

Knowing where a judgment debtor banks can also be extremely valuable, as you can order a sheriff, marshal, or constable to levy on a bank account and get whatever it contains at the time of the levy, subject to several exceptions. (See "Some Money Is Protected," below.) Of course, a bank account levy will only work once at a given bank, because the debtor is pretty sure to move the account when he or she realizes that you are emptying it.

Other types of property are normally much more difficult to grab. Why? Because all states have debtor's exemption laws that prohibit creditors from taking certain types of property to satisfy a debt. Items protected typically include a portion of or all equity in a family house, furniture, clothes, and much more. (*Solve Your Money Troubles: Strategies to Get Out of Debt and Stay That Way,* by Amy Loftsgordon and Cara O'Neill (Nolo), includes a list of the exempt property laws of all 50 states.)

Practically speaking, the only types of personal property (as opposed to real estate) other than wages and bank accounts that are normally worth going after are business receipts and property, and motor vehicles in which the judgment debtor has equity that's greater than your state's exemption amount. Theoretically, there are many other assets that you could reach—boats and planes, for example—but in most cases they are not worth the time and expense involved, considering that your judgment is for a modest amount.

Real estate is different. Even if the judgment debtor doesn't have much equity in the property, you will still want to record a judgment lien. Most people refinance or sell within a three-year period, at which time your lien will probably be paid in order to clear title to the property. (See "Property Liens," below.)

Writ of Execution

Before you can levy on a person's wages or other property, you must get court permission, usually in the form of a writ of execution, writ of garnishment, writ of attachment, or similarly titled document, which, for convenience, we'll refer to as a "writ." (See "Sample Writ of Execution," below.) Some courts also require that you complete a short application for the writ. If you have a small claims judgment, you are entitled to a writ. In most states, you get your writ from the small claims court clerk, who will often help you fill in part of the information. There is often a small fee, which is a recoverable cost.

Once the court issues your writ, take or send it to the sheriff, marshal, or constable in the county where the assets are located. Give the officer:

- The original writ and one to three or more copies, depending on the requirements of the sheriff, marshal, or constable. Keep a copy of the writ for your files.
- The required fees for collecting, which will vary as to the type of asset. Call ahead to inquire or check the county's website—many post information on collection procedures and fees.
- Instructions on what type of asset to collect and where it is located. The sheriff, marshal, constable, or small claims clerk may have a form to use when providing these instructions. Normally, however, they will accept a letter if it contains all the necessary information.

CAUTION
Don't delay in serving a writ of execution. A writ of execution expires if it is not served on the debtor by the sheriff, marshal, or constable within a certain number of days of the date it was issued by the court. If this time runs out, you will have to go back to the small claims clerk and get another writ of execution issued. So don't get a writ of execution until you have identified the property you want to take. That way, you won't use up part of the time holding a debtor's examination or trying other ways to locate property you can take.

Sample Writ of Execution

EJ-130

ATTORNEY OR PARTY WITHOUT ATTORNEY *(Name, State Bar number and address):*	*FOR COURT USE ONLY*

TELEPHONE NO.: FAX NO.:

E-MAIL ADDRESS:

ATTORNEY FOR *(Name):*

☐ ATTORNEY FOR ☐ JUDGMENT CREDITOR ☐ ASSIGNEE OF RECORD

SUPERIOR COURT OF CALIFORNIA, COUNTY OF

STREET ADDRESS:

MAILING ADDRESS:

CITY AND ZIP CODE:

BRANCH NAME:

PLAINTIFF:

DEFENDANT:

WRIT OF
☐ EXECUTION (Money Judgment)
☐ POSSESSION OF ☐ Personal Property ☐ Real Property
☐ SALE

CASE NUMBER:

☐ Limited Civil Case ☐ Small Claims Case
☐ Unlimited Civil Case ☐ Other_____

1. **To the Sheriff or Marshal of the County of:**

 You are directed to enforce the judgment described below with daily interest and your costs as provided by law.

2. **To any registered process server:** You are authorized to serve this writ only in accord with CCP 699.080 or CCP 715.040.

3. *(Name):*

 is the ☐ judgment creditor ☐ assignee of record whose address is shown on this form above the court's name.

4. **Judgment debtor** *(name, type of legal entity stated in judgment if not a natural person, and last known address):*

 ☐ Additional judgment debtors on next page

5. **Judgment entered** on *(date):*

6. ☐ **Judgment renewed** on *(dates):*

7. **Notice of sale** under this writ

 a. ☐ has not been requested.

 b. ☐ has been requested *(see next page).*

8. ☐ Joint debtor information on next page.

 [SEAL]

9. ☐ See next page for information on real or personal property to be delivered under a writ of possession or sold under a writ of sale.

10. ☐ This writ is issued on a sister-state judgment.

11. Total judgment $

12. Costs after judgment (per filed order or memo CCP 685.090) $

13. Subtotal *(add 11 and 12)* $

14. Credits . $

15. Subtotal *(subtract 14 from 13)* $

16. Interest after judgment (per filed affidavit CCP 685.050) (not on GC 6103.5 fees). . . $

17. Fee for issuance of writ $

18. **Total** *(add 15, 16, and 17)* $

19. Levying officer:

 (a) Add daily interest from date of writ *(at the legal rate on 15)* (not on GC 6103.5 fees) of. $

 (b) Pay directly to court costs included in 11 and 17 (GC 6103.5, 68637; CCP 699.520(i)) $

20. ☐ The amounts called for in items 11–19 are different for each debtor. These amounts are stated for each debtor on Attachment 20.

Issued on *(date):*

Clerk, by _____ , Deputy

NOTICE TO PERSON SERVED: SEE NEXT PAGE FOR IMPORTANT INFORMATION.

Page 1 of 2

Form Approved for Optional Use
Judicial Council of California
EJ-130 [Rev. January 1, 2012]

WRIT OF EXECUTION

Code of Civil Procedure, §§ 699.520, 712.010, 715.010
Government Code, § 6103.5
www.courts.ca.gov

Wages and Bank Accounts

To seize a person's wages, you will probably have to provide an official copy of the writ of execution form to the sheriff, marshal, or constable in the county where the assets are located, and a letter of instruction (see "Sample Letter Containing Wage Levying Instructions," below). The sheriff or marshal will serve a wage withholding order on the debtor's employer, and you should get some money soon. Typically, an earnings withholding order lasts for a set period of time, such as 90 days, or until the judgment is satisfied or expires.

> CAUTION
> **Discrimination against "garnishee" prohibited.** Federal law and the laws of some states prohibit an employer from firing an employee because the employee's wages are garnished to satisfy a judgment. (15 U.S.C. § 1674(a).)

To levy on a bank account, first contact the sheriff, marshal, or constable's office to be sure they handle this work (if not, contact a process server). You'll need the original and one or more copies of the writ, a letter of instruction, and the correct fee. If a bank account is in the name of the defendant and someone else, you may have to post a bond, depending on your state's laws.

Some Money Is Protected

Not all money in a debtor's bank account is up for grabs. Most states have laws that prohibit you from taking exempt funds, and if you do take exempt funds the judgment debtor can force you to return them. Typically, approximately 75% of wages placed in a bank account are exempt (100% if there has been a previous wage attachment involving the same money) for 30 days after payment. Generally, Social Security, certain retirement accounts, and financial aid for school are also exempt.

Sample Letter Containing Wage Levying Instructions

P.O. Box 66

Jackson, New York 12355

March 1, 20xx

Sheriff (Civil Division)

Mapleville, New York 12345

Re: *John Toller vs. Mildred Edwards*

 Small Claims Court No. 81-52

Dear Sheriff:

Enclosed you will find the original and one copy of a Property-Income Execution issued by the small claims court in the amount of $ _____ .
I also enclose a check for your fee in the amount of $_____ .

I hereby instruct you to execute on the wages of Mildred Edwards, who works at the Graphite Oil Co., 1341 Chester Street, Mapleville, New York. Please serve the Execution on or before March 15, 20xx. [*For a bank account, you would simply substitute "all monies in the accounts of Mildred Edwards, located at [address]." You generally do not need to know the account number—although some counties may require it—only the bank and branch, but your chance of collecting is probably better if you can supply the account number.*]

Very truly yours,

John Toller

John Toller

> **TIP**
> **Timing is key.** The amount of money in most of our bank accounts fluctuates over the course of a month or year. If the debtor is employed, the bank account is probably ripest for the picking around the first of the month. If the debtor has seasonal employment, certain times of the year are probably best for the levy. Before you write your instructions to the levying officer, think about when you are most likely to find the money.

Business Assets

In many states, it is possible to have someone from the sheriff's, marshal's, or constable's office sent to the business of a person who owes you money to collect it from the cash on hand. It is done with a till tap or a keeper. You will want to ask your court clerk about your local rules.

A till tap consists of a one-time removal of all cash and checks from the business. The fees are reasonable. For a keeper, a deputy from the sheriff's, marshal's, or constable's office goes to the place of business, takes all the cash and checks in the cash register, and then stays there for a set period of time (an eight-hour keeper, a 24-hour keeper, or a 48-hour keeper) to take more money as it comes in. Because you must pay the deputy to stay at the collection site, keepers' fees are relatively high. It is also possible for the business's property to be seized and sold. But the costs of doing so are usually prohibitive.

Talk to the sheriff, marshal, or constable in your area to get more details. This person will want an original and several copies of your writ, as well as instructions on where and when to go. You can get the judgment debtor to reimburse you for money you spend on collection processes, if enough money comes in to cover it.

Motor Vehicles

Seizing a person's motor vehicle tends to be difficult for several reasons, including the following:

- A portion of the equity in a car is exempt from your levy in many, though not all, states. The exempt amount ranges widely, from $1,000 to $20,000.

EXAMPLE: A judgment debtor in Oregon has a car worth $4,000 on which he owes $3,000 to a bank. This means his equity is $1,000—the bank owns the rest. Equity of up to $3,000 is exempt under Oregon law, so you would end up with nothing.

- The car must be parked in an accessible place, such as a street or driveway, unless you obtain a court order allowing entry into a garage or other private place.
- You can't always be sure that the judgment debtor owns the car he drives. It may be in someone else's name, or he may be leasing it.

Finding out whether a judgment debtor owns the car he or she drives can be tricky. You might get this information from the judgment debtor's statement of assets or by conducting a debtor's examination (see "Finding the Debtor's Assets," above). In addition, for a small fee, you may be able to find out from the Department of Motor Vehicles who owns the car, including whether or not a bank or finance company has an interest.

Once you have this information, you can determine whether the car is worth enough to levy against. If the car is sold, will the sale price be enough to pay off any car loan the debtor has, give the debtor his or her exemption, cover the costs of the sale, and leave enough to pay all, or at least a substantial part, of your judgment? If you are convinced that the vehicle is worth enough to cover these costs, as would be the case if it is relatively new and owned free and clear by the debtor, then have the sheriff pick up the car and sell it. But remember, the sheriff's fees to do this are relatively high and must be paid in advance. Also, the sale price at a public auction will fetch far less than at a private sale. If the car sells for enough, you can get back the money spent on sheriff's fees when the vehicle is sold.

Call the sheriff, marshal, or constable of the county in which the car is located to find out how much money is required as a deposit and how many copies of the writ you'll need. Then write a letter like the one below.

Sample Letter to Sheriff Requesting Levy

P.O. Box 66

Jackson, New York 12355

March 1, 20xx

Sheriff (Civil Division)

Cheyenne, New York 12345

Re: *John Toller vs. Mildred Edwards*

 No. SC 81-52

Dear Sheriff:

You are hereby instructed, under the authority of the enclosed Property-Income Execution, to execute upon and sell all of the right, title, and interest of Mildred Edwards, judgment debtor, in the following motor vehicle:

[*Enter the description of the car as it appears on the DMV report, including the license number.*]

The vehicle is registered in the name(s) of Mildred Edwards, and is regularly found at the following address(es):

[*List home and work address of owner. Remember that the car must be in a public place, such as parked on a street.*]

Enclosed is my check for $_____ to cover your costs of execution and sale.

Very truly yours,

John Toller

John Toller

CAUTION

Some states have no exemption for motor vehicles, and some exempt a higher amount of equity. Check your state's laws, call your local sheriff's or marshal's office, or consult *Solve Your Money Troubles: Strategies to Get Out of Debt and Stay That Way*, by Amy Loftsgordon and Cara O'Neill (Nolo), which contains an up-to-date list of all states' exemptions.

Stocks, Bonds, Mutual Funds, and Other Securities

If the judgment debtor owns stock or other securities that are not exempt as part of a retirement plan (see below), you may be able to force the debtor to sell these assets to pay your judgment. Your collection method will depend on whether the debtor personally holds the stock certificates or whether they're held by a stockbroker.

If the judgment debtor personally holds the certificates, you can levy against the certificates themselves as tangible personal property. However, you will first need to get a court order allowing you to reach property in a private home.

If, as is common, the certificates are held for the judgment debtor by a broker, generally you can initiate a third-party levy against the branch office of the stock brokerage firm. The sheriff, marshal, or constable will require a writ, written instructions, and fee to handle the levy.

Sometimes stock or mutual fund ownership is not manifested in certificates but is recorded in the computers of the company issuing the securities. In this case, it is usually possible to make a third-party levy at a company's in-state headquarters. If the company's headquarters are out of state, however, you will need to use different procedures, such as obtaining a court order assigning you the right to the securities. For assistance with this, ask the small claims clerk.

Small Items

Normally, it isn't worth the trouble to try to levy on small items of personal property, such as furniture or appliances, because they are commonly covered by one or another debtor's exemption laws. Even if property isn't exempt, selling it is usually more trouble (and produces less cash) than it's

worth. If you identify valuable nonexempt property, you will need a court order to allow a levying officer access to property in a private home.

Individual Retirement Plans

In many states, you can get at money in the judgment debtor's individual (for example, IRA) or self-employment (for example, Keogh) retirement plans held in banks or savings institutions. You'll need to check your state laws to find out whether individual retirement accounts are fair game. If you're entitled to go after this money, you can do so just as you would with any other money kept in a bank. Of course, you need to know where the money is. Also, some states allow you to collect up to 25% of the periodic payment from an individual retirement or Keogh type retirement plan, just the way you would get a wage garnishment.

Private company retirement plans and state or local government retirement plans generally can't be touched.

Federal government pension and retirement benefits may not generally be garnished to satisfy any debts for judgments you get in small claims court.

Judgments From Auto Accidents

In certain circumstances, a judgment debtor's driver's license may be suspended by the Department of Motor Vehicles if the debtor doesn't pay a judgment stemming from an auto accident. Check with your Department of Motor Vehicles for information.

TIP

First, try negotiation. If the debtor needs to drive to work, license suspension may cause the person to lose his or her job. To get rid of the debt and therefore avoid the suspension, the debtor might decide to declare bankruptcy. If you are a creditor and intend to ask the Department of Motor Vehicles to suspend the debtor's license, first negotiate with the debtor. You may be able to work out a payment plan, which is a win-win result: You get your money, and the debtor doesn't have to declare bankruptcy.

Property Liens

Another way to collect money from a person or business against whom you have a small claims judgment is by putting a lien on real estate owned by the debtor. In some states, the entry of a court judgment automatically creates a lien on any real property the debtor owns in the county where the judgment was obtained. In the rest of the states, you must record the judgment with the county to create a lien on the debtor's real property.

Once you have a lien on the judgment debtor's property, especially real property, there is a good chance you'll eventually be paid. It usually works like this: When the judgment debtor wishes to sell the real estate, the title will be clouded by your lien and the debtor will probably pay you off to be able to transfer clear title to a third party. Likewise, if the debtor wishes to refinance, it almost certainly will be contingent on all liens being paid off. Thus, sooner or later, you should get your money. Remember, however, that a portion of the debtor's equity in the home is exempt from collection.

Before you record your lien, make sure you wait until the time to appeal has passed. In many states, here's how to record a property lien against all the debtor's real estate that you know about:

1. Get an Abstract of Judgment form from the small claims clerk's office at the court where your case was heard (a small fee is required).
2. Take or mail the Abstract of Judgment form to the County Recorder's office in each county where property is located or you think the debtor might buy property, and pay the required fee. The recorder's office will record your lien and notify the judgment debtor.

Collection Costs

Using formal collection methods like wage garnishments and property liens to get a judgment debtor to cough up the money owed can be expensive. You will want to make the judgment debtor pay you back for these costs, if possible. You can be compensated for many—but not all—costs of collecting a judgment. Generally speaking, you can get your direct costs of collecting, which include costs like:

- sheriff, marshal, or constable fees
- costs to get copies of required court papers, like a writ of execution or abstract of judgment, and
- fees to file a lien against a debtor's real estate.

However, generally you won't be able to get compensated for indirect costs such as:

- babysitting costs
- lost wages
- transportation costs, or
- postage or photocopying.

You are entitled to collect interest on your judgment according to your state's law. Interest begins to accrue on the date the judgment was entered. If the judge has entered a judgment to be paid in installments, you can charge interest only on installments that have become due, unless the judgment specifically says interest is to be earned earlier. Apply any payments you receive first toward interest and then to the unpaid balance of the judgment. You cannot claim interest on accrued unpaid interest.

Renew Your Judgment

Judgments expire after a certain number of years—usually between five and 20, depending on the state. To find out your state's rule, see "Time Limits to Collect Court Judgments," below. Be aware that the expiration periods may differ if you are collecting on a judgment that was originally entered in another state.

Fortunately, most states allow you to renew your judgment—and any liens based on it—if you do so before the expiration date (a few states allow you to revive an expired judgment, too). For information on how to renew a judgment, contact your small claims court clerk's office.

Time Limits to Collect Court Judgments

These statutes explain how many years you have to collect a court judgment. Be aware that this chart doesn't address reviving a judgment, and rules for particular types of judgments might exist. Check your state statute or consult an attorney.

State	Statute	Time Limit
Alabama	Ala. Code § 6-2-32	20
Alaska	Alaska Stat. § 09.10.040	10
Arizona	Ariz. Rev. Stat. §§ 12-544, 12-1551	5
Arkansas	Ark. Code Ann. §§ 16-56-114, 16-19-1002	10; 5 in Justice of Peace Courts
California	Cal. Civ. Proc. Code § 683.020	10
Colorado	Colo. Rev. Stat. § 13-52-102	20; 6 in county courts
Connecticut	Conn. Gen. Stat. Ann. § 52-598	20 for execution, 25 to bring an action; in small claims court: 10 for execution, and 15 to bring an action
Delaware	Del. Code Ann. tit. 10, § 4711	10
District of Columbia	D.C. Code Ann. § 15-101	12
Florida	Fla. Stat. Ann. § 95.11	20
Georgia	Ga. Code Ann. §§ 9-3-20, 9-12-60	7
Hawaii	Haw. Rev. Stat. §§ 657-1, 657-5	10
Idaho	Idaho Code § 5-215	11
Illinois	735 Ill. Comp. Stat. §§ 5/12-108	7
Indiana	Ind. Code Ann. § 34-11-2-11	10
Iowa	Iowa Code § 614.1(6)	20
Kansas	Kan. Stat. Ann. § 60-2403	5 (with 5 year renewals possible)
Kentucky	Ky. Rev. Stat. Ann. § 413.090	15
Louisiana	La. Civ. Code Ann. Art. 3501	10; unlimited renewals
Maine	Me. Rev. Stat. Ann. tit. 14, § 864	20
Maryland	Md. Code Ann. [Cts. & Jud. Proc.] § 5-102(a)(3)	12
Massachusetts	Mass. Gen. Laws ch. 260, § 20	20
Michigan	Mich. Comp. Laws § 600.5809	10

Time Limits to Collect Court Judgments (continued)

State	Statute	Time Limit
Minnesota	Minn. Stat. Ann. § 541.04	10
Mississippi	Miss. Code Ann. § 15-1-43	7
Missouri	Mo. Rev. Stat. §§ 511.370, 516.350	10
Montana	Mont. Code Ann. § 27-2-201	10
Nebraska	Neb. Rev. Stat. §§ 25-205, 25-1515	5
Nevada	Nev. Rev. Stat. Ann. § 11.190	6
New Hampshire	N.H. Rev. Stat. Ann. § 508:5	20
New Jersey	N.J. Stat. Ann. § 2a:14-5	20
New Mexico	N.M. Stat. Ann. § 37-1-2	14
New York	N.Y. C.P.L.R. Law § 211	20
North Carolina	N.C. Gen. Stat. § 1-47	10
North Dakota	N.D. Cent. Code § 28-01-15	10
Ohio	Ohio Rev. Code Ann. §§ 2329.07, 2325.18	Generally 5 years to execute judgment
Oklahoma	Okla. Stat. Ann. tit. 12, §§ 95, 735	5
Oregon	Or. Rev. Stat. Ann. § 12.070	10
Pennsylvania	42 Pa. Cons. Stat. Ann. § 5525	4
Rhode Island	R.I. Gen. Laws § 9-1-17	20
South Carolina	S.C. Code Ann. §§ 15-3-600, 15-35-810	10
South Dakota	S.D. Codified Laws Ann. § 15-2-6	20
Tennessee	Tenn. Code Ann. § 28-3-110	10
Texas	Tex. Civ. Prac. & Rem. Code Ann. § 34.001	10
Utah	Utah Code Ann. § 78B-2-311	8
Vermont	Vt. Stat. Ann. tit. 12, § 506	8
Virginia	Va. Code Ann. § 8.01-251	20
Washington	Wash. Rev. Code Ann. § 4.16.020	10
West Virginia	W.Va. Code § 38-3-18	10
Wisconsin	Wis. Stat. Ann. § 893.40	20
Wyoming	Wyo. Stat. § 1-17-307	5

Legal Research

When you're involved in a dispute, there may come a time when you need to know more about the relevant law. Usually, all you'll need to know is how to find the local ordinances, state statutes, or judicial opinions that speak to your particular problem. City and county agencies and offices can often give you good advice and information. For example, a zoning or planning office may answer questions about fence height restrictions or building permits. Also, all state laws are available for free on the Internet, and you can also use the Internet to read many cities' local laws and some judicial decisions. Or, you can make a trip to your local law library.

Where's the Law Library?

Public law libraries are usually located in or near the main county courthouse. You can check the white pages' government listing under "Law Library" or visit www.publiclawlibrary.org to search for your nearest public law library. If that fails, call the clerk of the local court for information.

This chapter gives basic guidelines for using the Internet and libraries to find answers to legal questions that frequently arise in small claims disputes. If you wish to delve more deeply into the law, Nolo publishes a comprehensive book called *Legal Research: How to Find & Understand the Law,* by Stephen Elias and the Editors of Nolo. An excellent resource with links to small claims court information in all states is www.freeadvice.com/resources/smallclaimscourts.htm.

Local Laws

Most cities' and towns' official websites contain a large body of helpful information, including local ordinances available for searching and downloading. Most cities' and counties' websites follow these formats:

- County: www.co.<county name>.<state postal code>.us
 Example: www.co.hennepin.mn.us

- City: www.ci.<city name>.<state postal code>.us
 Example: www.ci.boulder.co.us.

Your state website also may have links to cities and counties.

If your city's website does not include the text of local ordinances, you may be able to find local laws on one of these sites:

- State and Local Government on the Net (www.statelocalgov.net), and
- the Municipal Code Corporation (www.municode.com).

If you don't have success with the Internet, your local laws may be available at your local public library or the city or county law library (usually located near the courthouse). You can also try getting a copy of local ordinances from the relevant city or county office or special district. For example, the zoning board may give you a copy of your town's zoning ordinances; your regional water district may have copies of local water usage ordinances. These departments usually charge a small fee to cover photocopying costs.

Once you've found a copy of your town's local laws, look for your topic in the index, if there is one, or in the table of contents. Be prepared to look under several different terms. Some indexes are not as helpful as they should be. For instance, if you're quarreling with neighbors about the excessive height of their new fence, you might start by looking under "height" and "fence." If you are unsuccessful, try "zoning laws."

Once you've found the law you need, make sure it hasn't been changed or repealed. If you're reading an ordinance online, the source will tell you what year's version of the law you're looking at. If you're not sure it's current, you can call the city or county clerk's office and ask when the law was last amended. At the library, check the front or back of the book of ordinances for updates, and ask the librarian when the library received its most recent update.

State Laws

The easiest way to find a copy of a state law (also called a statute) is if you already know its citation—that is, the number of the specific statute. If you don't know the statute's citation, there are both Internet and print resources to help you find statutes on a particular subject.

If You Know the Citation

Citations to state statutes normally refer to the title (or volume) and section numbers. The three examples shown in Figure 1 are typical.

<div style="border:1px solid black; padding:1em;">

Sample State Statute Citations

23 **Vt. Stat. Ann.** **§ 1185**

title (volume Vermont Statutes section
number) Annotated number

N.J. Stat. Ann. **2A:** **170-90.1**

New Jersey Statutes volume section
Annotated number number

Mich. Comp. Laws Ann. **421.27** **(c)(2)(ii)**

Michigan Compiled Laws section subsection
Annotated number letter

</div>

Figure 1

Some states' laws are divided up into several different topical sections. In states such as New York and California, citations look like those shown below.

<div style="border:1px solid black; padding:1em;">

Sample California and New York Citations

P.C. **§ 518**

Penal section
Code number

Penal Law **§ 14025**

Collection of section
Penal Statutes number

</div>

Figure 2

When you know the statute's citation, then you can use the Internet or a local law library to get a copy.

Using the Internet

Every state maintains its statutes on the Internet. The websites vary in their format, but almost all of them allow you to search for statutes by topic, keyword, or citation.

If your state's official website does not allow you to search by topic or keyword, then check the Cornell Legal Information Institute website (www.law.cornell.edu). It lets you search for statutes by topic as well as by name.

Finding Your State's Website

Every state has its statutes on the Internet. State websites usually use the following format:

> www.<state postal code>.gov
>
> Example: www.ny.gov

Within the state's site, look for a link to legislature or laws.

Using the Library

You can find state laws in your local public law library. Use the annotated version of the statute book if possible, because that version includes additional information that will help with research. These books also have subject indexes or tables of contents that you can use to find statutes on particular topics. For example, if someone has cut down your tree, you'd look under "trees." Nothing useful there? Try "timber" or "trespass"—anything you can think of. Sometimes finding a particular state statute is easy. But sometimes, depending on the subject and the particular state, it can take quite a bit of time and patience. A few states have pretty bad indexes.

Make Sure the Law Is Current

Once you've found the law you need, make sure it hasn't been changed or repealed. If you're reading an ordinance online, the source will tell you what year's version of the law you're looking at. At the library, check the front

or back of the book of statutes for updates. Just look for the number of the law in the update material. If nothing is there under that number, it means there has been no change. If you find a change, it replaces the law printed in the hardbound volume. If there is nothing but the word "repealed" after the number of the law, the law printed in the hardbound volume is no longer in effect.

Reading and Interpreting a Statute

When you find a statute on your subject, read it carefully. Remember that the laws are written by lawyers, many of whom seem unable to write in plain English. (How wonderful it would be if other states could learn from North Dakota. That state not only has a good index, but the laws are clearly written in a style that puts other state statutes to shame.)

Figure 3 shows a page from a volume of state statutes. This state law on spite fences is from the annotated laws of Massachusetts. Let's look at the different pieces of information on the page:

① the topic of the statute

② the section number of the statute

③ the name of the statute

④ the text of the statute

⑤ historical information including when the statute was enacted (1887), and when it was modified

⑥ a listing of reference materials that discuss the statute

⑦ a subject index of cases interpreting the statute

⑧ a citation to a case discussing the statute, and

⑨ the page number of the book in which the statute appears.

Sometimes you'll want to read a judicial decision interpreting a particular statute—for example, if the phrasing of the statute is unclear or if you want to know how the court applied the statute in a particular situation. To find cases interpreting a statute, check the listings after the text of the statute in an annotated version of your state's statutes, which you can find in the law library.

①

SPITE FENCES ③ ④

② § **21.** **Definition; remedy of injured occupant**

A fence or other structure in the nature of a fence which unnecessarily exceeds six feet in height and is maliciously erected or maintained for the purpose of annoying the owners or occupants of adjoining property shall be deemed a private nuisance. Any such owner or occupant injured in the comfort or enjoyment of his estate thereby may have an action of tort for damages under chapter two hundred and forty-three.

Historical Note ⑤

St.1887 c. 348. R.L.1902 c. 33 § 19.

Library References ⑥

Nuisance ⊜3(12).
C.J.S. Nuisance § 39.

Comment. Damnum absque injuria, see M.P.S. vol. 14, Simpson, § 1373.

Notes of Decisions

⑦
Constitutionality 1
Distance from boundary line 3
Motive in erecting fence 2
Persons liable 4
Subsequent proceedings 5
Validity 1

⑧ ———

1. Validity

St.1887, c. 348, declaring fences unnecessarily exceeding six feet in height for annoyance of adjoining owner to be private nuisances, applies to existing structures subsequently maintained as well as those afterward erected and is consti-

tutional. Rideout v. Knox (1889) 19 N. E. 390, 148 Mass. 368, 2 L.R.A. 81, 12 Am.St.Rep. 560; Smith v. Morse (1889) 19 N.E. 393, 148 Mass. 407.

2. Motive in erecting fence

Under St.1887, c. 348, purpose of annoyance must be dominant motive for erecting and maintaining fence. Rideout v. Knox (1889) 19 N.E. 390, 148 Mass. 368, 2 L.R.A. 81, 12 Am.St.Rep. 560.

3. Distance from boundary line

Where defendant maliciously erected fence unnecessarily more than 6 feet

5A M.G.L.A.—29 **449**

⑨

Figure 3

In the annotated code, one-sentence summaries of court cases that interpret the statute directly follow the notes on the statute's history. (See number 8 in Figure 3.) Some statutes have been interpreted by the courts so many times that the publisher includes a little index to the case summaries, which are organized by issues raised by the statute. (See number 7 in Figure 3.) It is often difficult to tell from such a brief summary whether or not a case is in fact relevant to your problem. Fortunately, the summaries also contain a case citation that allows you to look up the case and read it for yourself. It is essential that you read the case itself and not just rely on what it says in the annotation.

Annotated statutes are not available online except for a fee. At Westlaw (www.westlaw.com), you can pay a fee by credit card and then enter the citation for a statute and receive a list of all court cases discussing the law.

Case Law

A judicial opinion, decision, or case is a written opinion of a court, ruling on one or more issues of a particular lawsuit. These opinions are called case law. Often, they interpret the laws created by the legislature, which is why you may need to read them. Even if your state laws address a particular topic, the language of the law may not give you a clear-cut answer to your question. If you find a particular statute that looks as if it will help you, it's always helpful to know how courts have actually interpreted the law.

You may need to read a judicial decision for another reason, too. Although most common small claims court issues are addressed either by local law or state statute, some issues are governed entirely by the courts. When there are no state statutes or local ordinances to help you, you may find help in what's called the "common law." The common law is the body of law that is entirely developed by the courts through their written decisions.

Finding Cases on the Internet

Unfortunately, the full text of many judicial decisions is not available online unless you're able to pay a (usually reasonable) fee.

Free Research Sites

Google has state court cases going back to 1950. Go to "Google Scholar," select "Case law," and type in a case name.

In addition, all states make their more recent cases available free on the Internet—though usually not as far back as Google. To find these cases for your state:

Step 1: Go to www.law.cornell.edu/co.html.

Step 2: Locate the link to the court opinions for your state. This may be one link, or there may be separate links for your state's supreme court and your state's courts of appeal (the lower trial courts seldom publish their opinions, so you probably won't be able to find them).

Fee-Based Research Sites

If you can't find what you need for free, you'll need to try a site that charges for access to cases. A good place to start is VersusLaw, a fee-based system for finding both current and past (archived) state and federal cases. VersusLaw (www.versuslaw.com) offers state and federal court opinions that range from the most recent to those decided 75 years ago.

Other fee-based legal research sites include Westlaw (www.westlaw.com) and LexisNexis (www.lexis.com).

Finding Cases in the Library

Even if you start your legal research on the Internet, you may find yourself needing a law library, especially if you're looking for case law and are unable or unwilling to pay a fee for searching. In the law library, you can read the full text of court cases once you know the citation (see "Understanding Case Citations," below), or use reference materials to find cases on particular subjects.

Ask the librarian to point you to some reference books or to a general legal encyclopedia. These books can give you background information and may also mention cases that will bear on your situation.

Legal encyclopedias. Some states have their own; if yours doesn't, use a national one, such as *American Jurisprudence* (called "Am. Jur." for short). Like regular encyclopedias, these books are arranged alphabetically by topic. The encyclopedia articles discuss how courts have ruled in actual court cases.

Some encyclopedias have more than one series; you want the most recent. For instance, the current series of Am. Jur. is Am. Jur. 2d. Also be sure to check the back of the books (called pocket parts) for more recent updates.

Figure 4 shows a page from Am. Jur. 2d, discussing uncertain boundary lines—in this example, neighbors setting a boundary by building a fence. You can see the short summaries of court decisions that follow each issue that is raised. Let's look at the different sections of the page:

(1) the volume you're currently reading

(2) the topic

(3) the section number within that topic

(4) the name of the section

(5) explanatory text

(6) citation to a relevant case

(7) a cross-reference to A.L.R., a set of volumes whose full name is *American Law Reports*, where you'll find another article about this topic, and

(8) the page number.

American Law Reports is another national compilation of court decisions, books, and published articles concerning all areas of the law. A.L.R. also comes in several series—the 6th is the latest—and has updated material in the back. A.L.R. has separate index volumes that list the topics in alphabetical order.

Reading a Case

A court case contains a lot of information before you even get to the court's actual opinion. Let's look at an example. You find a case that says that a

① ② ③

mutual acquiescence and recognition by the adjoiners is essential to practical location, provided that there is, at the time of the location, a disputed, indefinite, or uncertain boundary line between the adjoining owners.[11] A practical location of a boundary line has been said to be simply an actual designation on the ground, by the parties, of the monuments and bounds called for by the conveyances,[12] and it has also been said that when a disputed or uncertain boundary line is fixed by practical location it is binding, not by way of transfer of title, but by way of estoppel.[13]

§ 88. Erection of fence. ④

Where there is doubt and uncertainty as to the location of the true boundary line[14] between adjoining landowners, they may agree that a fence may be the division line between their lands.[15] To constitute the fence the boundary line it is not necessary that the agreement be express; it may be inferred from or ⑤ implied by the conduct of the parties, especially where the fence is acquiesced to as the boundary line for the period of the statute of limitations.[16] It has

11. Drury v Pekar, supra, quoting Kincaid v Peterson, 135 Or 619, 297 P 833.

The practical location of a boundary line can be established in any one of three ways: (1) the location relied upon must have been acquiesced in for a sufficient length of time to bar a right of entry under the statute of limitations; (2) the line must have been expressly agreed upon between the parties claiming the land on both sides thereof and afterward acquiesced in; or, (3) the parties whose rights are to be barred must have silently looked on, with knowledge of the true line, while the other party encroached upon it or subjected himself to expense in regard to the land which he would not have done had the line been in dispute. Fishman v Nielson, 237 Minn 1, 53 NW2d 553.

12. Wells v Jackson Iron Mfg. Co. 47 NH 235.

Boundary lines may be determined by physical indications of the lines on the ground accepted by the parties over a period of time. Fallone v Gochee, 9 App Div 2d 569, 189 NYS2d 363, app den 9 App Div 2d 699, 191 NYS2d 560.

The actual location of a deed may be satisfactorily established, not only by the natural objects found on the ground, but by the fact that all the parties who knew the facts and were interested in the land located the deed in a certain way. Kenmont Coal Co. v Combs, 243 Ky 328, 48 SW2d 9 (holding that location of deed by grantor and his grantee, subsequently acquiesced in for more than 30 years, could not be disputed).

13. Adams v Warner, 209 App Div 394, 204 NYS 613, quoted with approval in Drury v Pekar, 224 Or 37, 355 P2d 598.

14. Uncertainty of or dispute as to the location of the true boundary line is essential in order that a fence built on a line agreed as the boundary line may operate to preclude the parties from later claiming a different boundary line. Vowinckel v N. Clark & Sons,

217 Cal 258, 18 P2d 58; Pederson v Reynolds, 31 Cal App 2d 18, 87 P2d 51; Blank v Ambs, 260 Mich 589, 245 NW 525; Talbot v Smith, 56 Or 117, 107 P 480, 108 P 125. Annotation: 170 ALR 1146.

But it is not necessary that there should be an actual dispute between the parties regarding the true division line; it is sufficient if it appears that they were uncertain as to the true line and therefore agreed to a designated and certain boundary upon which they constructed a fence and occupied and cultivated or improved their respective portions to that division fence for more than the statutory period. Martin v Lopes (Cal App) 164 P2d 321, superseded 28 Cal 2d 618, 170 P2d 881. ⑥

When the real boundary line between contiguous landowners is known to them, neither of them may acquire title by acquiescence beyond such line by merely building a fence upon the other's property and cultivating and claiming the land to that point, since title to land by acquiescence is founded on an agreement when an uncertainty exists as to the true line. Martin v Lopes, supra.

15. An oral agreement fixing an uncertain and disputed dividing line of lands, and execution thereof by the building of a fence thereon, is not in violation of the statute of frauds, since the parties do not thereby undertake to acquire and pass title to real estate, but merely fix the location of the boundary of the land that they already own, the purpose being to identify their several holdings and make certain that which they regard as uncertain. Holbrooks v Wright, 187 Ky 732, 220 SW2d 524.

Generally as to oral agreements fixing boundary lines, see §§ 78 et seq., supra.

16. Hannah v Pogue, 23 Cal 2d 849, 147 P2d 572; Roberts v Brae, 5 Cal 2d 356, 54 P2d 698; Kandlick v Hudek, 365 Ill 292, 6 NE2d 196.

Annotation: 170 ALR 1145.

623

⑦ ⑧

Figure 4

neighbor was not able to collect money for damage caused by a neighbor's healthy tree. The case is *Turner vs. Coppola,* 102 Misc.2d 1043, 424 N.Y.S.2d 864 (N.Y. Sup. Ct. 1980). Figure 5 shows a copy of this page. Let's look in depth at what you see there:

1. the page number
2. the name and volume of the reporter (collection of cases) you're reading
3. the official citation for the case
4. the name of the case
5. the name of the court
6. the date the opinion was decided
7. a summary of the case, including what this court ruled, and
8. a topic and key number.

The West Publishing Company has given thousands of discrete issues of law their own "key numbers," ordered under topic headings. The topic and key number of a particular rule can be used to find other cases on the same point.

All published cases begin with this kind of introductory information. Once you have gone over the introduction, it is time to read the opinion itself. Never depend on what a reference book, or even the case summary, tells you an opinion says. The people doing the research for these books are only human, and occasionally summaries are very misleading.

Make Sure the Case Is Still Valid

Once you've located a case that addresses the issue you're interested in, you'll want to make sure the case is still valid (that is, hasn't been overturned or reversed by another court decision) before you use the case in your small claims dispute. You can make sure a case is still good law by using an online service called KeyCite, which is available from Westlaw (www.westlaw.com) for a fee. You also get a complete list of all cases that refer to the case, which may lead you to additional cases on the subject you're interested in.

You can check a case's validity using books in the law library—it's an arcane process called Shepardizing. For instructions, see Nolo's book *Legal Research: How to Find & Understand the Law,* by Stephen Elias and the Editors of Nolo.

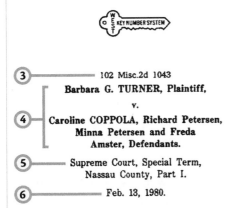

864　　424 NEW YORK SUPPLEMENT, 2d SERIES

"8. The instruction and supervision given * * * were so negligently given as to result in the * * * injuries sustained."

No other factual averment was made by plaintiff which in any way indicates a basis for his conclusion of negligence (*Koppers Co. v. Empire Bituminous Products, Inc.*, 35 A.D.2d 906, 316 N.Y.S.2d 858); and, such is not satisfied by a mere repetition of the complaint without factual evidence upon which to impose liability upon the movant (*Golding v. Weissman*, 35 A.D.2d 941, 316 N.Y.S.2d 522).

Defendant, Senior's motion is granted.

102 Misc.2d 1043

Barbara G. TURNER, Plaintiff,

v.

Caroline COPPOLA, Richard Petersen, Minna Petersen and Freda Amster, Defendants.

Supreme Court, Special Term, Nassau County, Part I.

Feb. 13, 1980.

Plaintiff, who alleged that branches on defendants' trees encroached on plaintiff's property, caused cosmetic damage to her garage and prevented her lawn from receiving adequate sunlight and that twigs, branches and buds from the trees constantly fell on her property, brought action for omnibus relief. On defendants' motion to dismiss complaint for failure to state cause of action, the Supreme Court, Nassau County, Special Term, B. Thomas Pantano, J., held that: (1) the trees were not a "nuisance per se," in such a sense as to sustain an action for relief; (2) complaint did not state cause of action for relief from private nuisance; (3) plaintiff did not have a cause of action in trespass; (4) plaintiff did not

have a cause of action in negligence; but (5) plaintiff could protect herself by self-help consisting of a reasonable cutting of branches to extent that they invaded her property.

Motion to dismiss complaint granted.

1. Nuisance ⟜1

Essence of a "private nuisance" is interference with the use and enjoyment of land amounting to an injury in relation to a right of ownership in that land.

See publication Words and Phrases for other judicial constructions and definitions.

2. Nuisance ⟜3(1)

In light of fact that defendants' trees, whose branches allegedly encroached on plaintiff's property and from which twigs, branches and buds were alleged to have constantly fallen onto such property, were not poisonous or noxious in their nature, the trees were not a "nuisance per se," in such a sense as to sustain an action for relief.

See publication Words and Phrases for other judicial constructions and definitions.

3. Nuisance ⟜42

Right to recover damages from overhanging branches depends on presence of actual injury to plaintiff or plaintiff's property.

4. Nuisance ⟜48

Complaint, in which it was alleged that branches on defendants' trees encroached on plaintiff's property, caused cosmetic damage to her garage and prevented her lawn from receiving adequate sunlight and that trees, branches and buds from the trees constantly fell on plaintiff's property, did not state cause of action for relief from private nuisance. RPAPL § 871.

5. Nuisance ⟜3(1)
 Trespass ⟜10

If an invasion of plaintiff's interest in exclusive possession of his land also deprives him of use and enjoyment of the land, trespass and nuisance would jointly arise, so long as the interference causes

Figure 5

Understanding Case Citations

A case's citation is like its address: It tells you exactly where to locate the published opinion. A citation will tell you the name of the case, the book it is published in, which court decided the case, and the year in which it was published.

Court cases are published in books called reporters. There are two kinds of reporters: One, called a state reporter, publishes just the court cases from a particular state; the second, called a regional reporter, includes cases from a group of states in the same book. A case's citation will usually give you information about where to find the case in either the state or the regional reporter.

Let's take an example: You find a citation for a case stating that a tree owner may have to pay for damage caused to his neighbor's property by his tree. The case citation is *Israel v. Carolina Bar-B-Que, Inc.*, 292 S.C. 282, 356 S.E.2d 123 (Ct. App. 1987). This tells you the name, the two different reporters the case is published in, plus the court and the date. Here's how to decode the information.

- The case name: Israel versus Carolina Bar-B-Que, Inc. (who sued whom)
- The first reporter information, 292 S.C. 282, means the case is published in volume 292 of the South Carolina Reporter, at page 282. Abbreviations for particular reporters are listed in the front of the volumes of reporters.
- The second reporter information, 356 S.E.2d 123, tells us the case is in volume 356 of the Southeastern Reporter, 2nd Series, at page 123.
- The court that published the opinion: We know the case is from South Carolina, because the South Carolina Reporter publishes only cases from that state. We can see that the case comes from a Court of Appeals of South Carolina from the "Ct. App." language in the parentheses.
- The date: 1987.

Small Claims Court Rules for the 50 States (and the District of Columbia)

CAUTION

Always check your small claims court rules for updates and changes. Laws may change after this book goes to press and local court rules may vary from one county to the next, so be sure to check your local small claims court rules before making any legal decisions. Whether you are a plaintiff or a defendant, you should either call your local small claims court clerk or see if the information you need is on the Internet. This appendix lists websites for each state's small claims information. (All links are accurate at the time of publication.) You will also find links to small claims courts on Nolo's website (www.nolo.com).

Alabama

Court: Small Claims Docket (district court).

Statutes: Ala. Code §§ 6-3-2; 6-3-7; 12-12-31; 12-12-70; 12-12-71.

Court rules: Alabama Small Claims Rules, Rules A to N; Alabama Small Claims Forms, 1 to 8.

Court information: www.alabamalegalhelp.org (click "Consumer Issues/Small Claims Actions").

Dollar limit: $6,000.

Where to sue: County or district where any defendant resides or where injury or property damage occurred. Corporation, where injury or property damage occurred, where principal place of business is located, or where plaintiff resides (if defendant does business there).

Service of process: Sheriff or other person approved by court; or certified mail, if requested.

Defendant's response: Defendant must file written answer within 14 days of service to avoid default.

Transfer: No provision.

Attorneys: Allowed; required for assignees (collection agencies).

Appeals: Allowed by either party within 14 days. Heard in circuit court as a new trial.

Evictions: No.

Jury trials: Not allowed.

Alaska

Court: Small Claims Procedure (district court or magistrate).

Statutes: Alaska Stat. §§ 22.15.040; 22.15.050.

Court rules: Alaska District Court Rules of Civil Procedure, Rules 8 to 22.

Court information: http://courts.alaska.gov/forms/#sc (see "Small Claims" heading) or www.commerce.alaska.gov/web/dcra/LocalGovernmentOnline/Administration/FilingSmallClaims.aspx.

Dollar limit: $10,000.

Where to sue: Court nearest to defendant's residence or place of employment, district in which injury or property damage occurred, district where defendant does business, or a place that will not cause unnecessary expense or inconvenience for defendant.

Service of process: Peace officer or registered or certified mail sent by court clerk. Certified or registered mail service is binding on defendant who refuses to accept and sign for letter. If defendant refuses service, clerk will send by regular first-class mail, and service is assumed.

Defendant's response: Defendant must file written answer within 20 days of service to avoid default.

Transfer: Defendant (or plaintiff against whom a counterclaim has been filed) or judge may transfer case to regular district court.

Attorneys: Allowed; required for assignees (collection agencies).

Appeals: Allowed by either party; heard in superior court on law, not facts.

Evictions: No.

Jury trials: Not allowed.

Arizona

Court: Justice of the Peace Court.

Statutes: Ariz. Rev. Stat. Ann. §§ 22-501 to 22-524.

Court information: www.azcourts.gov/AZ-Courts/Justice-Courts.

Dollar limit: $3,500.

Where to sue: Precinct where any defendant resides, transaction or injury occurred, or obligation was to be performed. Corporation, wherever it does business.

Service of process: Authorized officer or process server approved by court, or registered or certified mail with return receipt requested.

Defendant's response: Defendant must answer in writing within 20 days to avoid default.

Transfer: To justice court, if defendant in small claims division counterclaims over $3,500 or objects at least 10 days before hearing (for right of appeal and jury). For counterclaims over $5,000, transfer is allowed to superior court.

Attorneys: Allowed only if both parties agree in writing.

Appeals: Appeals are not allowed, but a party can file a "Motion to Vacate Judgment" asking the court to set aside the judgment based on certain reasons such as error.

Evictions: No.

Jury trials: Not allowed.

Notes: Justice Courts, similar to small claims court but with more procedures, have a limit of $10,000. Rules can be found at Ariz. Rev. Stat. Ann. §§ 22-201 to 22-284.

Arkansas

Court: Small Claims Division (district court).

Statutes: Ark. Const. amend. 80, § 7.

Court rules: Arkansas District Court Rule 10; Administrative Order 18.

Court information: www.arlegalservices.org/smallclaimspacket or arkansasag. gov/consumer-protection/resources/column-one/legal-resources/guide-to-small-claims-court.

Dollar limit: $5,000.

Where to sue: County where any defendant resides, transaction or injury occurred, or obligation was to be performed. Corporation, wherever it does business.

Service of process: Sheriff, sheriff's deputy, any person appointed by court; any person authorized to serve process under the law of the place outside this state where service is made; by the plaintiff or plaintiff's attorney via mail or commercial delivery company, with return receipt requested and delivery restricted to the addressee or the agent of the addressee.

Defendant's response: Defendant must file written answer within 30 days of service.

Transfer: If judge learns that any party is represented by attorney, case will be transferred to regular district court.

Attorneys: Not allowed.

Appeals: Allowed by either party within 30 days. Heard in circuit court as new trial.

Evictions: No.

Jury trials: Not allowed.

California

Court: Small Claims Division (superior court).

Statutes: Cal. Civ. Proc. Code §§ 116.110 to 116.950.

Court information: www.courts.ca.gov/selfhelp-smallclaims.htm or www.dca.ca.gov/publications/small_claims/index.shtml.

Dollar limit: $10,00 for individuals, except that a plaintiff may not file a claim over $2,500 more than twice a year. Limit for local public entity or for businesses is $5,000. $6,500 is the limit in suits by an individual against a guarantor that charges for its guarantor or surety services.

Where to sue: Judicial district where any defendant resides (or resided when promise or obligation was made), transaction or injury occurred, or obligation was to be performed. Corporation, wherever it does business.

Service of process: Certified or registered mail, return receipt requested, sent by court clerk; sheriff or disinterested adult.

Defendant's response: No written answer required.

Transfer: If defendant counterclaims over the dollar limit, case will be heard in higher court if the small claims court agrees to the transfer.

Attorneys: Not allowed.

Appeals: Allowed by defendant (or plaintiff who lost on a counterclaim) within 30 days. Heard in superior court as a new trial. Plaintiff may not appeal on a judgment but may make a motion to correct a clerical error or a decision that is based on a legal mistake.

Evictions: No.

Jury trials: Not allowed.

Colorado

Court: County Court (Small Claims Division).

Statutes: Colo. Rev. Stat. §§ 13-6-401 to 13-6-417.

Court rules: Colorado Rules of County Court Civil Procedure, Rule 411; Colorado Rules of Civil Procedure for Small Claims Courts, Rules 501 to 521.

Court information: www.courts.state.co.us/Forms/SubCategory.cfm?Category =Small.

Dollar limit: $7,500.

Where to sue: County in which any defendant resides, is regularly employed, is a student at an institution of higher education, or has business office.

Service of process: Sheriff or disinterested adult; or certified mail sent by court clerk.

Defendant's response: Defendant must file written and signed response on or before trial date.

Transfer: Allowed by defendant who has a counterclaim over $7,500.

Attorneys: No attorneys are allowed except for pro se or if the person is an authorized full-time employee of the entity bringing or defending the lawsuit or is an active general partner (partnership), authorized active member (union), a full-time officer (corporation), or active member (association), of the entity that is a party to the lawsuit. If an attorney does appear as permitted above, the other party can have one also.

Appeals: Allowed by either party within 14 days.

Evictions: No.

Jury trials: Not allowed.

Connecticut

Court: Small Claims (superior court).

Statutes: Conn. Gen. Stat. Ann. §§ 47a-34 to 47a-42; 51-15; 51-345; 52-259.

Court rules: Connecticut Superior Court Procedure in Civil Matters, Rules 24-1 to 24-33.

Court information: www.jud.state.ct.us/faq/smallclaims.html.

Dollar limit: $5,000 (except in landlord-tenant security deposit claims).

Where to sue: If plaintiff is corporation or company, county or geographical area where defendant resides or does business or where transaction or injury took place. If plaintiff is individual, where plaintiff resides, where defendant resides, or where transaction or injury took place.

Service of process: Priority mail with delivery confirmation, by certified mail return receipt requested or with electronic delivery confirmation, by a nationally recognized courier service providing delivery confirmation, or by a proper officer.

Defendant's response: Must file answer on or before the "answer date" that appears on a notice and answer form sent by the court clerk. The answer date will be between 15 and 45 days after the writ and accompanying documents are filed in the court.

Transfer: Allowed by either party to regular superior court docket upon counter-claim over $5,000, an affidavit stating that a good defense exists to the claim and setting forth with specificity the nature of the defense, or an affidavit stating that the case has been properly claimed for trial by jury.

Attorneys: Allowed; required for corporations.

Appeals: Appeals are not allowed in small claims court. However, a party can file a "motion to open judgment" to reopen the case for certain reasons such as a lack of actual notice.

Evictions: No.

Jury trials: Not allowed; case will be transferred to regular superior court.

Delaware

Court: Justice of the Peace Court (no small claims system).

Statutes: Del. Code Ann. tit. 10, §§ 9301 to 9640.

Court rules: Justice of the Peace Courts, Rules 1 to 72.1.

Court information: https://courts.delaware.gov/jpcourt.

Dollar limit: $15,000.

Where to sue: County where defendant resides; in eviction cases, county where property is located.

Service of process: Court serves by certified mail return receipt requested; or first class mail with certificate of mailing; sheriff, constable, or by special process server.

Defendant's response: In all debt or trespass claims, defendant must file written answer within 15 days after service is made to avoid default. If defendant files counterclaim above $15,000, can still pursue the counterclaim in Justice of the Peace Court. (There is no provision for transfer to higher court.) If defendant wins counterclaim, there are two options: (1) the court will note the outcome on the record and defendant may take the case to a higher court, or (2) defendant may waive the excess over $15,000 and accept $15,000 as the judgment.

Transfer: No provision.

Attorneys: Allowed.

Appeals: Allowed by either party within 15 days. Heard in superior court as new trial.

Evictions: Yes.

Jury trials: Generally not allowed. Permitted in eviction cases; defendant must make request within ten days of being served.

District of Columbia

Court: Small Claims and Conciliation Branch (superior court).

Statutes: D.C. Code Ann. §§ 11-1301 to 11-1323; 16-3901 to 16-3910; 17-301 to 17-307.

Court rules: District of Columbia Superior Court Rules of Procedure for Small Claims and Conciliation Branch, Rules 1 to 19.

Court information: www.dccourts.gov/services/civil-matters.

Dollar limit: $10,000.

Where to sue: District of Columbia Superior Court.

Service of process: U.S. Marshal or adult approved by court; or by registered or certified mail, return receipt requested, sent by court clerk. Certified or registered mail is binding on defendant who refuses to accept letter.

Defendant's response: No written response required, except where the defendant asserts a set-off or counterclaim.

Transfer: Transferable to regular superior court if justice requires, if defendant's counterclaim affects interest in real property (land or housing), or if either party demands jury trial.

Attorneys: Allowed; required for corporations. (Certified law students may also appear.)

Appeals: To court of appeals by either party within three days; reviewed on law, not facts.

Evictions: No.

Jury trials: Either party may demand one, but then case will transfer to regular branch of superior court.

Florida

Court: Small Claims Procedure or Summary Procedure (county court).

Court rules: Florida Small Claims Rules, Rules 7.010 to 7.350; Florida Rules of Appellate Procedure, Rules 7.070, 9.110.

Court information: www.flcourts.org/resources-and-services/family-courts/family-law-self-help-information/small-claims.stml.

Dollar limit: $5,000.

Where to sue: County where a defendant resides, transaction or injury occurred or property is located, or contract was entered into.

Service of process: Peace officer or adult approved by court; or (for Florida residents only) certified mail, return receipt requested, sent by court clerk or attorney of record.

Defendant's response: Must appear personally or by counsel at pretrial conference. No answer required, but must file any counterclaim in writing at least five days before pretrial conference.

Transfer: Allowed to regular county court if defendant counterclaims over $5,000.

Attorneys: Allowed; if attorneys are involved, parties are subject to discovery.

Appeals: Appeals may be filed by either party within 30 days. Heard in circuit court on law, not facts.

Evictions: Yes.

Jury trials: Either party may demand jury trial; plaintiff must make demand when filing suit; defendant must make demand within five days after service or notice of suit or at mediation/pretrial conference.

Georgia

Court: Magistrate Court.

Statutes: Ga. Code Ann. §§ 15-10-1; 15-10-2; 15-10-40 to 15-10-53; 15-10-80; 15-10-87.

Court information: consumer.georgia.gov/consumer-topics/magistrate-court.

Dollar limit: $15,000 (no limit in eviction cases).

Where to sue: County where defendant resides.

Service of process: Constable, any official or person authorized by law to serve process in the superior court, or by a disinterested adult authorized by judge.

Defendant's response: Defendant must answer within 30 days (either in writing or in person) to avoid default.

Transfer: To appropriate court if defendant's counterclaim is over $15,000; or defendant submits a written request for a jury trial.

Attorneys: Allowed.

Appeals: To the state court of the county or to the superior court of the county for new trial; no appeal if either party fails to appear in magistrate court.

Evictions: Yes.

Jury trials: Not allowed.

Hawaii

Court: Small Claims Division (district court).

Statutes: Haw. Rev. Stat. §§ 604-5; 633-27 to 633-36.

Court rules: Hawaii District Court Rules, Small Claims Division, Rules 1 to 13.

Court information: www.courts.state.hi.us/self-help/small_claims_info.

Dollar limit: $5,000; no limit in landlord-tenant residential security deposit cases. For return of leased or rented personal property, the property must not be worth more than $5,000.

Where to sue: Judicial district in which defendant resides, where transaction or injury occurred, or, in security deposit cases, where rental property is located.

Service of process: Certified or registered mail, restricted delivery, return receipt requested; sheriff, disinterested adult, or by either party personally.

Defendant's response: No formal written answer required. Counterclaims up to $25,000 are allowed.

Transfer: If a party entitled to a trial by jury in a case filed or pending files a jury trial demand, the case will be tried in the circuit court under the procedure provided for jury trials. Otherwise, the case can be transferred only if plaintiff agrees to transfer.

Attorneys: Allowed (except in landlord-tenant security deposit cases).

Appeals: Not allowed. Losing party may not appeal on a judgment but may seek to correct a mistake made in computing amount of judgment or present new evidence discovered after time of trial.

Evictions: No.

Jury trials: If a party entitled to a trial by jury in a case filed or pending files a jury trial demand, the case will be tried in the circuit court under the procedure provided for jury trials.

Idaho

Court: Small Claims Department of the Magistrate Division.

Statutes: Idaho Code §§ 1-2301 to 1-2315.

Court information: https://courtselfhelp.idaho.gov/small-claims.

Dollar limit: $5,000.

Where to sue: County where the defendant resides or where claim arose. Corporation, wherever it does business.

Service of process: Personal service; or certified or registered mail, return receipt requested, sent by court clerk.

Defendant's response: Must file written answer within 20 days and sign, complete, and file it with the court clerk to avoid default.

Transfer: No provision.

Attorneys: Not allowed.

Appeals: Allowed by either party within 30 days.

Evictions: No.

Jury trials: Not allowed.

Illinois

Court: Small Claims.

Statutes: 735 Ill. Comp. Stat. §§ 5/2-101 to 5/2-208; 705 Ill. Comp. Stat. § 205/11.

Court rules: Illinois Supreme Court Rules, Rules 281 to 289.

Court information: www.ag.state.il.us/consumers/smlclaims.html.

Dollar limit: $10,000.

Where to sue: County in which any defendant resides, or transaction or injury occurred. Private corporation, where it does business; public corporation, where its principal office is located.

Service of process: Sheriff, other law enforcement officer, licensed detective, or court-approved adult; or certified or registered mail, restricted delivery, return receipt requested, by court clerk.

Defendant's response: No formal written answer required. Must appear by date on court summons.

Transfer: No provision.

Attorneys: Allowed; required for corporations.

Appeals: Allowed by either party within 30 days. Heard in appellate court on law, not facts.

Evictions: Yes.

Jury trials: Either party may demand jury trial.

Notes: An alternative procedure exists for claims of $1,500 or less in Cook County Pro Se Court. Plaintiffs represent themselves, and lawyers are allowed for defendants. See www.cookcountyclerkofcourt.org/includes/pages/community _resources/pro_se_faqs.asp.

Indiana

Court: Small Claims Docket (circuit court, superior court, and county court); Marion County Small Claims Court.

Statutes: Ind. Code Ann. §§ 33-28-3-2 to 33-28-3-10 (circuit court); 33-29-2-1 to 33-29-2-10 (superior court); 33-30-5-1 to 33-30-5-10 (county court); 33-34-3-1 to 33-34-3-15 (Marion County Small Claims Court).

Court information: www.in.gov/judiciary/2710.htm.

Dollar limit: $6,000 ($8,000 in Marion County).

Where to sue: County in which any defendant resides or is employed, where transaction or occurrence took place, or where obligation arose or was to be performed by defendant. For landlord-tenant disputes, in county or town where property is located.

Service of process: Sheriff; or registered or certified mail, sent by court clerk. Marion County: Personal service or registered or certified mail.

Defendant's response: No formal written answer required.

Transfer: No.

Attorneys: Allowed.

Appeals: Within 30 days. Marion County: All appeals taken to the circuit court or superior court of the county and tried as a new trial.

Evictions: Yes, if total rent due does not exceed $6,000 ($8,000 in Marion County).

Jury trials: Defendant may request jury trial within ten days following service of complaint upon submitting an affidavit stating questions of fact that require

a jury trial. Once requested, transferred from small claims to formal court. Marion County: Defendant must file a jury duty request at least three calendar days before the trial date that appears on the complaint. Once filed, transferred from small claims to superior court.

Iowa

Court: Small Claims Docket (district court).

Statutes: Iowa Code §§ 631.1 to 631.17.

Court information: www.iowacourts.gov/Court_Rules_Forms/Small_Claims_Forms.

Dollar limit: $5,000.

Where to sue: County in which any defendant resides or if resident is out of state, where resident can be found, where transaction or injury occurred, or obligation was to be performed.

Service of process: Peace officer or disinterested adult; or certified mail, restricted delivery, return receipt requested, sent by court clerk. For eviction cases, must be served personally.

Defendant's response: The defendant must appear within 20 days after service is made to avoid default.

Transfer: At judge's discretion if defendant counterclaims over the dollar limit.

Attorneys: Allowed.

Appeals: Allowed by either party upon oral notice at end of hearing or by written notice within 20 days of judgment. Heard in district court; no new evidence on appeal.

Evictions: Yes.

Jury Trials: Not allowed.

Kansas

Court: Small Claims (district court).

Statutes: Kan. Stat. Ann. §§ 61-2701 to 61-2714.

Court information: www.kscourts.org/rules-procedures-forms/small-claims-information.

Dollar limit: $4,000.

Where to sue: County in which defendant lives, or county where plaintiff resides if defendant is served there, or defendant's place of business or employment, or county where the cause of action arose only if defendant was a resident of that county at the time the cause of action arose.

Service of process: Sheriff or party (party must notify clerk), or by return receipt delivery (including certified mail, priority mail, commercial courier service, etc.).

Defendant's response: No formal written answer required.

Transfer: If the defendant counterclaims over $4,000 but still within dollar limit of the regular district court, judge may either decide claim or allow defendant to bring claim in court of competent jurisdiction. The court is allowed to hear it or not; court has to allow defendant to file in the proper court or have court hear case up to small claims limit and sue in proper court for remaining amount.

Attorneys: Generally not allowed, but if one party has attorney, all other parties are entitled to attorney.

Appeals: Allowed by either party within 14 days. Heard in district court as new trial.

Evictions: No.

Jury trials: Not allowed.

Kentucky

Court: Small Claims Division (district court).

Statutes: Ky. Rev. Stat. Ann. §§ 24A.200 to 24A.360.

Court information: https://courts.ky.gov/courts/jefferson/smallclaims/Pages/default.aspx or https://courts.ky.gov/resources/publicationsresources/Publications/P6SmallClaimsHandbookweb.pdf.

Dollar limit: $2,500.

Where to sue: Judicial district in which defendant resides or does business, or if corporation, county of corporate headquarters.

Service of process: Certified or registered mail by court clerk first; if that fails, then by sheriff or constable.

Defendant's response: Must appear for hearing (20 to 40 days from service of process). Must file counterclaim within five days of hearing.

Transfer: Allowed to regular district court or circuit court if defendant's counterclaim is over $2,500, if defendant demands jury trial, or if judge decides the case is too complex for small claims division.

Attorneys: Allowed.

Appeals: Allowed by either party within ten days. Heard in circuit court.

Evictions: Yes.

Jury trials: Only if defendant makes a written request at least seven days before hearing date. Case is then transferred to regular district court.

Notes: Professional moneylenders and collection agents cannot sue in small claims court.

Louisiana

Court: Rural: Justice of the Peace; Urban: Small Claims Division (city court).

Statutes: La. Rev. Stat. Ann. §§ 13:5200 to 13:5211 (city court); La. Code Civ. Proc. Art. 4831, 4832, 4845, 4901 to 4925, and Art. 42 (Justice of the Peace Court).

Court information: lasc.libguides.com/c.php?g=463399&p=3167530brgov.com/dept/citycourt/civilfaqs.htm (Baton Rouge).

Dollar limit: $5,000 (city court); $5,000 (Justice of the Peace, but no limit in eviction cases).

Where to sue: Parish in which defendant resides. Corporation or partnership, in parish or district in which business establishment located.

Service of process: Certified mail with return receipt requested; or sheriff, marshal, or constable, if certified mail is unclaimed or refused.

Defendant's response: Must file written answer within ten days of service (15 days if served by secretary of state) to avoid default.

Transfer: Small claims may be transferred to regular city court if defendant files written request within ten days of service of process, or if counterclaim ("reconventional demand") is over dollar limit. In Justice of the Peace Court, if demand in amended or supplemental pleading ("incidental demand") exceeds jurisdictional amount, case will be transferred to court of appropriate jurisdiction.

Attorneys: Allowed.

Appeals: In Justice of the Peace Court, allowed by either party within 15 days; heard in parish court, or if there is no parish court, district court, as new trial. No appeal from small claims division of city court.

Evictions: Available in Justice of the Peace courts only.

Jury trials: Not allowed.

Maine

Court: Small Claims Proceeding (district court).

Statutes: Me. Rev. Stat. Ann. tit. 14, §§ 7481 to 7487.

Court rules: Maine Rules of Small Claims Procedure, Rules 1 to 18.

Court information: www.courts.maine.gov/maine_courts/small_claims/index.shtml.

Dollar limit: $6,000.

Where to sue: District court division in which defendant resides or has place of business, where the transaction occurred, or where registered agent resides if corporation.

Service of process: By first-class mail with two acknowledgment forms and prepaid envelope for the defendant; if acknowledgment not returned within 20 days, by registered or certified mail or personal service. Can arrange for court clerk to serve.

Defendant's response: No formal written answer required.

Transfer: No provision.

Attorneys: Allowed.

Appeals: Allowed by either party within 30 days. Heard in superior court. Plaintiff's appeal on questions of law only; defendant may request a new trial.

Evictions: No.

Jury trials: No provision.

Maryland

Court: Small Claims Court (district court).

Statutes: Md. Code Ann. [Cts. & Jud. Proc.] §§ 4-405; 6-403.

Court rules: Maryland Court Rules, Rules 3-701, 7-104, 7-112.

Court information: www.courts.state.md.us/legalhelp/smallclaims.html.

Where to sue: County in which any defendant resides, is employed, or does business; if multiple defendants from different counties, where injury to person or property occurred. Corporation may also be sued where it maintains principal office.

Service of process: Sheriff, constable, or disinterested adult, personally or by certified mail.

Defendant's response: Defendant has 15 days from receipt of summons to file "Notice of Intention to Defend" in order to avoid default (out-of-state defendant has 60 days).

Transfer: To regular civil docket if counterclaim exceeds $5,000 or if defendant demands jury trial.

Attorneys: Allowed.

Appeals: Allowed by either party within 30 days. Heard in circuit court as a new trial.

Evictions: Yes, as long as the rent claimed does not exceed $5,000.

Jury trials: Allowed if demand is filed; transferred to regular civil docket.

Massachusetts

Court: Small Claims Division, Boston Municipal Court; elsewhere, Small Claims Section (district court).

Statutes: Mass. Gen. Laws ch. 218, §§ 21 to 25; ch. 223, § 6; ch. 93A, § 9 (consumer complaints).

Court rules: Massachusetts Rules of Court, Uniform Small Claims Rules, Rules 1 to 10; Small Claims Standards, 1:00 to 9:05.

Court information: www.mass.gov/ago/consumer-resources/consumer-assistance/small-claims-court.html.

Dollar limit: $7,000; no limit for property damage caused by motor vehicle.

Where to sue: Judicial district in which plaintiff or defendant resides, is employed, or does business. Actions against landlords can also be brought in district in which property is located.

Service of process: First-class mail sent by court clerk for in-state defendants. For out-of-state defendants, sheriff or registered or certified mail.

Defendant's response: Written answer is optional, not required.

Transfer: Allowed to regular civil docket only at court's discretion.

Attorneys: Allowed.

Appeals: Allowed by defendant within ten days. Heard in superior court as new trial; jury allowed on appeal.

Evictions: No.

Jury trials: Not allowed except on appeal.

Notes: Consumer complaint small claims: (1) plaintiff must make written demand for relief at least 30 days before filing suit; (2) attorneys' fees available; (3) triple damages available.

Michigan

Court: Small Claims Division (district court).

Statutes: Mich. Comp. Laws §§ 600.8401 to 600.8427.

Court information: courts.mi.gov/administration/scao/forms/pages/small-claims.aspx or www.michiganlegalaid.org/library_client/resource.2006-03-07.5270199575.

Dollar limit: $5,000.

Where to sue: County where defendant resides or is employed, or where transaction or injury occurred.

Service of process: Court clerk shall serve defendant; otherwise, by certified mail, return receipt requested, or personal service.

Defendant's response: No formal written answer required.

Transfer: Either party may transfer to regular district court. If defendant's counterclaim is over $5,000 or if defendant wants attorney, case will be transferred.

Attorneys: Not allowed.

Appeals: Not allowed. Exception: If action is heard by district court magistrate, parties can appeal to small claims division for new trial within seven days.

Evictions: No.

Jury trials: Not allowed.

Minnesota

Court: Conciliation Court (district court).

Statutes: Minn. Stat. Ann. §§ 491A.01 to 491A.03.

Court rules: Minnesota General Practice Rules, Rules 501 to 525.

Court information: www.mncourts.gov/Help-Topics/Conciliation-Court.aspx.

Dollar limit: $15,000 ($4,000 for claims involving consumer credit transactions, $15,000 for claims involving money or personal property subject to criminal forfeiture).

Where to sue: County in which any defendant resides. Corporation, any county in which it has registered agent, place of business, or office; in certain circumstances, county in which plaintiff resides. Landlord-tenant disputes (other than evictions), county where rental property is located.

Service of process: First-class mail by court administrator; or by electronic means if party has agreed to or is required to accept electronic service. If claim is over $2,500, certified mail by plaintiff. If defendant is out-of-state, plaintiff must arrange service.

Defendant's response: No formal written answer required. Must file counterclaim within five days of the trial date. If defendant counterclaims over jurisdictional limit and files in another court, clerk will strike small claims case from calendar; plaintiff who is not served with counterclaim may reinstate small claims action after 30 days.

Transfer: To county court on demand for a jury trial or defendant's counterclaim above jurisdictional limit.

Attorneys: Allowed.

Appeals: Filed within 20 days. Heard in district court as new trial; jury trial permitted upon appeal.

Evictions: No.

Jury trials: Not allowed except on appeal to district court.

Notes: Educational institutions may bring actions to recover student loans, if loans were originally awarded in the county in which it has administrative offices, even though the defendant is not county resident.

Mississippi

Court: Justice Court.

Statutes: Miss. Code Ann. §§ 9-11-9 to 9-11-33; 11-9-101 to 11-9-147; 11-25-1; 11-51-85.

Court information: http://courts.ms.gov/trialcourts/justicecourt/justicecourt.html.

Dollar limit: $3,500.

Where to sue: County in which any defendant resides or where transaction or injury occurred; if nonresident, where transaction or injury occurred. Corporation, where registered office is located.

Service of process: Sheriff, constable, or disinterested adult (only in emergency with court's permission).

Defendant's response: No formal written answer required.

Transfer: No provision.

Attorneys: Allowed.

Appeals: Allowed by either party within ten days.

Evictions: Yes.

Jury trials: Either party may demand jury trial.

Missouri

Court: Small Claims Division (circuit court).

Statutes: Mo. Rev. Stat. §§ 482.300 to 482.365.

Court rules: Missouri Supreme Court Rules of the Small Claims Division of Circuit Court, Rules 140.01 to 152.

Court information: www.courts.mo.gov/page.jsp?id=704.

Dollar limit: $5,000.

Where to sue: County in which at least one defendant resides, or in which one plaintiff resides and at least one defendant may be found, or where transaction or injury occurred.

Service of process: Certified mail, return receipt requested. May be served personally by court if plaintiff requests.

Defendant's response: No formal written answer required. Must file counterclaim in person within ten days after service of process and any time before hearing.

Transfer: Allowed to regular circuit court if defendant counterclaims over $5,000, unless all parties agree to stay in small claims court. (Parties must be informed of right to consult attorney before giving consent.)

Attorneys: Allowed.

Appeals: Allowed by either party within ten days, for new trial in circuit court.

Evictions: No.

Jury trials: Not allowed.

Montana

Court: Small Claims Court (district court); Small Claims Division (justice court).

Statutes: Mont. Code Ann. §§ 25-2-118; 3-12-101 to 3-12-107 (district court); 25-33-101 to 25-33-306 (appeals); 25-35-501 to 25-35-807; 3-10-1001 to 3-10-1004 (justice court).

Court information: https://dojmt.gov/consumer/guide-to-small-claims-court.

Dollar limit: $7,000.

Where to sue: County or judicial district in which any defendant resides; if defendant does not live in state, where transaction or injury occurred.

Service of process: Sheriff or constable; other process server (justice court only).

Defendant's response: No formal written answer required. Defendant must serve counterclaim on plaintiff at least 72 hours before hearing. Counterclaims can't exceed $6,500 or if the court finds against plaintiff, defendant can pursue excess in justice or district court.

Transfer: Allowed by defendant to regular justice court if request filed within ten days of receipt of complaint.

Attorneys: Not allowed, unless all parties have attorneys.

Appeals: Allowed by either party within ten days. Heard in district court on law, not facts.

Evictions: No.

Jury trials: Not allowed. Defendant may request transfer to regular justice court for jury trial.

Nebraska

Court: Small Claims Court (county court).

Statutes: Neb. Rev. Stat. §§ 25-505.1; 25-2801 to 25-2807; 25-2734 (appeals).

Court information: https://supremecourt.nebraska.gov/self-help/small-claims/filing-small-claims-case-nebraska.

Dollar limit: $3,600 from July 1, 2015, through June 30, 2020 (adjusted every five years based on the Consumer Price Index).

Where to sue: County in which any defendant resides or works, or where injury or property damage occurred. Corporation, wherever it regularly conducts business.

Service of process: Personal service by disinterested adult, certified mail, or designated delivery service; return receipt requested.

Defendant's response: Written answer not required, unless the case is transferred to the regular docket. Counterclaim: must file and deliver to plaintiff at least two days prior to trial.

Transfer: Transferable to regular civil court on defendant's request at least two days prior to the hearing or counterclaim over $3,500. Defendant must file an answer when the case is transferred.

Attorneys: Not allowed.

Appeals: Allowed by either party within 30 days. Heard in district court as new trial; jury trial not permitted.

Evictions: No.

Jury trials: Not allowed in small claims court. Defendant may request transfer to regular docket of county court by giving notice at least two days before hearing. Defendant must file an answer when the case is transferred, and demand for a jury trial must be made on or before the date the answer is filed with the court.

Nevada

Court: Small Claims Action (justice court).

Statutes: Nev. Rev. Stat. Ann. §§ 73.010 to 73.060.

Court rules: Nevada Justice Court Rules of Civil Procedure, Rules 88 to 100.

Court information: www.lasvegasjusticecourt.us/divisions/small_claims/index.php (Las Vegas), www.washoecounty.us/rjc/divisions/civil/small-claims-civil.php (Reno).

Dollar limit: $10,000.

Where to sue: Township in which defendant resides, does business, or is employed.

Service of process: Court determines method. Either registered or certified mail, return receipt requested; or personal service by sheriff, constable, disinterested adult, or other person approved by court.

Defendant's response: No formal written answer required.

Transfer: No provision.

Attorneys: Allowed.

Appeals: Allowed by either party within five days.

Evictions: No.

Jury trials: No provision.

New Hampshire

Court: Small Claims Actions (district or municipal court).

Statutes: N.H. Rev. Stat. Ann. §§ 503:1 to 503:11.

Court rules: New Hampshire District Court Rules, Rules 4.1 to 4.28.

Court information: www.courts.state.nh.us/district/eclaims.

Dollar limit: $7,500.

Where to sue: Municipal court of town in which defendant or plaintiff resides; if no municipal court, in the district court in district in which either party resides. If defendant is not a state resident, where defendant does business or owns property, or transaction or injury occurred.

Service of process: First class mail sent by court; if returned as undelivered, plaintiff must complete service according to court clerk's instructions.

Defendant's response: Must respond to claim in writing within 30 days of return date given on summons to avoid default.

Transfer: To superior court if defendant requests a jury trial (claim must be more than $1,500).

Attorneys: Allowed.

Appeals: Allowed by either party within 30 days.

Evictions: No.

Jury trials: Not allowed, must transfer to superior court. Defendant must file request for jury trial within five days of plaintiff's claim; only permitted for claims over $1,500.

New Jersey

Court: Small Claims Section (Superior Court, Special Civil Part).

Statutes: NJR LAW DIV CIV PT RULE 6:1-2.

Court rules: New Jersey Rules of Court, Rules 6:1 to 6:12-2; Rule 2:4-1.

Court information: www.judiciary.state.nj.us/courts/scco.html.

Dollar limit: $3,000 ($5,000 for claims relating to security deposits); certain landlord-tenant suits cannot be brought.

Where to sue: County in which any defendant resides or, if defendants do not reside in New Jersey, county where transaction or injury occurred. For security deposit claims, county where property is located. Corporation, wherever it does business.

Service of process: Certified and regular mail by the court; if service not made, court officer or other adult approved by the court.

Defendant's response: No written answer required. Defendant must file counterclaim within 35 days of service of the complaint.

Transfer: Allowed to special civil part if recovery or counterclaim will exceed the monetary limit, or if defendant demands jury trial.

Attorneys: Allowed.

Appeals: Allowed by either party within 45 days. Heard in appellate division of superior court.

Evictions: No.

Jury trials: Defendant must submit demand at least five days before return of summons (case is then transferred to special civil part).

Notes: The Special Civil Part, like the small claims court but with more procedures, has a limit of $15,000. See www.judiciary.state.nj.us.

New Mexico

Court: Metropolitan Court (Bernalillo County); Magistrate Court.

Statutes: N.M. Stat. Ann. §§ 34-8A-1 to 34-8A-10 (metropolitan court); 35-3-3, 35-3-5, 35-8-1, and 35-8-2 (magistrate court); 35-11-2, 35-13-1 to 35-13-3 (appeals).

Court rules: New Mexico Rules of Civil Procedure for the Magistrate Courts, Rules 2-101 to 2-804; New Mexico Rules of Civil Procedure for the Metropolitan Court, Rules 3-101 to 3-804.

Court information: www.nmcourts.gov/Self-Help/self-help-guide.aspx.

Dollar limit: $10,000.

Where to sue: County in which defendant resides or may be found, or where transaction or injury occurred.

Service of process: Personal service or service by mail to defendant's attorney or if unrepresented, to defendant.

Defendant's response: Must file answer on or before appearance date in summons.

Transfer: No provision.

Attorneys: Allowed.

Appeals: Allowed by either party within 15 days; heard in district court as new trial.

Evictions: Yes.

Jury trials: Allowed at either party's request. Plaintiff must make jury trial request in the complaint, and defendant must make request in the answer.

New York

Court: Small Claims Part (civil court, cities—including New York City; district court, Nassau and Suffolk counties; justice court, rural areas). Commercial Small Claims (city courts and district courts).

Statutes: N.Y. Uniform City Ct. Act §§ 1801 to 1815, 1801-A to 1814-A (commercial claims); N.Y. Uniform Dist. Ct. Act §§ 1801 to 1815, 1801-A to 1814-A (commercial claims); N.Y. Uniform Just. Ct. Act §§ 1801 to 1815; N.Y. City Civ. Ct. Act §§ 1801 to 1815; 1801-A to 1814-A (commercial claims).

Court rules: N.Y. Uniform Trial Court Rules, Rules 208.41, 208.41-A, 210.41, 210.41-A, 212.41, 212.41-A, 214.10.

Court information: www.courts.state.ny.us/courthelp/smallClaims/index.shtml.

Dollar limit: $5,000 (town and village justice courts, $3,000).

Where to sue: Political subdivision in which defendant resides, is employed, or has business office.

Service of process: Certified mail, return receipt requested, or ordinary first-class mail by court clerk. If after 21 days not returned as undeliverable, then notice is presumed.

Defendant's response: No written answer required. Defendant to file counterclaim within five days of receiving plaintiff's claim. If counterclaim in excess of $5,000, cannot be brought in small claims court.

Transfer: Allowed by court's discretion.

Attorneys: Allowed.

Appeals: Allowed only on the ground that "substantial justice" was not done. Must file appeal within 30 days if received judgment in court or by personal delivery, or within 35 days of the mailing date if mailed by the court clerk. Heard in county court or appellate division of supreme court (for New York City) on law, not facts. There is no appeal from arbitrator's decision.

Evictions: No.

Jury trials: Defendant may request jury trial at least one day prior to hearing. Must file affidavit stating issues that require jury trial.

Notes: Corporations and partnerships cannot sue in small claims court, but may appear as defendants. (Does not apply to municipal and public benefit corporations and school districts.) Instead, they can bring commercial claims, which have similar rules to small claims courts but are subject to these additional restrictions: (1) Same limits and procedures as regular small claims except claim is brought by corporation, partnership, or association. (2) Business must have principal office in New York state. (3) Defendant must reside, be employed, or have a business office in the county where suit is brought.

North Carolina

Court: Small Claims Court (district court).

Statutes: N.C. Gen. Stat. §§ 7A-210 to 7A-232; 42-29.

Court information: www.nccourts.org/Courts/Trial/SClaims.

Dollar limit: $10,000.

Where to sue: County in which defendant resides. Corporation, where it maintains place of business.

Service of process: Personal service, registered or certified mail, signature confirmation, or designated delivery service. (Alternate method is permitted in eviction cases; see N.C. Gen. Stat. § 42-29.)

Defendant's response: Defendant has option to file written answer any time before trial; no particular form required. If answer is not filed, general denial of all claims is assumed. Counterclaims over $10,000 not allowed.

Transfer: No provision; but defendant can bring separate action in proper court.

Attorneys: Allowed.

Appeals: Allowed by either party within ten days. Heard in district court as new trial; jury trial allowed if request made within ten days of appeal notice.

Evictions: Yes.

Jury trials: Not allowed in small claims court. If case is not assigned to a magistrate, it is treated as a regular civil case. Plaintiff may request jury trial within five days of receiving notice of nonassignment, and defendant may make request either before or at the same time as filing an answer.

North Dakota

Court: Small Claims Court (district court).

Statutes: N.D. Cent. Code §§ 27-08.1-01 to 27-08.1-08.

Court information: www.ndcourts.gov/ndlshc/SmallClaims/SmallClaims.aspx.

Dollar limit: $15,000.

Where to sue: County where defendant resides. For bad checks or less than $1,000 owed on credit: county where defendant resides, has place of business, or where act or transaction occurred. For claims related to defendant's lease of property or dispute over earnest or money deposit related to a contract to purchase property, where defendant resides or property is located unless parties consent in writing to a different county. Corporations, LLCs, or partnerships, where place of business is located or where the subject of the claim arose.

Service of process: Disinterested adult or; certified mail.

Defendant's response: Defendant must return form requesting hearing within 20 days of service. Defendant must file and serve counterclaim at least 48 hours before hearing.

Transfer: Defendant may transfer case to regular civil court procedure if request is made within 20 days of service.

Attorneys: Allowed.

Appeals: Not allowed.

Evictions: No.

Jury trials: Not allowed.

Notes: Plaintiff may not discontinue once small claims process is begun; if plaintiff seeks to discontinue, claim will be dismissed with prejudice (plaintiff cannot refile claim).

Ohio

Court: Small Claims Division (municipal and county courts).

Statutes: Ohio Rev. Code Ann. §§ 1925.01 to 1925.18.

Court rules: Ohio Rules of Civil Procedure, Rules 3 and 4.1; Ohio Rules of Appellate Procedure, Rule 4.

Court information: www.supremecourt.ohio.gov/jcs/interpretersvcs/forms/ english/5.pdf or www.ohiolegalservices.org/public/legal_problem/courts-hearings /representing-yourself-in-court/small-claims/qandact_view.

Dollar limit: $3,000.

Where to sue: County in which defendant resides or has place of business, or where obligation arose.

Service of process: Sheriff; or certified mail by clerk, return receipt requested.

Defendant's response: No written answer required. Must file and serve counterclaim at least seven days before trial date.

Transfer: To regular civil court upon defendant's counterclaim over $3,000 or court's motion. Defendant (or plaintiff if counterclaim is made) may request transfer, but must file affidavit stating grounds of defense.

Attorneys: Allowed.

Appeals: Must be filed within 30 days. Heard in court of appeals.

Evictions: No.

Jury trials: Not allowed.

Oklahoma

Court: Small Claims Procedure (district court).

Statutes: Okla. Stat. Ann. tit. 12, §§ 131 to 141; 1751 to 1773.

Court information: www.oklahomacounty.org/158/Small-Claims.

Dollar limit: $7,500.

Where to sue: County in which defendant resides, or if defendant is nonresident, where defendant can be found. In automobile or boat accident cases, where one or more party resides or where accident occurred. For open account or collection on a note cases, can also sue where contract was entered into. Corporations, in a county in which it has principal office or place of business or where transaction or injury occurred.

Service of process: Certified mail by clerk, return receipt requested. Plaintiff may request personal service by sheriff or other disinterested adult.

Defendant's response: No formal written answer required. Defendant must file counterclaim at least 72 hours before appearance date.

Transfer: Allowed with court approval.

Attorneys: Allowed.

Appeals: Allowed by either party within 30 days. Heard by Oklahoma Supreme Court on law only, not facts.

Evictions: Yes.

Jury trials: Not allowed unless claim or counterclaim is more than $1,500. Then either party may demand jury trial at least two working days before time set for defendant's appearance.

Notes: Collection agencies may not sue in small claims court.

Oregon

Court: Small Claims Department (circuit or justice court).

Statutes: Or. Rev. Stat. §§ 46.405 to 46.570; 55.011 to 55.140.

Court information: www.osbar.org/public/legalinfo/1061_SmallClaims.htm.

Dollar limit: $10,000.

Where to sue: County where defendant resides or can be found, where injury or damage occurred, or where contract or obligation was to be performed.

Service of process: Certified mail, or sheriff or court-approved adult. (In justice court, if claim is over $50, must use personal service.)

Defendant's response: Defendant must answer within 14 days of service to avoid default, and must request hearing. If counterclaim is over $10,000, must file motion to transfer to regular circuit court or counterclaim will be ignored. Plaintiff must reply to defendant's counterclaim within 20 days of service.

Transfer: To regular docket or other appropriate court if counterclaim is more than $10,000 and defendant requests transfer; or if defendant demands jury trial and counterclaim is for more than $750.

Attorneys: Not allowed without judge's consent.

Appeals: From circuit court, no appeal. From justice court, allowed by defendant (or plaintiff, on counterclaim) within ten days. Heard in circuit court.

Evictions: No.

Jury trials: If claim is over $750, defendant may request jury trial. Request must be made at same time as answer, within 14 days of service. Case is then transferred to appropriate court.

Pennsylvania

Court: District Justice Court; Philadelphia Municipal Court.

Statutes: 42 Pa. Cons. Stat. Ann. §§ 1123, 1515.

Court rules: Pennsylvania Rules of Civil Procedure, Rules 400 to 405, 1002, 1006, 2179; Pennsylvania Rules of Civil Procedure Governing Actions and Proceedings Before Magisterial District Judges, Rules 201 to 324; Philadelphia Municipal Court Rules of Civil Practice, Rules 101 to 144.

Court information: www.courts.phila.gov/municipal/civil (Philadelphia), or www.pabar.org/clips/bringingsuitbeforeDJ.pdf.

Dollar limit: $12,000.

Where to sue: Individual, wherever defendant can be served, where cause of action arose or act or transaction occurred, or in any other county authorized by law. Corporation or partnership, where it regularly conducts business or has principal place of business or where cause of action arose or act or transaction occurred.

Service of process: Sheriff, or first-class mail, with returned acknowledgment from defendant.

Defendant's response: Defendant must file counterclaim at least five days before hearing (district justice court); at least ten days before trial (Philadelphia Municipal Court), but defendant's counterclaim can't exceed court's dollar limit.

Transfer: If defendant's counterclaim is over $10,000, defendant must bring suit in court of common pleas within 30 days or anything over $10,000 is considered waived and case will proceed as small claim (Philadelphia Municipal Court). There is no provision for transfer from district justice court.

Attorneys: Allowed.

Appeals: Allowed by either party within 30 days (ten days in eviction cases). Heard in court of common pleas as a new trial.

Evictions: Yes.

Jury trials: Either party can request jury trial and case will be transferred (district justice court). Not allowed except on appeal (Philadelphia Municipal Court).

Notes: If claiming more than $2,000 personal injury or property damage, must submit statement of claim signed under oath (Philadelphia Municipal Court).

Rhode Island

Court: Small Claims Court (district court).

Statutes: R.I. Gen. Laws §§ 10-16-1 to 10-16-16; 9-4-3; 9-4-4; 9-12-10 (appeals).

Court rules: Rhode Island District Court Rules of Small Claims Procedure, Rules 1.00 to 7.01; Rhode Island District Court Rules of Civil Procedure, Rule 73.

Court information: www.courts.ri.gov/Courts/districtcourt/Pages/Small%20 Claims%20Court.aspx.

Dollar limit: $2,500.

Where to sue: District where either party resides or where defendant can be found; if plaintiff is corporation, where defendant resides or can be found.

Service of process: If plaintiff is represented by an attorney, attorney shall serve by registered or certified mail. Otherwise, court clerk shall serve by mail. If defendant does not claim notice, plaintiff must serve with process server. Defendant's refusal of certified mail is still valid service.

Defendant's response: Defendant must file written answer, defense, or counterclaim either before or on date set for answering.

Transfer: If defendant's counterclaim is for over $2,500 and judge finds for defendant, defendant can still file claim in district court. Alternatively, judge can dismiss both claims to be refiled in district court.

Attorneys: Allowed; required for all corporations other than close corporations with assets under $1 million.

Appeals: Defendant has right to appeal on plaintiff's claim (plaintiff has right to appeal on defendant's counterclaim). Must file within two days. Heard in superior court as new trial. Exception: In consumer plaintiff claim, if manufacturer or seller defendant loses by default, no appeal is allowed.

Evictions: No.

Jury trials: No provision.

South Carolina

Court: Magistrates Court.

Statutes: S.C. Code Ann. §§ 22-3-10 to 22-3-320; 15-7-30; 18-7-10 to 18-7-30.

Court rules: South Carolina Administrative and Procedural Rules for Magistrates Court, Rules 1 to 19.

Court information: www.sccourts.org/selfhelp/FAQMagistrate.pdf.

Dollar limit: $7,500.

Where to sue: County where at least one defendant resides or where the most substantial part of the cause of action arose. Against a domestic corporation, county where it has principal place of business.

Service of process: Sheriff, the sheriff's deputy, a magistrate's constable, or other disinterested adult; commercial delivery service; personal service or certified mail, return receipt requested and delivery restricted to the addressee.

Defendant's response: May answer in writing or orally and file counterclaims within 30 days or time period stated in summons.

Transfer: Counterclaims over $7,500 will be transferred to the circuit court of the county, unless the defendant waives the excess of the counterclaim over the $7,500.

Attorneys: Allowed.

Appeals: Must be filed within 30 days. Heard in county or circuit court on law, not facts.

Evictions: Yes.

Jury trials: Either party may request jury trial in writing at least five days before trial date.

South Dakota

Court: Small Claims Procedure (Circuit or Magistrates Court).

Statutes: S.D. Codified Laws Ann. §§ 15-39-45 to 15-39-78; 16-12B-6; 16-12B-12; 16-12B-16; 16-12C-8; 16-12C-13 to 16-12C-15.

Court information: ujs.sd.gov/Small_Claims.

Dollar limit: $12,000.

Where to sue: County in which any defendant resides, or where transaction or injury occurred. Corporation, partnership, or LLC, any county where defendant has place of business.

Service of process: Certified or registered mail first, return receipt requested (service is binding on defendant who refuses to accept and sign for the letter).

If undeliverable, then service must be made by another method, determined by court. If plaintiff elects not to pursue further notification of the defendant or if the further notification is unsuccessful after 90 days, the clerk may dismiss the action without prejudice.

Defendant's response: No formal written answer required.

Transfer: Allowed at judge's discretion on defendant's petition for regular civil or jury trial. (Plaintiff may request transfer in response to counterclaim.) Must make petition at least five days before appearance date and provide affidavit giving reasons that justify transfer. Appeals are allowed by both plaintiff and defendant if case transferred.

Attorneys: Allowed.

Appeals: Not allowed. However, a party can file a "Motion to Vacate Judgment" asking the court to set aside the judgment based on certain reasons such as error or reasons for missing a court appearance.

Evictions: No.

Jury trials: Not allowed. Defendant must apply for transfer to circuit court five days before trial date.

Tennessee

Court: Court of General Sessions.

Statutes: Tenn. Code Ann. §§ 16-15-501 to 16-15-505; 16-15-710 to 16-15-735; 16-15-901 to 16-15-905; 20-4-101; 20-4-103.

Court rules: Tennessee Rules of Civil Procedure, Rule 38.03.

Court information: tncourts.gov/programs/self-help-center.

Dollar limit: $25,000. No limit in eviction suits or suits to recover personal property.

Where to sue: County where defendant resides or where the cause of action arose. In certain cases involving property, county where the real property, or any portion of it, or where any part of the personal property is located.

Service of process: Disinterested adult, plaintiff's attorney, or certified mail, with return receipt.

Defendant's response: No formal written answer required.

Transfer: Defendant may request transfer to circuit court at least three days before hearing (must provide affidavit that defense is either substantial, complex, or expensive enough to require transfer).

Attorneys: Allowed.

Appeals: Allowed by either party. Heard in circuit court as new trial. May demand jury trial within ten days after appeal filed.

Evictions: Yes.

Jury trials: Not allowed except on appeal or transfer.

Notes: Tennessee has no actual small claims system, but trials in general sessions court are normally conducted with informal rules.

Texas

Court: Justice Court.

Statutes: Tex. Gov't. Code Ann. § 27.060.

Court rules: Texas Rules of Civil Procedure, Rules 500 to 507.

Court information: www.texasattorneygeneral.gov/cpd/filing-in-small-claims-court.

Dollar limit: $10,000.

Where to sue: County and precinct in which defendant resides; or county where obligation was to be performed, incidents giving rise to the claim occurred, or property at issue is located. If the defendant is a nonresident of Texas, or if defendant's residence is unknown, file the suit in the county and precinct where the plaintiff resides.

Service of process: Sheriff, constable, process server, or (with court approval) disinterested adult. Certified mail by court clerk, upon request by plaintiff. Service by publication in a newspaper if the defendant can't be found.

Defendant's response: Defendant must file a written answer with the court and serve a copy on the plaintiff. If the defendant was not served by publication, the answer is due by the end of the 14th day after the day the defendant was served with the citation. If the defendant was served by publication, the answer is due by the end of the 42nd day after the citation was issued. In either case, there are exceptions for weekends, holidays, and days the court is closed before 5:00 p.m.

Transfer: Transfer allowed to another precinct in same county upon written motion of defendant based on improper venue, by either party with affidavits of two credible people that the party can't get a fair and impartial trial in the precinct or in front of a specific judge, or by consent of both parties.

Attorneys: Allowed.

Appeals: Allowed by either party within 21 days. Heard in county court as new trial.

Evictions: Separate small claims courts have been abolished as of August 2013; both small claims cases and evictions are heard in Justice Court. Evictions cases are governed by Rules 500–507 and 510 of Part V of the Rules of Civil Procedure.

Jury trials: Either party may demand jury trial by filing a request no later than 14 days before the trial date.

Notes: No professional moneylenders or collection agents may sue in small claims court.

Utah

Court: Small Claims Department (district court).

Statutes: Utah Code Ann. §§ 78A-8-101 to 78A-8-109.

Court rules: Utah Rules of Small Claims Procedure, Rules 1 to 12, A to K.

Court information: www.utcourts.gov/howto/smallclaims.

Dollar limit: $11,000.

Where to sue: County in which defendant resides or debt was incurred.

Service of process: Sheriff, constable, marshal, or their deputy; a person over 18 years old who is not a party or a party's attorney; courier service or mail, return receipt requested.

Defendant's response: No answer required. Must file counterclaim at least 15 days before trial.

Transfer: No provision.

Attorneys: Allowed.

Appeals: Either party may appeal within 28 business days of entry of judgment. Heard in district court as new trial.

Evictions: No.

Jury trials: No provision.

Vermont

Court: Small Claims Procedure (superior court).

Statutes: Vt. Stat. Ann. tit. 12, §§ 5531 to 5541; 402.

Court rules: Vermont Rules of Small Claims Procedure, Rules 1 to 14.

Court information: www.vermontjudiciary.org/SRL/smallclaims/default.aspx.

Dollar limit: $5,000.

Where to sue: County in which either party resides.

Service of process: Court will serve by first-class mail; if defendant does not return form acknowledging receipt, plaintiff must arrange service by sheriff or another person authorized to serve process.

Defendant's response: Answer required within 30 days of mailing date by plaintiff or receipt of service. Answer may include any related counterclaim but judgement can't exceed small claims limits.

Transfer: A claim or counterclaim cannot be transferred.

Attorneys: Allowed.

Appeals: Allowed by either party within 30 days. Heard in superior court on law, not facts.

Evictions: No.

Jury trials: Defendant may request jury trial at least one day prior to appearance.

Virginia

Court: Small Claims Division (district court).

Statutes: Va. Code Ann. §§ 8.01-262; 16.1-76; 16.1-77; 16.1-106; 16.1-113; 16.1-122.1 to 16.1-122.7.

Court information: www.courts.state.va.us/resources/small_claims_court_procedures.pdf or www.courts.state.va.us/courts/gd/home.html.

Dollar limit: $5,000.

Where to sue: District in which defendant resides, is employed, or regularly conducts business; where transaction or injury occurred; or where property is located. For a nonindividual defendant, where its principal office or principal place of business is located, or where the defendant has a registered office or agent for service.

Service of process: Court shall serve defendant.

Defendant's response: No formal written answer required. May file counterclaim any time before trial, counterclaim cannot exceed $5,000.

Transfer: To circuit court if defendant wants attorney representation.

Attorneys: Not allowed in small claims division; if defendant wants attorney representation, can request transfer.

Appeals: Allowed by either party within ten days (on cases over $20). Heard in circuit court as new trial; on appeal either party may request jury trial.

Evictions: No.

Jury trials: Not allowed (except on appeal, if requested).

Notes: General district courts, similar to small claims court but with more procedures, can hear claims up to $25,000. See Va. Code Ann. §§ 16.1-77 to 16.1-80.

Washington

Court: Small Claims Department (district court).

Statutes: Wash. Rev. Code Ann. §§ 12.36.010 to 12.40.120; 3.66.040.

Court information: www.atg.wa.gov/small-claims-court-0.

Dollar limit: $5,000.

Where to sue: County where any defendant resides or, if residence cannot be determined by reasonable efforts, place of employment. Corporation, where it transacts business or has office.

Service of process: Sheriff, deputy, or disinterested adult; or certified or registered mail, return receipt requested.

Defendant's response: No formal written answer required. Defendant with counterclaim over $4,000 may file separate suit in superior court while plaintiff's case proceeds in small claims court.

Transfer: Allowed only upon judge's decision, following a hearing.

Attorneys: Not allowed without judge's consent, unless case transferred from regular civil court.

Appeals: Within 30 days. The party who files a claim or counterclaim can't appeal unless the amount exceeds $1,000; no party can appeal unless amount claimed is $250 or more. Heard in superior court as new trial.

Evictions: No.

Jury trials: No provision.

West Virginia

Court: Magistrate Court.

Statutes: W. Va. Code §§ 50-2-1 to 50-6-3; 56-1-1.

Court rules: Rules of Civil Procedure for Magistrate Courts, Rules 1 to 21.

Court information: www.courtswv.gov/lower-courts.

Dollar limit: $5,000.

Where to sue: County in which any defendant resides or can be served, or where transaction or injury occurred. West Virginia corporations, where principal office is located; other corporations, where they do business. For eviction suits, county where property is located.

Service of process: Sheriff or disinterested adult; certified or registered mail by court at plaintiff's request, return receipt requested.

Defendant's response: Defendant must appear or file written answer within 20 days of service to avoid default (30 days if service is made on defendant's attorney or agent). Defendant can also file a counterclaim for $5,000 or less.

Transfer: Allowed if all parties agree to remove to circuit court, or by any party for claims over $2,500. Also allowed at magistrate's discretion if defendant requests transfer to another venue in her answer or within reasonable time.

Attorneys: Allowed.

Appeals: Allowed by either party within 20 days. Heard in circuit court. If original trial was by jury, appeal is on law only, not facts; if original trial was without a jury, appeal is new trial (also without a jury).

Evictions: Yes.

Jury trials: Either party may demand jury trial if claim is over $20 or involves possession of real estate. Must be made in writing within 20 days of service of defendant's answer, or in eviction cases, five days after service of complaint.

Wisconsin

Court: Small Claims Action (circuit court).

Statutes: Wis. Stat. §§ 799.01 to 799.445; 421.401; 801.50; 808.03.

Court information: www.wicourts.gov/services/public/selfhelp/smallclaims.htm.

Dollar limit: $10,000. No limit in eviction suits.

Where to sue: County in which any defendant resides or does substantial business, where transaction or injury occurred, or where property is located. County where contract claim arose or, if claim arose from consumer transaction, county where contract was signed or where purchase or loan took place. For landlord-tenant claims, county where property is located.

Service of process: Sheriff, process server, or disinterested adult; or by certified mail by court clerk, return receipt requested.

Defendant's response: No formal written answer required.

Transfer: Upon defendant's counterclaim over $10,000, case will be tried according to regular circuit court civil procedure.

Attorneys: Allowed.

Appeals: Allowed by either party within 15 days. No appeal from default judgment.

Evictions: Yes.

Jury trials: Either party may request a jury trial.

Wyoming

Court: Small Claims Case (circuit court).

Statutes: Wyo. Stat. Ann. §§ 1-21-201 to 1-21-205; 5-9-128; 5-9-136.

Court rules: Wyoming Rules and Forms Governing Small Claims Cases, Rules 1 to 7, Forms 1 and 2.

Court information: www.courts.state.wy.us/legal-assistances-and-forms/court-self-help-forms.

Dollar limit: $6,000.

Where to sue: County in which defendant has an address.

Service of process: Sheriff, deputy, or disinterested adult; or by certified mail, return receipt requested (by court clerk if defendant lives in the same county as court).

Defendant's response: No answer is required.

Transfer: No provision.

Attorneys: Allowed. If one party appears with an attorney, the other party is entitled to a continuance to obtain one.

Appeals: Allowed by either party. Heard in district court on law only, not facts.

Evictions: No.

Jury trials: Either party may request a jury trial.

Legal Jargon for Small Claims Court

Mercifully, there is not a great deal of technical language used in small claims courts. But there are a few terms that may be new to you and that you will have to become familiar with. Don't try to learn all of these terms now. Refer back to these definitions when you need them.

Abstract of Judgment. An official document you get from the small claims court clerk's office that indicates that you have a money judgment in your favor against another person. Filing it with the County Recorder places a lien on real property owned by the judgment debtor. (For more information about property liens, see Chapter 24.)

Appeal. In the small claims context, a request that the superior court rehear the case from scratch and reverse the decision of the small claims court. Some states allow only a defendant to appeal; others allow the parties to appeal based only on law—not facts. Many require you to post a bond when you file an appeal. (See Chapter 23 and the appendix.)

Calendar. A list of cases to be heard by a small claims court on a particular day. A case taken "off calendar" is removed from the list. This usually occurs because the defendant has not received a copy of the plaintiff's lawsuit or because the parties jointly request that the case be heard on another day.

Claim of Exemption. A procedure by which a judgment debtor can claim that, under federal or state law, certain money or other property is exempt from being grabbed to satisfy a debt.

Conditional Judgment. When a court issues equitable relief (such as the return of a piece of property), it has power to grant a conditional judgment. A conditional judgment consists of certain actions or requirements that are contingent on other actions (for instance, return the property in ten days or pay $2,000).

Continuance. A court order that a hearing be postponed to a later date.

Counterclaim. When a defendant responds to a plaintiff's lawsuit by countersuing the plaintiff for damages arising from the same act or failure to act that the plaintiff's lawsuit is about; also known as a Claim of Defendant or a Cross-Complaint.

Default Judgment. A court decision in favor of the plaintiff (the person filing suit) when the defendant fails to show up (that is, defaults).

Defendant. The person or party being sued.

Defendant's Claim. A claim by a defendant that the plaintiff owes him or her money. The claim is filed as part of the same small claims action that the plaintiff started.

Dismissed Case. A dismissal usually occurs when a plaintiff drops the case. If the defendant has not filed a counterclaim, the plaintiff simply files a written request for dismissal. If the defendant has filed a counterclaim, both plaintiff and defendant must agree in writing before the court will allow a dismissal. A judge may also dismiss a case if a defendant successfully claims that a case was filed in the wrong court. (See Chapter 9.) Also, if a plaintiff does not show up in court on the appointed day, the judge may dismiss the case. Most cases are dismissed without prejudice, which is legal jargon meaning they can be refiled. But if a case is dismissed with prejudice, it means that it can't be refiled unless the plaintiff successfully appeals the dismissal.

Equitable Relief. There are several areas in which a small claims court judge has the power to issue judgment for something other than money damages—that is, to order a party to return unique property, end a fraudulent contract, fix a mistaken contract, or do one or more of the acts discussed in more detail in Chapter 4. This type of judgment is called equitable relief (as opposed to monetary relief).

Equity. The value of a particular piece of property that you own. For example, if a car has a fair market value of $10,000 and you owe a bank $8,000 on it, your equity is $2,000.

Eviction. See Unlawful Detainer Proceeding, below.

Exempt Property. Under federal and state law, certain personal and real property is exempt from being taken to pay (satisfy) court judgments if the debtor follows certain procedures. (See Chapter 24.)

Formal Court. As used here, this term refers to the regular state courts other than small claims court. The states call their trial courts by all sorts of names (municipal, superior, district, circuit, supreme, civil, and so on). In California, for example, claims too large to qualify for small claims court are heard in superior court. All of these courts require considerable attention to often confusing legal language and procedures, and you will want to do some homework if you decide to bring a case there. If your claim really is too big for small claims court, see *Represent Yourself in Court: How to Prepare & Try a Winning Case,* by Paul Bergman and Sara Berman (Nolo). With or without a lawyer, you'll find guidance on certain important pretrial procedures in *Nolo's Deposition Handbook,* by Paul Bergman and Albert Moore (Nolo).

Garnish. To attach (legally take) money—usually wages, or commissions, or a bank account—for payment of a debt.

Hearing. The court trial.

Homestead. Homestead laws allow homeowners to protect a certain amount of the equity in their homes from attachment and sale to satisfy most debts. Homestead laws can work in one of two ways. In some states, the homeowner must file a paper called a Declaration of Homestead. In other states, simply owning a home (and having the deed recorded) is enough to entitle the homeowner to homestead protection. (See Chapter 24.)

Judge Pro Tem. A lawyer who pinch-hits for a regular judge on a temporary basis. Because this person isn't an elected or officially appointed judge, he or she can only hear your case with your written consent, which will normally be requested on the day you go to court.

Judgment. The decision given by the court. A judgment must be written down and signed by a judge.

Judgment Creditor. A person to whom money is owed under a court decision.

Judgment Debtor. A person who owes money under a court decision.

Jurisdiction. A court's authority to hear and decide a case. To properly hear a case, a court must have jurisdiction over the type of dispute and over the parties. A small claims court has jurisdiction to hear cases involving money damages up to a certain amount—for example, $10,000 in Alaska, $4,000 in Kansas. (This is often called the "jurisdictional amount" or "jurisdictional limit.") Some small claims courts also have jurisdiction over certain types

of nonmonetary cases, such as unlawful detainer (eviction) actions, and some may award nonmonetary remedies (equitable relief), as discussed in Chapter 4. Generally, small claims courts have jurisdiction over parties who live in the state, were present in the state when the dispute arose, or who purposefully do business in the state. (For more information about the courts' jurisdiction over people, see Chapter 8.)

Jury Trial. All small claims cases and appeals are heard by judges or commissioners—you're generally not entitled to a jury. Some small claims courts allow jury trials, although most do not. (See the appendix for your state's rules.)

Levy. A legal method to seize property or money for unpaid debts under court order. For example, a sheriff can levy on (take and sell) your automobile if you refuse to pay a judgment.

Lien. A legal right to an interest in the real estate (real property) of another for payment of a debt. To get a lien, you first must get a court judgment and then take proper steps to have the court enter an Abstract of Judgment. To establish the lien, you then take the abstract to the County Recorder's office in a county where the judgment debtor has real estate.

Magistrate. Another word for judge.

Mediation. A process encouraged in many small claims courts by which the parties to a dispute meet with a neutral person (the mediator) who attempts to help them arrive at their own solution to the problem. If mediation succeeds, it's normally not necessary to argue the case in court; if it fails, the dispute can still go to court to be decided on by a judge.

Motion to Vacate Judgment. The motion the defendant must file to reopen a proceeding in which the judge entered a default judgment because the defendant didn't show up. (See Chapter 15.)

Order of Examination. A court procedure allowing a judgment creditor to question a judgment debtor about the extent and location of assets.

Party. A participant in a lawsuit. The plaintiff or defendant may be referred to as a party—and both together as the parties—to a small claims suit.

Plaintiff. The person or party who starts a lawsuit.

Prejudice. A term used when a case is dismissed. A case dismissed without prejudice can be refiled at any time as long as the statute of limitations period

has not run out (see Chapter 5). However, a case dismissed with prejudice is dead (can't be refiled) unless the dismissal is first successfully appealed.

Process Server. The person who delivers court papers to a party or witness. (See Chapter 11.)

Recorder (Office of the County Recorder). The county office that records and files important legal documents, such as deeds to real property. The County Recorder's office is usually located in the main county courthouse.

Release. A written agreement in which a person agrees to waive a right or responsibility; for example, a release of liability.

Replevin. A type of legal action in which the owner of movable goods is given the right to recover them from someone who shouldn't have them. It is commonly used in relation to buyers and sellers; for example, a seller might bring a replevin action if the seller delivered goods to a buyer who then failed to pay for them. Some states' small claims courts allow replevin actions.

Satisfaction of Judgment. A written statement filed by the judgment creditor when the judgment is paid. (See Chapter 23.)

Service. The formal delivery of court papers to a party or witness, which must be done in a manner specified by statute. Also called service of process.

Statute of Limitations. The time period during which you must file your lawsuit. It normally starts on the date the act or failure to act giving rise to the lawsuit occurred, and ends one or more years later, with the number of years depending on the type of suit. (See Chapter 5.)

Stay of Enforcement. When a defendant appeals a small claims court judgment to the superior court, enforcement (collection) of the judgment is stayed (stopped) until the time for appeal has expired.

Stipulation. An agreement on any topic relevant to a case, entered into by the parties and then presented to the judge.

Submission. When a judge wants to delay deciding a case until a later time, he or she takes it under submission. Some judges announce their decision as to who won and who lost right in the courtroom. More often, they take the case under submission and mail out a decision later.

Subpoena. A court order requiring a witness to appear in court. It must be delivered to the person subpoenaed to be valid. (See Chapter 14.)

Subpoena Duces Tecum. A court order requiring that certain documents be produced in court.

Substituted Service. A method by which court papers may be delivered to a defendant who is difficult to reach by other means. (See Chapter 11.)

Transfer. The procedure by which the defendant can have a small claims case transferred to a formal court. In most states this can be done when the defendant has a claim against the plaintiff for an amount greater than the small claims maximum. In a few states, the defendant can transfer a case simply to get out of small claims court. In many states, a defendant who wants a jury trial can also transfer to formal court. See the appendix for details.

Trial de Novo. The rehearing of a small claims case from scratch after a defendant appeals. In this situation, the previous decision by the small claims judge has no effect, and the appeal takes the form of a new trial (trial de novo). This is allowed only in some states. Check the appendix.

Unlawful Detainer Proceeding. Legalese for eviction. Also known as summary dispossession and forcible entry and detainer in some states. Unlawful detainer proceedings may be brought in small claims court in some states but are not allowed in most. Check the appendix.

Venue. This basically refers to the proper location (courthouse or county) in which to bring a suit and is discussed in detail in Chapter 9. If a suit is brought in the wrong county or court (one that is too far from where the defendant lives or a key event in the case occurred), it can be transferred to the right court or dismissed. If it is dismissed, the plaintiff must refile in the right court. However, the case can be heard even in the wrong court if both parties appear and agree to it.

Wage Garnishment. After a judgment has been issued (and the defendant's time to appeal has elapsed), the small claims court clerk will issue a Writ of Execution on the judgment creditor's request. This may be turned over to a sheriff, marshal, or constable with orders to collect (garnish) a portion of the judgment debtor's wages directly from an employer.

Writ of Execution. An order by a court to the sheriff, marshal, or constable to collect a specific amount of money due.

Index

⚖ NOLO | *Online Legal Forms*

Nolo offers a large library of legal solutions and forms, created by Nolo's in-house legal staff. These reliable documents can be prepared in minutes.

Create a Document

- **Incorporation.** Incorporate your business in any state.
- **LLC Formations.** Gain asset protection and pass-through tax status in any state.
- **Wills.** Nolo has helped people make over 2 million wills. Is it time to make or revise yours?
- **Living Trust (avoid probate).** Plan now to save your family the cost, delays, and hassle of probate.
- **Trademark.** Protect the name of your business or product.
- **Provisional Patent.** Preserve your rights under patent law and claim "patent pending" status.

Download a Legal Form

Nolo.com has hundreds of top quality legal forms available for download—bills of sale, promissory notes, nondisclosure agreements, LLC operating agreements, corporate minutes, commercial lease and sublease, motor vehicle bill of sale, consignment agreements and many more.

Review Your Documents

Many lawyers in Nolo's consumer-friendly lawyer directory will review Nolo documents for a very reasonable fee. Check their detailed profiles at **Nolo.com/lawyers**.

⚖ NOLO *Save 15%* off your next order

Register your Nolo purchase, and we'll send you a
coupon for 15% off your next Nolo.com order!

Nolo.com/customer-support/productregistration

On Nolo.com you'll also find:

Books & Software

Nolo publishes hundreds of great books and software programs for consumers and
business owners. Order a copy, or download an ebook version instantly, at Nolo.com.

Online Legal Documents

You can quickly and easily make a will or living trust, form an LLC or corporation, apply
for a trademark or provisional patent, or make hundreds of other forms—online.

Free Legal Information

Thousands of articles answer common questions about everyday legal issues
including wills, bankruptcy, small business formation, divorce, patents,
employment, and much more.

Plain-English Legal Dictionary

Stumped by jargon? Look it up in America's most up-to-date source for
definitions of legal terms, free at nolo.com.

Lawyer Directory

Nolo's consumer-friendly lawyer directory provides in-depth profiles of lawyers all
over America. You'll find all the information you need to choose the right lawyer.

NSCC17